PRAISE FOR

Reviving Ophelia

"[A] compelling account."
—*Roanoke Times & World-News*

"Pipher is an eloquent advocate. . . . With sympathy and focus
she cites case histories to illustrate the struggles required of
adolescent girls to maintain a sense of themselves. . . . Pipher
offers concrete suggestions for ways by which girls can
build and maintain a strong sense of self."
—*Publishers Weekly*

"Pipher integrates literature, memoirs, and memories of her
own adolescence and that of her daughter; she also has a
deft way of summing up psychological phenomena
in layperson's terms. . . . Serious and thoughtful material
presented with the fluidity of good fiction."
—*Kirkus Reviews*

"A must-read for all of us who care about the young women
in our lives. . . . *Reviving Ophelia* arms us with information
we can use in helping our daughters grow to adulthood
with their strength intact."
—*Lincoln Journal Star*

Saving the Selves
of Adolescent Girls

Reviving
Ophelia

Mary Pipher, Ph.D.,
and Sara Pipher Gilliam

RIVERHEAD BOOKS

New York

RIVERHEAD BOOKS
An imprint of Penguin Random House LLC
penguinrandomhouse.com

Copyright © 1994 by Mary Pipher, Ph.D.
Copyright © 2019 by Mary Pipher, Ph.D., and Sara Pipher Gilliam
Penguin supports copyright. Copyright fuels creativity, encourages
diverse voices, promotes free speech, and creates a vibrant culture.
Thank you for buying an authorized edition of this book and
for complying with copyright laws by not reproducing, scanning,
or distributing any part of it in any form without permission.
You are supporting writers and allowing Penguin to continue
to publish books for every reader.

Library of Congress Cataloging-in-Publication Data

Names: Pipher, Mary Bray, author. | Gilliam, Sara Pipher, author.
Title: Reviving Ophelia : saving the selves of adolescent girls /
Mary Pipher, Ph.D., and Sara Pipher Gilliam.
Other titles: Saving the selves of adolescent girls
Description: Riverhead 25th anniversary edition. | New York City : Riverhead Books, 2019. |
An updated edition of the 1994 Putnam publication.
Identifiers: LCCN 2019003400 (print) | LCCN 2019006433 (ebook) |
ISBN 9780525537052 (ebook) | ISBN 9780525537045 (pbk.)
Subjects: LCSH: Teenage girls--Psychology. | Teenage girls--Family relationships. |
Self-esteem in adolescence. | Girls--United States--Social conditions--21st century. |
Girls--United States--Social life and customs--21st century.
Classification: LCC HQ798 (ebook) | LCC HQ798 .P57 2019 (print) | DDC 305.235/2--dc23
LC record available at https://lccn.loc.gov/2019003400

G. P. Putnam's Sons hardcover edition: April 1994

First Ballantine Books trade paperback edition: March 1995

First Riverhead trade paperback edition: July 2005

Riverhead 25th Anniversary edition: June 2019

Riverhead 25th Anniversary edition ISBN: 978-0-525-53704-5

Printed in the United States of America
3   5   7   9   10   8   6   4   2

Book design by Marysarah Quinn

All clients are composite characters drawn from the authors' life
experiences and clinical work. Names and details have been
changed to protect confidentiality.

Acknowledgments

The following people helped us with the 2019 edition of the book: Francis Baty, Pam Barger, Ina Bhoopalam, La'Rae Bonebright, Ashlee Brimage, Dawn Brown, Blake Carrichner, Eric Crump, Danika and Sequoia Davis, Anaka Evans, Niki Figard, Grace Fitzgibbon, Patty Forsberg, Sandy Gallentine, Nijole Gedutis, Sarah Gervais, Julia Haack, Rachel Halliday, Beth Hardy, Sophie Holz, Ellen James, Gillian Burrow Jenkins, Ann and Grace Kaseman, Neva Kushner, Frank McPherson, Mary Kon, Lynda Madison, Laurel Maslowski, Megan May, Helen Meyer, Anna Musgrave, Abbie Radenslaben, Jesse Reed, Meghan Renz, Abbie Rosauer, Shari Stenberg, Paige Trevarrow, Emma Went, and Ken and Helen Winston.

Our granddaughter/niece Kate Pipher read and edited this book multiple times and we are grateful for her knowledge and thoughtfulness.

We thank our agent, Susan Lee Cohen; *Reviving Ophelia*'s original editor, Jane Isay; and our editor at Penguin USA, Jake Morrissey.

To the rebels and the shy girls, the
activists and the poets, the big sisters
and the little sisters, the daughters
and dreamers. We believe in you.

Contents

Introduction

MARY

REVIVING OPHELIA WAS MY attempt to understand my experiences as a mother of a teenage daughter and a therapist for adolescent girls. I wrote it in 1994 to sound an alarm about the poisonous culture that adolescent girls were experiencing. At the time, my goals seemed grandiose: I wanted to educate therapists, teachers, and parents; to help girls heal; and to change the culture. Yet, in some ways, I feel as if the book accomplished its aims. It was widely read and loved by many teenagers and their parents. Mothers told me that it helped them understand their daughters. Psychologists gradually moved away from attributing teenagers' problems to their dysfunctional families and turned instead to helping adolescents and their parents cope with a difficult cultural environment. Educators developed ways to encourage and sustain girls' interest in math and science. All over the country organizations such as the Ophelia Project, Girl Scouts, and the YWCA worked to empower young women.

I am deeply grateful to my readers, the communities that hosted me for speaking events, and the many people who contacted me to share their reactions to the book. My greatest reward has been to hear of all the positive changes that *Reviving Ophelia* inspired.

Twenty-five years later, I am honored to work with my daughter, Sara, to update that edition. In this book we explore what has and hasn't changed for girls, and we will examine the effects of American culture on the lives of girls today. We hope this new edition will be of use to girls and to the adults who want to help them grow into bold, kind, competent women.

In the 1990s, my office was swamped with girls with serious, even life-threatening, problems, such as anorexia or the desire to harm themselves. Others had problems that ranged from refusing to go to school, to intentionally underachieving, to constantly provoking fights with their parents. These kinds of issues were less dangerous than suicide threats but more puzzling. Many of my clients were victims of sexual violence. As I talked with these girls, I became aware of how little I really understood about the world of adolescent girls in the 1990s. My adolescent experiences from the early 1960s weren't helpful. Girls in the 1990s were living in a whole new world, a world of increasingly violent and sexualized television, MTV videos, and blatantly sexualized advertising.

As a therapist, I often felt bewildered and frustrated. These feelings led to questions: Why are so many girls in therapy? What is the meaning of lip, nose, and eyebrow piercings (which were new phenomena at that time)? How can I help thirteen-year-olds deal with herpes or genital warts? Why are drugs and alcohol common in the stories of seventh graders? Why do so many girls say they hate their parents?

Meanwhile, Sara and her friends were riding a roller coaster. Sometimes they were happy and interested in their world; other times they just seemed wrecked. They were hard on their families and one another. Junior high seemed like a crucible where confident, well-adjusted girls were transformed into sad and angry failures.

When my friends and I talked about our adolescent daughters, we felt angry and unsure how to proceed. Many of us were frustrated by our daughters, who became upset with us for the smallest things. We had raised our girls to be assertive and confident, yet they seemed to be insecure and concerned with their looks and femininity. Several dilemmas came up again and again: How could we encourage our daughters to be independent and autonomous and still keep them safe? How could we inspire them to take on a world that included kidnappers and date rapists? How could we offer them guidance and support without making them mad? Even in our small city with its mostly middle-class population, girls often experienced trauma. How could we help girls heal from it? What could we do to prevent it?

As a mother and therapist, I struggled to make sense of what I was observing. My friends and I had unleashed our share of adolescent angst yet, for the most part, we didn't develop eating disorders, threaten suicide, cut ourselves, or run away from home. Why were girls having more trouble in the 1990s?

At first blush, it seemed life for teenage girls should have felt better in 1994. After all, we had embraced the women's movement. Hadn't that helped? The answer turned out to be yes and no. Many of my friends—middle-aged and middle-class women like myself—were fortunate in ways few women had been since the beginning of time. We had opportunities our mothers never imagined possible. However, in specific ways, girls felt more oppressed. They were coming of age in a more dangerous, sexualized, and media-saturated culture. They faced incredible pressure to be beautiful and sophisticated, which in junior high meant using drugs and alcohol and being sexually active. As they navigated a more dangerous world, girls were less protected.

The more I looked around, the more I listened to the music, watched television and movies, and examined sexist advertising, the more convinced I became that, as a society, we were on the wrong path with our daughters. American culture was poisonous to teenage girls. The messages girls received about sex, beauty, and their place in the world truncated their development and left many of them traumatized. With the onset of puberty, girls were crashing into a junk culture that was just too hard for them to understand and master. Many became overwhelmed, depressed, and angry.

In 1963, Betty Friedan wrote of "the problem with no name." She pointed out that many women were miserable but couldn't articulate the source of that misery. Adolescent girls in the 1990s faced a similar unnamed problem. They knew that something was very wrong, but they looked for the source within themselves or their families. I wanted to help them see their lives in the context of larger cultural forces. With *Reviving Ophelia*, I named the problem I was seeing.

Now, twenty-five years later, adolescent girls are doing better than girls were in the 1990s, but they too are coming of age in a new world: the digital world. As I reflect on fifty years of girls' lives, I realize how the culture has not only changed for girls. In 1959, I turned thirteen with all the shyness, pimples, hormones, and self-consciousness that age implies. In the 1990s, I was the mother of a teenage daughter and a therapist working primarily with adolescent girls. Now I have two teenage granddaughters.

Kate, Sara, and I are all members of brink generations. Born right after World War II ended and living in rural Nebraska, I was a member of the last American generation to grow up without television. Born right after the official end of the Vietnam War, my daughter was in the last generation to be raised without cell phones, computers, or digital devices. And my granddaughter Kate, born in July 2001, two months before 9/11, is a member of the first generation of digital natives.

I grew up in a slow time and place, and my world was my family and the tiny town of Beaver City, Nebraska. Most of the news was local and most of our entertainment was locally manufactured and face-to-face. Children had little to do but play together, read, and talk to people.

Sara's generation negotiated the transition from a local culture to a global one. The sense of community that had sheltered girls of my generation was rapidly vanishing. Girls still maintained face-to-face relationships, but their common culture was generated far away by corporate entities with no interest in their health and well-being. My daughter and my adolescent therapy clients in 1994 were part of a generation running headfirst into a toxic culture with little help from the adults in their lives. Teenagers were rebellious, unsettled, and angry at their parents for not understanding their experiences and not protecting them.

Today, adults and teenagers are more sophisticated about the effects of corporate culture, but now we find ourselves confronted with new waves of technology that none of us understand how to manage. With the rare exception of girls who are off-line by intention or circumstance, digital devices have replaced face-to-face interactions. Teens are more likely to stay home or go places with their parents than they are to venture out on their own or with their friends. Now they spend their weekends watching Netflix and communicating with friends via texts, Snapchat, or Instagram.

Girls today are less likely to be in trouble for their drinking, drug use, sexual behavior, or party-going, but they are more likely to be depressed, anxious, and suicidal. Many girls sense that something is wrong in the digitally driven culture they inhabit. They sleep with their phones on and describe pressure to stay connected at all times. Yet they also feel a deep loneliness and a lack of connection to their families, communities, and to the natural world. They express nostalgia for the "olden days" of dating, reading books, and phone calls with friends. They seem fragile and afraid of being out on their own.

In my small town in the 1950s and 1960s, I felt safe. We know now that sexual assaults and domestic violence were not reported and that many people of color were victims of violence, but the children I knew moved about the world freely and danger seemed far away. My daughter's generation was more aware of sexual assaults, incest, and violent crimes from all over the country. Television reported such events;

crime rates were higher; and milk cartons featured grainy photos of missing children. Yet 1994 was pre-Columbine and other school shootings; it predated 9/11, the Iraq War, Al Qaeda and ISIS, the opioid epidemic, the climate crisis, the global refugee crisis, the political and social polarization of our country, and the rise of white supremacism.

Primarily because of the nonstop coverage of crime and danger, today's teens and their parents are more frightened and risk averse than earlier generations. Teens are less likely to go out on their own than were teens in 1994 despite the fact that—according to the Pew Research Council—by 2016, violent crime rates had decreased by 50 percent since 1993.

Between 1960 and today, two great force vectors have been operative. Americans have become much more fearful, and we have moved from a person-to-person, community-based style of living to one that relies primarily on digital connections. A professor friend of mine told me that students used to be so loud between classes that it was almost impossible to hear. He said that now, between classes, the halls are absolutely silent. Students aren't flirting or chatting; they are looking at their phones.

Still, many aspects of life have changed for the better since 1994. Divorce rates have dropped. Fewer teenagers have unplanned pregnancies. This generation is more open to the LGBTQ community and less likely to be racist. Girls are less frequently in trouble for their behaviors and more inclined to be activists and feminists.

Girls, especially once they reach high school, also report strong feelings of love and respect for their parents. In our recent interviews and focus groups, we observed very little of the surliness and angry attitudes that were so prevalent in the 1990s. Parents also report that they feel close to their daughters and have few discipline issues.

I suspect there are many reasons for these improvements in relationships between parents and teens. These include increasingly harsh economic conditions and the perception that the world is a dangerous place. Families tend to stick together when the going gets tough. Also, as real communities disappear, what's left is the family unit. Since teens today aren't causing as much trouble, parents tend to be warmer and more accepting of their children. In addition, fathers are much more engaged in their daughters' lives than they were even twenty-five years ago. Girls appreciate that they have a family that shelters them from the storms of today's world.

Most of what I learned about social media while researching this new edition of *Reviving Ophelia* was negative. Since 2007, when iPhones arrived on the scene, girls as a group have become more isolated. Critical developmental processes are being disrupted. I acknowledge that digital technology has an upside, but even the positive arguments for social media can be overstated. For example, I often hear a variant of, "A daughter can stay in touch with her grandmother by texting." My reply is, "Well, sure, but she and her grandmother would probably be closer if they talked on the phone or visited face-to-face."

On the other hand, we have witnessed the power of social media and networking in nascent youth-built activist movements, such as #MeToo and #NeverAgain, the latter of which originated following the school shooting in Parkland, Florida, in February 2018. Middle-school and high-school students nationwide "found" one another on Twitter and Instagram and used those platforms to organize rallies and positive actions for such groups as Sí Se Puede and Black Lives Matter.

And, of course, I use social media myself. I have a professional website and an author page on Facebook. Sara checks her Twitter and Instagram accounts several times each day. I know many people depend on social media for entertainment and we all need a break from the harsh global political realities that define the world today. I judge no one for their use of social media. Rather, I want to suggest ways in which parents and their daughters can be more intentional in their online use. I assume most of us don't want our epitaph to read "She had 2,000 followers."

Sara and I were fortunate to find just the research we needed from monitoring the future and in psychologist Jean Twenge's book *iGen*. Twenge examines research from 1974 to 2016 on everything from suicide and crime rates to incidence of television watching, time spent online, and books read per year. By comparing one generation to another on hundreds of dimensions, she was able to make insightful points about how times and teens have changed.

In this updated edition, we conducted interviews with girls from much the same demographic groups as my therapy clients in the early 1990s and we held focus groups for teenage girls and for mothers. I interviewed therapists while Sara, a former middle-school teacher, interviewed teachers and school counselors.

In the first edition of *Reviving Ophelia*, I wrote about therapy clients I had seen over the years. Most of the girls we discuss in this update, we met only once. These interviews and focus group girls cannot capture growth across time the way that therapy stories did, but they do highlight the unique challenges that girls face today and they offer us snapshots of their lives. Our interviews and research reveal those challenges that have changed and the perils and joys that have remained the same.

We also invited girls from diverse communities around the country to read *Reviving Ophelia* and share their reactions. We asked them what felt dated and what still felt relevant to their lives. We encouraged them to illustrate the text with captions, margin notes, and slash marks and to candidly report to us what they thought we needed to discuss in the new edition. Not surprisingly, we found that girls still struggle with misogyny, eating disorders, sexism, peer pressure, and identity issues.

What they all agreed had changed the landscape of adolescence was social media. Every girl wrote in almost every chapter, "Include social media."

In this update, we kept many of the compelling stories from the original book and we have added new stories of modern girls. We reflect on the changes in girls' lives and include up-to-date research and advice tailored to this moment in time. We kept some of the language from the earlier edition, even though it now reads as dated. (For example, girls in the 1960s and '90s attended junior highs. Now they attend middle schools.)

I wrote "Then and Now, 1959–2019" and "What I've Learned from Listening." Sara conducted and penned almost all the interviews. We added one new chapter on anxiety. In chapter 16, "A Fence at the Top of the Hill," we offer concrete suggestions for parents, teens, and all those who work with teenagers. Our afterword offers hope and guidance for thriving in an age of disruption.

When I reread *Reviving Ophelia*, I was struck by how relevant it still felt. Girls continue to grapple with peer troubles, family discord, and anxiety about their appearance. While the culture has changed, the developmental needs of girls have stayed the same. Girls still need what they have long needed—loving parents, decent values, friends, physical safety, freedom to move about independently, respect for their own uniqueness, and encouragement to grow into productive adults. They need protection from the most harmful aspects of our culture and connection to its most wholesome and beautiful aspects.

In 1994, I suggested that we work together to strengthen girls so that they will be prepared for the culture they actually live in. Sara and I reached that same conclusion today. We can encourage emotional resilience and self-protection. We can support and guide girls through the tumult of adolescence, but most important, we can work together to build a culture that is less complicated and more nurturing, less violent and sexualized, and more growth producing. Our daughters deserve a world in which all their gifts can be developed and appreciated. We hope this book fosters a conversation about how we can build that world with them.

Introduction

SARA

*Reflections from
the Original Ophelia*

IF REBELLION AND RISK-TAKING defined my generation of adolescent girls—those who graduated from high school in the early- to mid-1990s—then I could have been a poster child for my peers. I was as snarky and rebellious as a middle-class Nebraska girl could be, which is to say that while taking risks I also earned good grades and remembered to handwrite thank-you notes to my grandmother for birthday and Christmas presents. My stomping ground was Lincoln, Nebraska, a pleasant college town in a flyover state smack in the middle of the country. Several of my close friends appeared in the original *Reviving Ophelia*, and my mother called upon me to edit dialogue for "teen accuracy."

Highlights of my adolescence included forays into vegetarianism and animal rights activism, an eyebrow ring at seventeen, remarkably unnatural hair colors, grunge attire, and sneaking out to raves and concerts in cities several hours from home. I sneered at mainstream culture and used the word *Muffy* to describe my preppy, cheerleading counterparts. I was at once atypical and fairly representative of early-'90s girls and their peccadilloes. I remember one comically dark moment from my freshman year of college when I heard an uncharitable neighbor mutter in my direction at the grocery store, "*Reviving Ophelia?* More like *Drowning Ophelia.*"

It's funny now but, in fact, that busybody was missing the point. We adolescent girls weren't drowning, we were cannonballing off the high diving board. The Ophelias in my social circle were limit pushers, riot grrrls, budding feminists, and haters of conformity. We listened to all-female punk rock, road-tripped to the Lilith Fair, and aimed for androgyny in our style. The last thing we wanted was the approval of the cardigan-wearing, cookie-baking book club set.

We were also, unsurprisingly, leading lives not fully understood by our mothers. Teenage girls will always keep secrets, and that is both fair and developmentally appropriate. We kept under wraps our crushes, our experimentation with drugs and alcohol, our rule breaking. We cursed like sailors, reclaiming words like *pussy* and *cunt* as empowering and powerful. I loved my mother fiercely but nearly perished from embarrassment every time she made small talk with my friends. We were busy with the work of distancing ourselves from our families of origin and embracing our emerging identities as independent young women.

My friends and I got away with a lot, by virtue of our middle-class white privilege, our family connections, and our intelligence. While I spent my fair share of time grounded for missing curfew, I also soloed in youth symphony and volunteered at a homeless shelter. One friend and I skipped orchestra for a month during our junior year of high school, instead spending sixth period downtown playing pool and drinking Italian sodas at a coffee shop. I'm pretty sure I still earned an A that semester. My peers and I cared about schoolwork and assumed we were going to college. The higher education conversations in our household weren't *if* but rather *where?*

In 1994, some of my friends were having sex and some weren't. Sex wasn't a coolness-defining act, and in my peer group it tended to occur in the context of long-term relationships. I was envious of my friends who were having sex, mainly because it meant they also had a guaranteed prom date and someone to hold hands with in the cafeteria. I have no doubt that sexual assaults occurred, but I didn't hear much about them. We were all a bit in awe of our first friends to lose their virginity, and we were also aware of the slut versus stud double standard and supported one another accordingly.

In the evenings, we made time for *Beverly Hills, 90210* between music lessons and homework. We were the MTV generation, setting our clocks by the debuts of new videos, *Total Request Live*, and *Headbanger's Ball*. We wanted Julia Roberts's legs, Winona Ryder's style, and the ability to wail like Tori Amos. We longed for a boyfriend who reflected the perfect, broody combination of Patrick Swayze, Eddie Vedder, Luke Perry, and our dreamy philosophy teacher, Mr. Jundt.

Darkness flitted around the fringes of our comfortable Nebraska lives. During my junior year of high school, a local college student named Candice Harms was abducted, tortured, and murdered. In the frightening time after her disappearance but before her captors were apprehended, our teachers urged us never to walk to our cars alone and to shine flashlights into our backseats before driving anywhere at night. It was the first time such violence hit close to home, and my classmates and I were terrified. Around that same time, my best friend, Sarah, and I discovered a clunky, dial-in local chat room and spent every waking hour (at five cents per minute) calling in and typing to new friends, mostly other awkward high school kids around town. It was months later that we learned we'd shared virtual space—and occasionally messaged with—Candi's murderer. It was an early and abrupt lesson in the dangers of online "relationships."

Depression, often unnamed, touched many of us. Though as a group we were less fretful about grades and test scores than our present-day counterparts, we shared their predilection for poor self-image and social anxiety. Most of us wanted to be thinner, and thin girls wanted more curves. We fell apart when we didn't get accepted to our first-choice universities (I'm looking at you, Macalester College) and soothed our bruised hearts with marijuana or Boone's Farm wine coolers. Looking back, our challenges seem so much simpler than those experienced by girls today. My generation predated Columbine, 9/11, ISIS, and Snapchat. Our problems tended to be local, family or school based, or internal.

To an extent, every generation is written off as apathetic by those who paved the way, and mine was no exception. We were third wave feminists enjoying the fruits of our foremothers' efforts, but my peers and I were not entitled princesses content to eat macaroons while popular culture and politics rocketed past us. We wanted to create change in our own lives and communities.

Nineteen nineties girls were cultural critics, ushering in a new era of openness and advocacy. Friends and I at our high school formed GLOBE, the Gay/Lesbian Organization for the Betterment of Everyone, an early iteration of gay/straight alliances. We encouraged our administrators to create a recycling program, and we wore black armbands to school after the 1991 beating of Rodney King by Los Angeles police officers. We cared about causes, but we also existed in a haze of unselfconscious myopia. Our feelings, our friendships, were of paramount importance. Activism was an extracurricular activity.

If we floundered significantly in our awareness, it was around race. Lincoln High School was, at the time, the largest and most diverse school in the state, yet most of my friends were white. Our cafeteria seating was de facto segregated, and Rainbow Club—an organization celebrating diversity and our student body's rich breadth of cultural backgrounds—was generally led by students of color and sparsely attended by white kids. I remember noticing these divides and disliking them, but I didn't generate ideas for how to change things.

Looking back from my current vantage point—that of a forty-one-year-old mother of two—there are many aspects of my adolescence that I am grateful for. I am grateful that my most awkward years coincided with the popularity of oversized flannel shirts; skinny jeans and crop tops would have ensured the annihilation of my fragile shards of self-confidence. I am relieved that I had to endure bullies only during the school day; their ridicule didn't follow me home on social media. I'm thankful for a cadre of female musicians who growled about their anger and made me feel understood. I am appreciative of loving parents who, with both exasperation and grace, rode out my moodiness and predilection for body jewelry.

I am inspired, as well, by the girls I interviewed for this book. They are getting many things right in this new century. They have bypassed tolerance in favor of acceptance—and often, celebration—of people different from themselves. They are insightful about their own mental health. They are activists for causes they believe in. They are weathering adolescence with humor and sincerity. Today's girls need love, guidance, deep friendships, respectable limits, and time to figure out life on their own terms.

So did I.

Reviving
Ophelia

ONE

Saplings
in the Storm

WHEN MY COUSIN Polly was a girl, she was energy in motion. She danced, did cartwheels and splits, played football, basketball, and baseball with the neighborhood boys, wrestled with my brothers, biked, climbed trees, and rode horses. She was as lithe and as resilient as a willow branch and as unrestrained as a lion cub. Polly talked as much as she moved. She yelled out orders and advice, shrieked for joy when she won a bet or heard a good joke, laughed with her mouth wide open, argued with kids and grown-ups, and insulted her foes in the language of a construction worker.

We formed the Marauders, a secret club that met over her garage. Polly was the Tom Sawyer of the club. She planned the initiations and led the spying expeditions and hikes to haunted houses. She showed us the rituals to become blood "brothers" and taught us card tricks and how to smoke cigarettes.

Then Polly had her first period and started junior high school. She tried to keep up her old ways, but she was called a tomboy and chided for not acting more ladylike. She found herself excluded by her boy pals and by the girls, who were moving into makeup and romances.

This left Polly confused and shaky. She had temper tantrums and withdrew from both the boys' and girls' groups. A few months later, she reentered her community as Becky Thatcher, Tom Sawyer's quiet, well-behaved girlfriend. She wore stylish clothes and watched from the sidelines as the boys dominated the classroom and playground. Once again she was accepted and popular. She glided smoothly through our small society. No one spoke of the changes or mourned the loss of our school's most dynamic citizen. I was the only one who felt that a tragedy had transpired.

Girls in what Freud called the latency period, roughly age six or seven through puberty, are anything but latent. I think of my daughter, Sara, during those years—performing chemistry experiments and magic tricks, playing her violin, starring in her own plays, rescuing wild animals, and biking all over town. I think of her friend Tamara, who wrote a three-hundred-page novel the summer of her sixth-grade year. I remember myself at that age, reading every children's book in the library of my town. One week I planned to be a great doctor like Albert Schweitzer. The next week I wanted to write like Louisa May Alcott or dance in Paris like Isadora Duncan. I have never since had as much confidence or ambition.

Most preadolescent girls are marvelous company because they are interested in everything—sports, nature, people, music, and books. Almost all the heroines of time-tested girls' literature come from this age group—Anne of Green Gables, Heidi, and Pippi Longstocking. Girls this age bake pies, solve mysteries, and go on quests. They can take care of themselves and are not yet burdened with caring for others. They have a brief respite from the female role and can be tomboys, a word that conveys courage, competence, and irreverence.

They can act adaptively in any situation regardless of gender-role constraints. In the 1990s, girls between seven and eleven rarely came to therapy; they didn't need it. I could count on my fingers the girls this age whom I had seen: Coreen, who was physically abused; Anna, whose parents were divorcing; and Brenda, whose father killed himself. These girls were courageous and resilient. During one session Brenda said, "If my father didn't want to stick around, that's his loss." Coreen and Anna were angry, not at themselves, but rather at the grown-ups they felt were making mistakes. It was amazing how little help these girls needed from me to heal and move on.

A horticulturist at a university told me a revealing story. Twyla led a tour of junior high girls who were attending a math and science fair on her campus. She showed them big blue grass, delicate snowdrops, maple and willow trees. The younger girls interrupted one another with their questions and tumbled forward to see, touch, and smell everything. The ninth graders were different. They hung back. They didn't touch plants or shout out questions. They stood primly to the side, looking bored and even a little disgusted by the enthusiasm of the younger girls. Twyla asked herself, *What's happened to these girls? What's gone wrong?* She told me, "I wanted to shake them, to say, 'Wake up, come back. Is anybody home at your house?'"

One summer morning, as I sat outside my favorite ice cream store, a mother and her teenage daughter stopped in front of me and waited for the pedestrian light to change. I heard the mother say, "You have got to stop blackmailing your father and me. Every time you don't get what you want, you tell us that you want to run away from home or kill yourself. What's happened to you? You used to be able to handle not getting your way."

The daughter stared straight ahead, barely acknowledging her mother's words. The light changed and they crossed the street. I licked my ice cream cone. Another mother approached the same light with her preadolescent daughter in tow. They were holding hands. The daughter said to her mother "This is fun. Let's hang out all afternoon."

Something dramatic happens to girls in early adolescence. Just as planes and ships disappear mysteriously into the Bermuda Triangle, so do the selves of girls go down in droves. They crash and burn in a social and developmental Bermuda Triangle. They lose their resiliency and optimism and become less curious and inclined to take risks. Their assertive, energetic, and "tomboyish" personalities fade away and they become more deferential, self-critical, and depressed. They report great unhappiness with their own bodies.

Psychology documents but does not explain the crashes. Girls who once rushed to drink in experiences in enormous gulps sit quietly in the corner. Writers such as Sylvia Plath, Margaret Atwood, and Olive Schreiner have described the wreckage. Diderot, writing to his young friend Sophie Volland, described his observations harshly: "You all die at 15."

Fairy tales capture the essence of this phenomenon. Young women eat poisoned apples or prick their fingers with bewitched needles and fall asleep for a hundred years. They wander away from home, encounter great dangers, and are rescued by princes and transformed into passive and docile creatures.

The story of Ophelia, from Shakespeare's *Hamlet*, shows the destructive forces that affect young women. As a girl, Ophelia is happy and free, but with adolescence she loses herself. When she falls in love with Hamlet, she lives only for his approval. She has no inner direction; rather, she struggles to meet the demands of Hamlet and her father. Her value is determined utterly by male approval. Ophelia is torn apart by her efforts to please. When Hamlet spurns her because she is an obedient daughter, she goes mad with grief. Dressed in elegant clothes that weigh her down, she drowns in a stream filled with flowers.

Girls know they are losing themselves. One of my clients said, "Everything good in me died in junior high." Wholeness is shattered by the chaos of adolescence. Girls become fragmented with their integrated personalities split into mysterious contradictions. They are sensitive and tenderhearted, mean and competitive, superficial and idealistic. They are confident in the morning and overwhelmed with anxiety by nightfall. They rush through their days with wild energy and then collapse into lethargy. They try on new roles every week—this week the good student, next week the delinquent, and the next, the artist. And they expect their families to keep up with these changes.

My teenaged clients in the 1990s were elusive and slow to trust adults. They were easily offended by a glance, a clearing of the throat, a silence, a lack of sufficient enthusiasm, or a comment that didn't meet their immediate needs. Their voices had gone underground—their speech was more tentative and less articulate. Their moods swung widely. One week they loved the world and their families, the next they were critical of everyone. Much of their behavior was unreadable. Their problems were complicated and metaphorical—eating disorders, school phobias, and self-inflicted injuries. I found that I needed to ask again and again in a dozen different ways, "What are you trying to tell me?"

Michelle, for example, was a beautiful, intelligent seventeen-year-old. Her mother brought her in after she became pregnant for the third time in three years. I tried to talk about why this was happening. She smiled a Mona Lisa smile to all my questions. "No, I don't care all that much for sex." "No, I didn't plan this. It just happened." When Michelle left a session, I felt like I'd been talking in the wrong language to someone far away.

Holly was another mystery. She was shy, soft-spoken, and slow-moving, pretty under all her makeup and teased red hair. She was a Prince fan and wore only purple. Her father brought her in after she attempted suicide. She wouldn't study, do chores, join any school activities, or find a job. Holly answered questions in patient, polite monosyllables. She really talked only when the topic was Prince. For several weeks we talked about him. She played me his tapes. Prince somehow spoke for her and to her.

Daniella burned and cut herself when she was unhappy. Dressed in black, thin as a straw, she sat silently before me, her hair a mess, her ears, lips, and nose all pierced with rings. She spoke about the civil war in Bosnia and the hole in the ozone layer and asked me if I liked rave music. When I asked about her life, she played with her earrings and sat silently.

I did my best for these girls, but I was in new territory. Eventually, Michelle, Holly, and Daniella made progress but, in the process, I was learning as much as they were about what was helpful.

My clients were not that different from girls who were not seen in therapy. They came into therapy in crisis, but many teenagers had similar crises and did not see therapists. At that time, I taught at a small liberal arts college and the young women in my classes had essentially the same experiences as my therapy clients. One student worried about her best friend who'd been sexually assaulted. Another missed class after being hit by her boyfriend. Another asked what she should do about obscene calls from a man threatening to rape her. When stressed, another student stabbed her hand with paper clips until she drew blood. Many students asked for advice on eating disorders.

When I spoke at high schools, girls approached me afterward to say that they had been raped, they wanted to run away from home, or that they had a friend who was anorexic or alcoholic. At first all this trauma surprised me. Then I expected it.

Psychology has a long history of ignoring girls in this age group. Until the early 1990s, adolescent girls hadn't been studied by academics, and they had long baffled therapists. Because they were secretive with adults and full of contradictions, they were difficult to study. So much was happening internally that's not communicated on the surface.

Simone de Beauvoir described the trouble that girls fall into this way: girls who were the subjects of their own lives became the objects of others' lives. She wrote, "Young girls slowly bury their childhood, put away their independent and imperious selves and submissively enter adult existence."

Adolescent girls experience a conflict between their status as human beings and their vocation as females. De Beauvoir said, "Girls stop being and start seeming."

Girls become female impersonators who fit their whole selves into small, crowded spaces. Vibrant, confident girls become shy, doubting young women. Girls stop thinking, *Who am I? What do I want?* and start thinking, *What must I do to please others?*

This gap between girls' true selves and our cultural prescriptions for what is properly female creates enormous problems. To paraphrase a Stevie Smith poem about swimming in the sea, "They are not waving, they are drowning." And just when they most need help, girls are unable to take their parents' hands.

Olive Schreiner wrote of her experiences as a young girl in *The Story of an African Farm.* "The world tells us what we are to be and shapes us by the ends it sets before us. To men it says, work. To us, it says, seem. The less a woman has in her head the lighter she is for carrying." She described the finishing school that she attended in this way: "It was a machine for condensing the soul into the smallest possible area. I have seen some souls so compressed that they would have filled a small thimble."

Anthropologist Margaret Mead believed that the ideal culture is one in which there is a place for every human gift. By her standards, our

Western culture is far from ideal for women. So many gifts are unused and unappreciated. So many voices are stilled. Stendhal wrote, "All geniuses born women are lost to the public good."

Psychologist Alice Miller wrote of the pressures on some young children to deny their true selves and assume false selves to please their parents. *Reviving Ophelia* suggests that adolescent girls experience a similar pressure to split into true and false selves, but this time the pressure comes not from parents but from the culture. Adolescence is when girls experience social pressure to put aside their authentic selves and to display only a small portion of their gifts.

This pressure disorients and depresses most girls. One girl put it this way: "I'm a perfectly good carrot that everyone is trying to turn into a rose. As a carrot, I have good color and a nice leafy top. When I'm carved into a rose, I turn brown and wither."

Adolescent girls are saplings bent to the ground in a hurricane of changes. Three factors make young women vulnerable to the hurricane. One is their developmental level. Everything is changing—their body shapes, hormones, skin, and hair. Equanimity is replaced by imbalance. Their thinking is evolving. Far below the surface they are struggling with the most basic of human questions: What is my place in the universe? What is my meaning?

Second, American culture has always smacked girls on the head in early adolescence. This is when they move into the broader culture that is rife with girl-hurting "isms," such as sexism, capitalism, and lookism, which is the evaluation of a person solely on the basis of appearance.

Third, American girls are expected to distance themselves from parents just at the time when they most need their support. As they struggle with countless new pressures, they must relinquish the protection and closeness they've felt with their families in childhood. They turn to their none-too-constant peers for support.

Parents know only too well that something is happening to their daughters. Calm, considerate, and confident daughters grow moody, demanding, and distant. Girls who loved to talk are sullen and secretive. Girls who liked to hug now bristle when touched. Mothers complain that they can do nothing right in the eyes of their daughters. Involved fathers bemoan their sudden banishment from their daughters' lives. But few parents realize how universal their experiences are. Their daughters are entering a new land, a dangerous place that parents can scarcely comprehend. Just when they most need a home base, they cut themselves loose without communication systems.

Parents want to keep their daughters safe while they grow up and explore the world. Their job is to protect. The daughters' job is to explore. Generally, parents are more protective of their daughters than is corporate America. Parents aren't trying to make money off their daughters by selling them designer jeans or cigarettes; they just want them to be well-adjusted. They don't see their daughters as sex objects or consumers but rather as real people with talents and interests. However, daughters turn away from their parents as they enter the new land. They rely on their peers, who are their fellow inhabitants of the strange country and who share a common language and set of customs. They often embrace the junk values of mass culture.

This turning away from parents occurs partly for developmental reasons. Early adolescence is a time of physical and psychological change, self-absorption, preoccupation with peer approval, and identity formation. It's a time when girls focus inward on their own fascinating changes. It's partly for cultural reasons. In America, we define adulthood as a moving away from families into broader culture. Adolescence is the time for cutting bonds and breaking free. Adolescents may claim great independence from parents, but they are hyperaware of their parents' behavior and ashamed of their smallest deviations from the norm. They don't like to be seen with them and find their imperfections upsetting. A mother's haircut or a father's corny joke can ruin their day. Teenagers are furious at parents who say the wrong things or do not respond with perfect answers. Adolescents claim not to listen to their parents, but with their friends they discuss endlessly all parental attitudes. With amazing acuity, they sense nuance, doubt, ambiguity, discrepancy, and hypocrisy.

Adolescents still have some of the magical thinking of childhood and believe that parents have the power to keep them safe and happy. They blame their parents for their misery, yet they make a point of not telling their parents how they think and feel. They keep secrets. For example, girls who are raped may not tell their parents. Instead, they become hostile and rebellious. In 1994, parents brought their daughters to therapy because of their anger and out-of-control behavior. When I heard about this unexplainable anger, I asked about rape. Ironically, girls were often angrier at their parents than at the rapists. They felt their parents should have known about the danger and been more protective; afterward, they should have sensed the pain and helped.

Most parents felt like failures. They felt shut out, helpless, and misunderstood. They often attributed the difficulties of this time to their daughters and their own failings. They didn't understand that these problems came with the developmental stage, the culture, and the times.

Parents experienced an enormous sense of loss when their girls entered this new land. They missed the daughters who sang in the kitchen, read them their school papers, and accompanied them on fishing trips and to basketball games. They missed the daughters who liked to bake cookies, play Pictionary, and be kissed good night. In place of their lively, affectionate daughters they now lived with changelings—new girls who were sadder, angrier, and more complicated. Everyone was grieving.

Fortunately, adolescence is time-limited. By late high school most girls are stronger and the winds are dying down. Some of the worst problems—cliques, confusion about identity, and struggles with parents—are on the wane. But the way each girl handles the problems of adolescence can have implications for her adult life. Without some guidance, the loss of wholeness, self-confidence, and self-direction can last well into adulthood. Many of my adult clients in the 1990s wrestled with the same issues that overwhelmed them as adolescent girls. Thirty-year-old accountants and Realtors, forty-year-old homemakers and doctors, and thirty-five-year-old nurses and schoolteachers asked the same questions as their teenage daughters.

Even sadder were the women who were not struggling, who had forgotten that they had selves worth defending. They had repressed the pain of their adolescence and the betrayals of self in order to be pleasing. These women had come to therapy with the goal of becoming even more pleasing to others. They came to lose weight, to talk about their depression, or to rescue their marriage. When I asked them about their own needs, they were confused by the question.

Most women struggled alone with the trauma of adolescence and they lived for years of adult life with their adolescent experiences unexamined. Many tried to forget painful memories of their own adolescence. Then perhaps their daughter's pain awakened their own pain. Some were addicted to pills or alcohol or had stress-related illnesses such as ulcers, colitis, migraines, or psoriasis. Many had tried and failed to be perfect women. Even though they followed the rules and did as they were told, the world had not rewarded them. They felt angry, betrayed, taken for granted, and used rather than loved.

Women I saw in therapy often knew how everyone in their family felt except themselves. They were great at balancing the needs of their coworkers, husbands, children, and friends, but they had forgotten to put themselves into the equation. They struggled with adolescent questions that were still unresolved in their lives: How important were looks and popularity? How do I care for myself and not be selfish? How can

I be honest and still be loved? How can I achieve but not threaten others? How can I be sexual but not a sex object? How can I be responsive but not responsible for everyone?

When I worked with women, the years fell away. We traveled back to their junior highs with the cliques, the shame, the embarrassment about bodies, the desire to be accepted, and the doubts about ability. So many adult women thought they were stupid and ugly. Many felt guilty if they took time to care for themselves. They did not express anger or ask for help.

We pieced together a picture of childhood lost. We reviewed each woman's particular story, her own time in the hurricane. Memories flooded in. Often there were tears, angry outbursts, sadness for what had been lost. So much time had been wasted pretending to be who others wanted. But also, we created a new vibrancy that comes from making connections, from choosing awareness over denial, and from the telling of secrets.

We worked twenty or thirty years behind schedule. We reestablished each woman as the subject of her life, not as the object of others' lives. We answered Freud's patronizing question, "What do women want?" Each woman wanted something different and particular and yet each woman wanted the same thing—to be who she truly was and to become who she could become.

Before I studied psychology, I studied cultural anthropology. I have always been interested in that place where culture and individual psychology intersect, in why cultures create certain personalities and not others, in how they pull for certain strengths in their members, in how certain talents are utilized while others atrophy from lack of attention. I'm interested in the role cultures play in the development of individual pathology. I believe as Gregory Bateson did that "the self is the individual plus her environment."

For a student of culture and personality, adolescence is fascinating.

It's an extraordinary time when individual, developmental, and cultural factors combine in ways that shape adulthood. It's a time of marked internal development and massive cultural indoctrination. In my therapy and writing, I have tried to connect each girl's story with larger cultural issues—to examine the intersection of the personal and the political. It's a murky place; the personal and political are intertwined in all our lives. Our minds, which are shaped by the society in which we live, can oppress us. And yet our minds can also analyze and work to change the culture.

An analysis of the culture cannot ignore individual differences in women. Some women blossom and grow under the most hostile conditions while others wither after the smallest storms. And yet we are more alike than different in the issues that face us. The most important question is, Under what conditions do most young women flower and grow?

Adolescent clients intrigued me as they struggled to sort themselves out. But I wouldn't have written this book had it not been for my clients in the early 1990s. My schedule was packed with girls with eating disorders, alcohol problems, post-traumatic stress reactions, sexually transmitted diseases, self-inflicted injuries, and strange phobias. I met many girls who had tried to kill themselves or run away from home. These clients showed me that something dramatic was happening to adolescent girls in America, something unnoticed by those not on the front lines.

At first, I was surprised that girls were having more trouble in 1994. After all, since the '60s, we'd had a consciousness-raising women's movement. More women were working in traditionally male professions and playing competitive sports. Many fathers helped with housework and child care. It seemed that these changes should count for something. Of course they did, but the progress toward women's empowerment was not even close to complete. The Equal Rights

Amendment had never been ratified, feminism was a pejorative term to many people, and, while some women had high-powered jobs, many women worked hard for low wages and did most of the "second shift" work. The lip service paid to equality made the reality of discrimination even more confusing.

The pressures girls had always faced intensified in the 1990s. Many elements contributed to this intensification: more divorced families, addictions, casual sex, and violence against women. Because of the media, which columnist Clarence Page called "electronic wallpaper," girls all lived in one big town—a sleazy, dangerous metropolis overrun with liquor stores and shopping malls. Increasingly, women had been sexualized and objectified, their bodies marketed to sell tractors and toothpaste. They were more likely to have been traumatized. This combination of old stresses and new was poison for my daughter's generation of young women.

Parents were attempting to manage unprecedented stress as well. For the preceding half century, parents had worried about their sixteen-year-old daughters driving, but in a time of drive-by shootings and carjackings, parents in the 1990s were panicked. Parents had always worried about their daughters' sexual behavior, but in an era of date rapes, herpes, and AIDS, they felt frightened. Traditionally parents had wondered what their teens were doing, but teens in the '90s were much more likely to be doing things that could get them killed. The protected place in space and time that we once called childhood had grown shorter. Parents, teachers, counselors, and nurses realized that girls were in trouble, but they did not realize how universal and extreme the suffering was. *Reviving Ophelia* was an attempt to share what I have seen and heard. It was a hurricane warning, a message to the culture that something important was happening. It was a National Weather Service bulletin from the storm center.

The process of evolving from a happy, emotionally sturdy girl to an anxious and cautious teenager has not changed dramatically over the decades. Puberty in the twenty-first century is essentially the same process it was in 1959 and 1994. Middle schools still host the social and emotional traumas they always have. Fun-loving, curious girls still fly into a Bermuda Triangle and go from Simone de Beauvoir's "being to seeming."

What has changed is that girls are less rebellious and hostile with their parents. Mother/daughter relationships are closer. Also, in the twenty-first century, women are more empowered than were women in the 1990s. They have not been trained to be nonstop full-service nurturers and often have reasonable boundaries and self-care skills. Their daughters respect this about them.

Daughters also have more language to describe the pressures of adolescence. They have some awareness of what they are up against in the culture. High schools host girls' empowerment clubs and teach all students about sexual harassment. Many women and girls, among them the US Olympic gymnasts, actresses Salma Hayek and Cara Delevingne, and musicians Janelle Monáe and Alicia Keys, have become outspoken role models for courage and empowerment.

Most girls today go online in early adolescence. We even have a new word for teenagers: *screenagers*. Almost immediately after girls receive a cell phone, they are exposed to pornography and other inappropriate material. One girl in seventh grade told us, "The first words all my friends googled were 'blow job' and 'anal sex.'" Once girls are online, childhood ends quickly and what replaces it isn't as healthy.

We think of Carson as we write this. She is an authentic, joyful twelve-year-old, just on the cusp of adolescence. She wears her hair in braids and favors colorful tights and T-shirts. Her favorite activities are playing with her two cats and creating art. For hours at a time, she sews and creates origami. Even though she is in middle school, she is still easygoing, curious, and physically affectionate with her parents and little sister. Her friends call her Miss Innocent.

Carson has resisted activities and conversations that push her toward adolescence. However, when she flew to St. Louis alone to visit her grandmother, her parents bought her a cell phone. As soon as she arrived at her grandmother's house, Carson climbed the stairs to the attic, found her American Girl dolls and antique tea set, and played happily while her grandmother fixed lunch.

While she was playing, Carson received a text message from her neighbor from home. Madison's parents had just told her that they were divorcing and she blamed herself because she had been mouthy and difficult at home. Madison told Carson that she wanted to kill herself and begged her not to tell anyone.

The text created a real dilemma for Carson. Her joyful mood was shattered and she felt frightened and overwhelmed. She showed the text to her grandmother and they talked about how to handle the message. Carson decided she would call Madison's mother. She also texted Madison that she loved her and didn't want her to die. She told her, "I need you for a best friend."

Fortunately, Carson and her grandmother were able to talk to Madison's mother who immediately took her daughter to a counselor. But this incident suggests that social media brings complicated situations into girls' lives when they are still children playing with dolls.

Some girls can't afford smartphones or internet access. Some parents ban social media until their daughters are older and a few girls resist it entirely, although statistics reveal that 80 percent of eighth graders are online and 98 percent of high-school students use social media. Adolescent girls check their phones an average of eighty times a day and spend six hours a day online. This is more than any other demographic group.

When a girl owns a device, her transition from child to adolescent can take place in minutes. She is vulnerable to her first image of an anorexic model or text requesting a picture of her in a bikini. As one girl put it: "You are a child and then wham, you are a sexual being. On Facebook in middle school, my peers would make comments about my boobs. I was twelve." Another girl told me, "My mom let me make an Instagram account in sixth grade. She really regrets that. I was not ready for the viciousness of online chatter."

Facebook and the iPhone arrived in the first decade of this century and, in less than twenty years, teens are spending almost all their leisure time online. In 2015, twelfth graders spent twice as much time online as teens did in 2006. Many girls sleep with their phones and check social media during the night. All that screen time alters their physical, social, cognitive, and emotional development.

Over millions of years, our species evolved from a primate line into hominids and then to our current status as *Homo sapiens*. This evolution occurred with us living in groups and cooperating to stay alive and connected. Disconnection for early humans literally meant death. Only in the last century has this pattern of living within communities changed significantly. For just over one decade, humans have used digital devices as a primary means of communication.

We humans are hardwired to be together—to see, hear, touch, and even smell one another. When this stops happening, we lose that most precious of all human resources, our connection to our tribe.

Today because of digital technology, most parents know where their daughters are and girls can quickly access their parents. However, many girls are more attached to their phones than they are to their families. Their digital lives disrupt the critical attunement necessary for deep learning and growth. Russian psychologist Lev Vygotsky discovered that children learn best when they are in a close relationship with their teachers. Attunement and, he would argue, even love, are necessary to grow into whole, authentic humans.

Much of the learning that comes from face-to-face conversation no longer happens. The satisfying feeling of being with a group of beloveds doesn't necessarily occur either. Consequently, both teens and adults are experiencing the deepest levels of loneliness ever recorded.

Today's families exhibit more harmony in part because members are interacting less. Girls feel less need to distance themselves from their parents with mouthiness and troublemaking because their devices are so easily distancing them. Unless parents protect time for family conversations and activities, even at dinner, family members are often texting. Most of the time when girls are home, they are in their rooms on social media. Sometimes parents are too busy with their own devices to protest much about their daughters' time online. In 2019, families are living alone together.

Of course, not all families and not all girls fit the description above. We know girls who work, play in orchestras, volunteer at animal shelters, or spend their time in creative pursuits. Some parents set clear limits for cell phone and computer use. They share hobbies and other activities with their daughters. They belong to communities of families who spend intentional time together at potlucks or sporting events. However, it's important to remember that in 1994, no one fit the description of a device-laden family.

Teenagers can often articulate the negative effects of social media and many say they wish they could control their own use, but social media is designed to be addictive. By nature, humans seek stimulation, news about their friends and family, and positive reinforcement. Social media delivers this positive reinforcement on what psychologists call an "intermittent reinforcement schedule." This schedule for receiving rewards is highly addictive. Fishing and gambling both offer the same kind of intermittent reinforcement.

Neurologists have shown that notifications on social media light up the same dopamine pathways in the brain as alcohol or cocaine. It's easy to become hooked on our own dopamine and, when we are hooked, it's harder to make conscious choices about our behavior. Instead, we act for that dopamine rush.

Other factors such as the fear of missing out (FOMO) and the need for personal validation keep girls on social media. In *Psychotherapy Networker*, psychologist Sharon Begley reported that, in an experiment, when teens were separated from their cell phones, they experienced elevated heart rates and other signs of anxiety. When they could check their iPhones, they calmed back down.

The irony is that, while cell phones may decrease short-term anxiety, they increase long-term anxiety and depression. Like drug and alcohol addictions, they cause short-term rewards and long-term damage. This is true of all addictive behaviors. Teens feel the need to be online, but social media does nothing to assuage their very real anxieties and sorrows.

Kimberly Young's research found that heavy users of social media manifest all the hallmarks of addicts. They had cravings for the phones when they weren't available. They lied about how much time they spent online and, when they tried to limit it, they couldn't. In fact, like all addictions, withdrawing from social media caused serious side effects: irritability, anxiety, sleeplessness, and cravings. Teens who were able to control their behavior and return to a less virtual life did so after a considerable detox program. Only then was the brain sufficiently resilient to break free of the addiction.

As we understand more about online addictions, we are developing treatment centers for Americans addicted to social media and gaming.

The first center was reSTART in Washington State, but by now there are many more such centers across the country.

This continual and increasing dependence on social media worries teachers, doctors, therapists, and parents. Girls receive frequent admonitions to control their use of social media but, in fact, well-meaning adults have trouble controlling their own use of social media and they don't really know how to help teenagers. Computers and cell phones exacerbate an already difficult life stage. Girls today have less protected space, quiet time, and quality time with parents than did their mothers. Meanwhile, they are more susceptible to online bullying, doctored images of beauty, and pressure to be perfect.

Polly (in 1994) and Carson (in 2019) are similar in many ways. They face the physical, social, and emotional changes that go along with becoming an adolescent. They are thoughtful and kind girls, unprepared for the new world they are entering. They are surrounded by loving adults, but adults can't protect them from the larger world they're moving into. They are struggling to adapt and most likely they will eventually succeed in becoming confident, centered women. Meanwhile, they are rudderless and unmoored in the Bermuda Triangle of adolescence, trying not to capsize.

TWO

False Selves, True Selves

CAYENNE (15)

In a home video made when she was ten, Cayenne was wiry and scrappy, all sixty-eight pounds of her focused on the ball as she ran down the soccer field. Her red ponytail bobbed and her face shone with sweat as she ducked in and around the other players, always hustling. When she scored a goal, she held her arms over her head in a moment of self-congratulation. She tossed her parents a proud smile and moved into position for another play.

Her parents loved her willingness to tackle the universe. One day she dressed up like a belly dancer, the next like an astronaut. She liked adults and babies, boys and girls, dogs and sparrows. An absolute democrat, Cayenne treated everyone with respect, and she expected the same from others.

When outraged, she took on the world. She once got a black eye from fighting with a boy who said that girls couldn't play soccer. At a lake on a school picnic, she dunked a much older boy who was throwing rocks at a little turtle. She threatened to hit kids who used racist language or bullied their peers. Because Cayenne was good at standing up for herself and concerned with justice, her teachers predicted she'd go to law school.

In elementary school Cayenne didn't fret much about her appearance. She weighed in once a year at the doctor's office and was pleased with gains in her height and weight chart. She wore jeans and T-shirts unless forced to dress up. Her mother had to beg her to go shopping and remind her to brush her hair.

She walked to school every day with her best friend, Chelsea. She and Chelsea biked together, played on the same ball teams, and helped each other with chores. They talked about everything—parents, school, sports, and their pets. They shared their dreams. Chelsea wanted to be a pilot, and Cayenne wanted to be a doctor. They made up elaborate fantasies in which Chelsea would fly Cayenne into a remote Alaskan village to deliver a baby or amputate the leg of a fisherman.

Cayenne liked school. Her grades were good and she loved projects, especially science projects. She was captain of her school's Destination Imagination team, a group that learned science and technology in fun and creative ways. She'd known most of the kids in her class since kindergarten. She'd played ball with them and gone to their houses for birthday parties.

Cayenne got along well with her parents. Marla, her older sister, had been the moodier and more disobedient child. As an adolescent, Marla used to sneak out of the house to drink with her friends. Cayenne felt sorry for her parents when Marla yelled or made them worry, and she promised she would never act that way.

Of course, Cayenne wasn't perfect. She hated to clean her room and was fidgety in church. She preferred junk food to fruits and vegetables. About twice a year, Cayenne would be cranky and sullen for a day, but mostly she was easygoing. Bad days were so rare that they were events, like Groundhog Day. Her parents came to depend on Cayenne as their emotional centerboard, and they jokingly called her "Old Faithful."

At twelve, Cayenne had her first period. As her body grew rapidly, it became awkward and unpredictable. She gained weight, especially in her hips, and she developed acne. Cayenne moved from her neighborhood school to a junior high with two thousand students. She was nervous the first day because she'd heard rumors that seventh graders' heads were stuffed in the toilets and that boys snapped girls' bras. Fortunately, these things didn't happen, but she came home upset that some boys teased her and that the girls wore makeup and expensive clothes. She was criticized for her JCPenney jeans, and even Chelsea begged her to give up soccer practice and spend Saturday with her at the mall.

Cayenne grew quieter and less energetic. For the first time, she needed to be coaxed into spending time with her family. She stopped wanting hugs from her parents and brushed them away when they approached her. She rarely laughed or talked to them.

Her parents expected some of this. When Cayenne became self-conscious about her appearance, it saddened them, but they knew this was "normal." They were more upset when she quit playing soccer and when her grades dropped, even in science, which Cayenne considered hard and boring.

Meanwhile Chelsea's parents divorced and Chelsea fell in with a wild crowd. She invited Cayenne to join and called her a coward when she hesitated. Eventually Cayenne became part of the group. Her parents suspected that this crowd might be using alcohol or drugs. They encouraged Cayenne to do more with other girls, but she complained about cliques. They tried to steer her toward sports and school activities, but she felt these activities were for nerds.

I met Cayenne the winter of her ninth-grade year. I believed that Cayenne and her parents needed help. During our first meeting, Cayenne scrunched between her parents wearing a T-shirt that said, IF YOU DON'T LIKE LOUD MUSIC, YOU'RE TOO FUCKING OLD. Her body posture signaled, "My parents can force me to be here but nobody can make me talk." When I offered her a soda, she rolled her eyes and said, "Color me excited."

Her mother said, "Cayenne acts like she's allergic to us. Everything we do is wrong."

Her father talked about her grades, her friends, the herpes she'd contracted, and depression, but most of all he mourned their lost relationship. Cayenne had been so close to them and so much fun. She was no longer "Old Faithful"—her bad days outnumbered her good. He thought that even Marla, Cayenne's older sister, had been easier to deal with. At least she hadn't contracted a sexually transmitted disease. After he shared his concerns, he asked, "Does Cayenne need to be hospitalized, or is she just acting like a fifteen-year-old?" *Good question*, I thought to myself.

Later, I met with Cayenne alone. Her blue eyes were icy under her frizzy red hair. She glared at me, almost daring me to make her talk. I sensed that while her surface behavior was angry and withdrawn, underneath she was hurting. I searched for a way to begin.

Finally Cayenne asked, "Do shrinks analyze dreams?"

"Do you have one?"

Cayenne told me of a recurring dream in which she was asleep in her upstairs bedroom. She heard footsteps on the stairs and knew who was coming. She listened, terrified, as the steps grew louder. An old man leading a goat walked into her room. He had a long, sharp knife. Cayenne lay in her bed unable to move while he began slicing at her toes. He sliced off pieces of her and fed them to the goat. She usually awoke when he reached her knees. She'd be covered with sweat and her heart would be racing wildly. Afterward she was afraid to go back to sleep for fear the man would return.

When she finished, I asked her what she thought the dream meant.

She said, "It means I'm afraid of being cut up and eaten alive." Over the next few months Cayenne talked in fragments, almost in code. Sometimes she talked so softly that I couldn't hear her. She wasn't happy in junior high and missed her old school. She missed her sister, Marla, who was away at college. Although she was sure it was they, not she, who had changed, Cayenne missed the closeness she had had with her parents.

Cayenne's demeanor was cautious and her speech elliptical, but she kept coming to therapy. She hated her looks. She thought her hair was too bright, her hips and thighs too flabby. She tried to lose weight but couldn't. She dyed her hair, but it turned a weird purple color and dried out. She thought every girl was prettier than she was. "Let's face it, I'm a dog," she said. She didn't feel comfortable around her old friends.

We talked about the girls in her class who teased her about her clothes and about the boys who gave her a hard time. Everything was unpredictable. One week she felt reasonably comfortable and accepted, the next she felt like a pariah. She told her friends secrets only to have them spread all over the school. She was included one day in a clique and left out the next. Some days guys called her a slut, other days these same boys would flirt with her.

She felt pressure to use drugs and alcohol. "I was the perfect angel in grade school," she said. "I never planned to smoke or drink, but all of a sudden, alcohol was everywhere. Even the president of the Just Say No Club got loaded all the time."

School, which had once been fun, was now a torment. Cayenne groaned, "School's just the way the government babysits kids." We talked about her parents' rules, which had become much stricter after her herpes diagnosis. Her protests were surprisingly weak. She felt ambivalent about her parents—part of her felt guilty about all the fights with them, while another part blamed them for not understanding the pressure she was under and not keeping her safe.

I recommended she write down three things every day that she felt proud of. I asked her to write me a letter telling me her good qualities. She wrote that she was proud of mowing the lawn, doing dishes, and going to church with her grandmother. As for good qualities, she liked her belly button and her feet. When I pressed her for personality characteristics, she said that she liked her courage and directness. At least, she could remember being that way.

One session, dressed in sweats and red-nosed from a bad cold, Cayenne told me that Chelsea was afraid she was pregnant. She had missed a period and tested positive on a home test. We had a general discussion of girls getting pregnant, teenage mothers, and birth control. Cayenne was happy to discuss her friend's sexual behavior, but she volunteered nothing about her own.

The next session she said that Chelsea was not pregnant and had renounced sex until she was sixteen. She and Chelsea had gone to the movies to celebrate her decision. We talked about *Mermaids*, the movie they had seen in which a teenage girl has graphic sex with a guy she barely knows. I asked Cayenne what she thought of that. She said, "It tells it like it is."

When I told Cayenne about the MTV videos I had watched in a hotel room in Chicago, she shrugged. I had been shocked by the sexual lyrics and scenes. In the first video, openmouthed and moaning women writhed around the male singer. In the second video, four women with vacant eyes gyrated in low-cut dresses and high black boots. It seemed that male singers weren't complete without an entourage of "Video Vixens."

We talked about the film *The Silence of the Lambs*. Much to my dismay, she insisted on describing to me the images of skinned women and oozing body parts. Violence that upset me didn't bother her. In fact, Cayenne was proud of being able to watch scary and graphic scenes—it proved she wasn't a wimp. Despite our different reactions to media, the talk raised important issues—lookism, sexism, cultural stereotypes of men and women, and the prevalence of violence and casual sex in movies.

Finally Cayenne was ready to talk about her own sexual experiences, at first in a tentative way, and later in a more relaxed manner. She made fun of the school's sex education films with their embryos and cartoon sperm that looked like tadpoles. She said her parents told her to wait for sex until she was out of high school and involved with someone whom she loved.

I asked, "How does your experience fit with what your parents told you?"

Cayenne looked at me wide-eyed. "My parents don't know anything about sex."

She pushed back her frizzy bangs. "In seventh grade everyone was sex-crazy. Kids kept asking me if I did it, if I wanted to get laid, stuff like that. Guys would grab at me in the halls. I was shocked, but I didn't show it. Later I got used to it."

By the middle of her eighth-grade year, Cayenne wanted to have sex. Her friends said it was fun and they teased her about being a virgin. But she was scared—she wondered if it would hurt, if she would get AIDS or become pregnant, or if the boy would lose respect for her. She told me she knew that "boys who have sex are studs, but girls who do it are sluts." The summer before ninth grade she and Chelsea went to an unsupervised party. A guy she knew from the Destination Imagination team was there. Tim had been innocent and clean-cut in sixth grade. Now he was a sophomore with long hair pulled back in a headband and he had a sarcastic sense of humor.

Tim's friend had invited ten girls and nine guys. He opened his parents' liquor cabinet and poured cinnamon schnapps for the girls and scotch for the guys. Cayenne hated the cough-syrup taste, but because she was nervous, she drank it. Tim came over and sat by Cayenne. He complimented her shirt and joked about all the geeks at the party. He poured refills. Tim's friend put on a Depeche Mode album and turned off all the lights.

Cayenne was nervous and excited. Tim put his arm around her and kissed her on the forehead. They whispered for a while, then made out. All the other kids were doing the same thing. Some moved off into other rooms.

"I knew this would be the night," Cayenne said softly. "I was surprised by how fast things happened. We had sex in the first hour of the party."

After that night, she and Tim called each other for the next month. They talked about school, music, and movies—never sex. They lived in different parts of town and couldn't figure out how to meet each other. Twice they made elaborate plans that fell through. After a while, both became interested in kids at their own schools and they drifted apart.

I asked her how she felt about Tim now. Cayenne rubbed her forehead. "I wish it had been more romantic."

Cayenne was a typical therapy client. She'd had a reasonably happy childhood. With puberty, the changes and challenges in her life overwhelmed her, at least temporarily. Her grades fell, she dropped out of sports, and she relinquished her dream of being a doctor. As she moved from the relatively protected space of an elementary school into the more complex world of junior high, all her relationships grew turbulent. She had decisions to make about adult issues such as alcohol and sex. And after having sex with Tim, she contracted herpes.

When I first worked with girls like Cayenne, I was lost myself. I had been educated by male psychologists in the 1970s. With the exception of Carol Gilligan's work, almost all theory about teenagers had been authored by men who had mainly studied boys.

I found girls to be preoccupied with complicated and intense relationships. They felt obligated and resentful, loving and angry, close and distant, all at the same time with the same people. Sexuality, romance, and intimacy were all jumbled together and they needed sorting. My clients' symptoms seemed connected to their age and their common experiences. Certain themes, such as concern with weight, fear of rejection, and the need for perfection, seemed rooted in cultural expectations for women rather than in the "pathology" of each individual girl. Girls struggled with mixed messages: Be beautiful, but beauty is only skin deep. Be sexy, but not sexual. Be honest, but don't hurt anyone's feelings. Be independent, but be nice. Be smart, but not so smart that you threaten boys.

Adolescent girls in therapy presented me with all kinds of problems that my education and experience didn't help me solve. When I stubbornly tried traditional methods of psychotherapy, they didn't work. Girls dropped out of therapy, or even worse, they came in obediently, chatted obligingly, and accomplished nothing. I thought a great deal about my adolescent clients. I wanted to conceptualize their problems in ways that actually led to positive action, and I tried to connect their surface behaviors with their deeper struggles. I found help from the writings of Alice Miller.

Miller was an expert on the sacrifice of wholeness. In *The Drama of the Gifted Child*, she describes how some of her patients lost their true selves in early childhood. She believed that, as young children, her patients faced a difficult choice: They could be authentic and honest, or they could be loved. If they chose wholeness, they were abandoned by their parents. If they chose love, they abandoned their true selves.

Her patients' parents taught their children that only a small range of thoughts, emotions, and behaviors would be tolerated. The children disowned that which wasn't tolerated. If anger was not tolerated, they acted as if they felt no anger. If sexual feelings were not permitted, they acted as if they had no sexual urges. As children, Miller's patients chose parental approval and experienced a loss of their true selves. They stopped expressing unacceptable feelings and engaging in the unacceptable behaviors, at least in front of adults. They stopped sharing unsanctioned thoughts. The part of them that was unacceptable went underground and eventually withered from lack of attention. Or the part that was unacceptable was projected onto others.

Miller believed that as the true self was disowned, the false self was elevated. If others approved, the false self felt validated and the person was temporarily happy. With the false self in charge, all validation came from outside the person. If the false self failed to gain approval, the person was devastated.

This loss of the true self was so traumatic that her patients repressed it. They had only a vague recollection of what was lost, a sense of emptiness and betrayal. They felt vulnerable and directionless—happy when praised and devastated when ignored or criticized. They were like sailboats with no centerboards. Their self-worth changed with the direction of the wind.

Miller contrasted adults with false selves to authentic adults who experienced all feelings in an honest way. Authentic adults accepted themselves rather than waiting for others to accept them. She called this state of psychological health vibrancy. Her weapon against mental illness was "the discovery and emotional acceptance of the truth of each individual." She encouraged her patients to recognize, grieve for, and eventually accept what happened to them as young children. Only then could they become authentic adults.

Of course, this process is not an either-or phenomenon. In fact, the creation of a false self follows a continuum that ranges from basic socialization to abuse. It is present in all families: All parents accept and reject some of their children's behaviors and teach children to sacrifice some wholeness to social acceptability. And even the most authoritarian parents usually don't succeed in totally destroying the true selves of their children.

Miller wrote in a different time and place. What is timeless and important about Miller's work is her description of the process by which the self splits. With great clarity she describes the splitting into false versus true selves and documents the damage that this splitting can do. She also describes the therapeutic process for reclaiming the true self.

Something analogous to Miller's splitting occurs for girls in early adolescence. Whereas Miller sees the parents as responsible for the splitting in early childhood, I see the culture as splitting adolescent girls into true and false selves.

Often parents are fighting hard to save their daughters' true selves. Parents encourage their daughters to stay with their childhood interests and argue with them over issues such as early sexual activity, makeup, diets, and dating. They encourage athletics and math and science classes. They resist cultural definitions of their daughters as consumers or sex objects. They do not want their daughters to sell their souls for popularity. They are fighting to preserve wholeness and authenticity.

As daughters move into the broader culture, they care what their friends, not their parents, think. They model themselves after media stars, not parental ideals. Because of girls' developmental stage, parents have limited influence. Cayenne, for example, would barely speak to her parents. And when they did speak, they argued. As Cayenne's mother put it, "When I ask her a question, it's like I am tossing a hand grenade into a fireworks store."

With puberty, girls face enormous cultural pressure to split into their false selves. It comes from advertising, television, music, and peers. Girls can be true to themselves and risk abandonment by their peers, or they can reject their true selves and be socially acceptable. In public, most girls become who they are supposed to be.

Authenticity is an "owning" of all experience, including emotions and thoughts that are not socially acceptable. Girls lose confidence as they "disown" themselves. They suffer enormous losses when they stop expressing their true thoughts and feelings.

Cayenne exemplified the process of disowning the true self. With puberty she moved from being a whole, authentic person into a diminished, unhappy version of herself. Her dream of being cut into pieces and fed to a goat reflected quite emphatically her loss of wholeness. Many girls I worked with in the 1990s reported dreams like Cayenne's. They dreamed of drowning, of being paralyzed, and of being stuck in quicksand. A common dream was of being attacked and unable to scream or fight back in any way. The attackers varied: men, schoolmates, insects, or snakes. The important elements of the dream are the attack, the paralysis, and the imminent destruction of the self.

With adolescence, Cayenne began to operate from a false self. When she said, "Let's face it, I'm a dog," she accepted society's right to define her solely on the basis of her appearance. She even defined herself that way. Earlier, she had fought to save a turtle and defend her ideals, now she stopped protesting even when her bodily integrity was threatened.

As she adopted a false self, Cayenne lost her confidence, calmness, and direct speech. She distanced from her parents, who encouraged her to remain true to herself. Her surface behavior and her deeper feelings were not congruent. She no longer behaved in a way that met her true needs. Her decisions were not thoughtful, conscious choices, but rather reactions to peer pressure. Cayenne was off course and unfocused. She abandoned her plan to be a doctor.

Cayenne experienced what all girls experienced in the 1990s—rigorous training for the female role. In early adolescence, girls were expected to sacrifice parts of themselves on the altar of social acceptability and to shrink their souls down to a petite size that fits societal expectations. The rules for women were: be attractive, be a lady, be unselfish and of service, make relationships work, and be competent without complaint.

Girls learned to be nice rather than honest. Cayenne told me, "The worst punishment is to be called a bitch. That will shut anyone up." She continued, "If I'm having a bad day, teachers and kids tell me to smile. I've never heard them say that to a guy."

The rules for girls were confusing and the deck was stacked against them, but they soon learned that this was the only game in town. One high school client remembered that when she was in seventh grade, she wished someone would tell her what was expected of her. She said, "It was so hard to play the game correctly without knowing the rules."

While the rules for proper female behavior weren't clearly stated, the punishment for breaking them was harsh. Girls who spoke frankly were labeled as bitches. Girls who were not attractive were scorned. The rules were reinforced by the visual images in soft- and hard-core pornography, by song lyrics, by casual remarks, by criticisms, by teasing and jokes.

Many of the young women I taught at the university remembered their choices—to be quiet in class rather than risk being called a brain, to diet rather than eat when they were hungry, to go out with the right crowd rather than the girls they liked, and to be pretty rather than have fun. One girl put it this way: "You have to suffer to be beautiful." But generally, at the time it happens, girls are inarticulate about the trauma.

The issues that '90s adolescent girls struggled with were barely discussed in the culture. Language didn't fit their experiences. Protest was called delinquency, frustration was called bitchiness, withdrawal was called depression, and despair was labeled hormonal. Many battles for the self were won and lost without reports from the front lines.

There were many different experiences that caused girls to relinquish their true selves. In early adolescence, girls learned how important appearance was in defining social acceptability. Attractiveness was both a necessary and a sufficient condition for girls' success. This was an old, old problem: Helen of Troy didn't launch a thousand ships because she was a hard worker. Juliet wasn't loved for her math ability.

The Ladies' Guide to Health, written in 1888, pointed out that while boys were dressed for winter in wool pants, jackets, and sweaters, girls were dressed in silks and laces that fell gracefully from their shoulders and left their arms exposed. The author bemoaned the deaths of girls from diphtheria and pneumonia.

Teen magazines in the 1990s were a good example of the training in lookism that girls received. Once when Sara was sick I wanted to buy her some light reading. When I picked up her antibiotics at the drugstore, I leafed through the magazines. The models all looked six feet tall and anorexic. The emphasis was on makeup, fashion, and weight. Girls were encouraged to spend money and to diet and work out to develop the looks that would attract boys. Apparently attracting boys was the sole purpose of life, because the magazines had no articles on careers, hobbies, politics, or academic pursuits. I couldn't find one that wasn't preaching the message, "Don't worry about feeling good or being good, worry about looking good."

Girls come of age in a misogynistic culture in which men have most political and economic power. Girls read a history of Western civilization that is essentially a record of men's lives. As the Australian scholar Dale Spender wrote, "Women's accomplishments are relegated to the lost and found." As girls study Western civilization, they become increasingly aware that history is the history of men. History is His Story, the story of Mankind.

I discovered this when I read H. G. Wells's *Outline of History* and Winston Churchill's *History of the Western World*. Both are primarily histories of war and the distribution of property. Women's lives were ignored except as they influenced the course of men's lives. Sara made the same observation about her high school history text. "It's so boring, just a bunch of kings and generals fighting each other. What were the women and kids doing anyway?"

Girls move into a culture with a Constitution that originally gave property-owning white men, not all Americans, the right to vote, and that has yet to pass an Equal Rights Amendment. They join a culture in which historical documents proclaim the rights of man. Women's voices have been silenced through the ages, and the silencing continues in the present.

By junior high, girls in the 1990s sensed their lack of power, but usually they could not articulate what they sensed. They saw that most congressmen, principals, bankers, and corporate executives were men. They noticed that most famous writers, musicians, and artists were men. But they did not focus on the political—their complaints were personal.

What girls said about gender and power issues depended on how they are asked. When I asked my therapy clients if they were feminists, most said no. To them, *feminism* was a negative word, like *communism* or *fascism*. But if I asked if they believed men and women should have equal rights, they said yes. When I asked if their schools were sexist, they were likely to say no. But if I asked if girls were ever harassed sexually at their school, they said yes and told me stories. If I asked who wrote most of the material they studied at school, they knew it's men. If I asked who is more likely to be a principal, they said a man.

I encouraged my adolescent clients to bring me examples of discrimination. One girl noticed that the mountains in Colorado that were named for men had their last names. She brought in a map to point out Mount Adams, Mount Audubon, Babcock Peak, Mount Edwards, Mount Garfield, Hilliard Peak, and Mount Sneffels. The few natural features that are named for women are named with only the woman's first name, such as Mount Alice, Mount Emma, Mount Eva, Lake Emmaline, Lake Agnes, Maggie Gulch, and Mount Flora.

I remember the trouble I had with misogynistic writers. I loved Tolstoy, but realized when I read *The Kreutzer Sonata* that he detested women. Later I had the same experience with Schopenhauer, Henry Miller, and Norman Mailer. Sara read Aristotle in a philosophy class. One night she read a section aloud and said, "This guy doesn't respect women." I wondered what it meant to her that one of the wisest men of the ages was misogynistic.

It was important for girls to be exposed to more women writers, but, equally important, we needed to change the way women were portrayed in the media. Not many girls read Tolstoy in the 1990s, but almost all watched television. On the screen they saw women mainly depicted as half-clad and half-witted, often awaiting rescue by quick-thinking, fully clothed men. I asked many clients to study the ways women were portrayed on television. We talked about their observations and I'd inquire, "What does this teach you about the role of women?"

"Men are the doctors and scientists who give product endorsements," Cayenne noted. "Women's bodies sell products that have nothing directly to do with women—tires, tractors, liquor, and guns."

She also noticed that television almost never featured old, heavy, or unattractive women and that, even if a woman was a doctor or a scholar, she looked like a Playboy bunny. Many movie plots had to do with women being raped, beaten, chased, or terrorized by men. Sex scenes often had scary music, and violent scenes had sexy music so that sex and violence were all mixed up.

Another client hated the Old Milwaukee beer ads that feature the

Swedish Bikini Team, in which a group of bikini-clad women parachuted onto a beach to fulfill the sexual thirsts of a beer-drinking man. She said, "Women are portrayed as expensive toys, as the ultimate recreation." She brought in cologne ads. A Royal Copenhagen ad showed a seminaked woman kissing a man. The tagline was: "Some of the wildest things happen below deck." She showed me an ad for liquor showing a woman in a short, tight skirt sitting on a man's lap locked in a passionate embrace. She said, "It looks like he'll get sex if he buys this alcohol."

To my embarrassment, one client brought in a magazine from my own waiting room. It was an alumni magazine that featured the arts and sciences. In the glossy thirty-five-page magazine, there were forty-five photographs, forty-four of which pictured males. The one female pictured was on the last page in an article on ballet classes. A male teacher posed with a young girl in a tutu.

Ironically, bright and sensitive girls are most at risk for problems. They are likely to understand the implications of the media around them and be alarmed. They have the mental equipment to pick up our cultural ambivalence about women, and yet they don't have the cognitive, emotional, and social skills to handle this information. Often they are paralyzed by complicated and contradictory data that they cannot interpret. They struggle to resolve the unresolvable and to make sense of the absurd. It's this attempt to comprehend the whole of adolescent experience that overwhelms bright girls.

These bright girls often look more vulnerable than their peers who have picked up less or who have chosen to deal with all the complexity by blocking it out. Later, bright girls may be more adaptive and authentic, but in early adolescence they just look shell-shocked.

Girls have four general ways in which they can react to the cultural pressures to abandon the self. They can conform, withdraw, be depressed, or get angry. Whether girls feel depression or anger is a matter of attribution—those who blame themselves feel depressed, while those who blame others feel angry. Often they blame their parents. Of course, most girls react with some combination of the four general ways.

To totally accept the cultural definitions of femininity and conform to the pressures is to kill the self. Girls who do this are the "Barbie dolls" with hair and smiles in place and a terrible deadness underneath. They are the ones who make me want to shout, "Don't give up, fight back!" Often girls who try to conform overshoot the mark. For example, girls with anorexia try too hard to be slender, feminine, and perfect. They become thin, shiny packages, outwardly carefully wrapped and inwardly a total muddle.

Girls have long been trained to be feminine at considerable cost to their humanity. They have been evaluated on the basis of appearance and caught in myriad double binds: achieve, but not too much; be polite, but be yourself; be aware of our cultural heritage, but don't comment on the sexism. Another name for this training could be false-self training. Girls are educated to be what the culture wants of its young women, not what they themselves want to become.

America is a girl-destroying place. Everywhere, girls are encouraged to sacrifice their true selves. Their parents may fight to protect them, but their parents have limited power. Many girls lose contact with their true selves, and when they do, they become extraordinarily vulnerable to a culture that is all too happy to use them for its purposes.

Alice Miller said, "It is what we cannot see that makes us sick." It's important for girls to explore the impact the culture has on their growth and development. They can all benefit from consciousness-raising. Once girls understand the effects of the culture on their lives, they can fight back. They learn that they have important choices to make and ultimate responsibility for those choices. Intelligent resistance keeps the true self alive.

Today, the culture for adolescent girls feels both totally different and exactly the same as it did in 1994. Girls today struggle with all the developmental challenges that puberty brings. There are still girls in as much trouble as Cayenne, but the proportion of girls like her is much smaller. Teen pregnancy, drug and alcohol use, and lawbreaking behavior are on the wane. We found in our interviews and focus groups that many adolescent girls are more likely to go to dinner and a movie with their parents than sneak out to a keg party. One vivid example of the changes is that in 1994, the greatest punishment a girl could receive was to be grounded from going out with friends. Now it is taking away her smartphone.

The rules for girls around femininity have loosened considerably since the 1990s. Girls have more permission to dress and act in what used to be considered tomboyish ways. At home and at school, adults encourage girls to be all they can be. However, there are still many constraints, including the glass ceiling and harsh condemnation of angry women. Hillary Clinton, Lindy West, and Serena Williams are examples of strong women who have been treated differently than men and have been demonized for their assertive personalities.

Most girls look on screens rather than in magazines for their fashion tips, but the standards for beauty remain the same. Fashion, movies, and music have changed. Tori Amos has been replaced by Lorde, and Beyoncé sits on Madonna's throne, but the cultural messages to girls remain: be sexy, but not a slut; be attractive at all costs; be who others want you to be. If anything, in the last twenty years, the gap between the true and the false selves has widened.

There's a simple reason for this: girls spend a great deal of their lives online, and their online presence is extraordinarily different from reality. The online world runs on pretense, with doctored selfies and videos, created personas, always-positive personalities, and sexualized presentations. Online presentation pushes girls toward promoting a perfect and utterly false self. Meanwhile, the true self is buried at best or, at worst, not even developed.

In our focus groups, many girls could articulate what is wrong with social media but said, in the same breath, that they couldn't live without it.

"When you're a kid, you're not self-conscious about what you look like when you are doing things," Aspen said. "But after you go online . . . look out!"

"Every post or selfie has to be an advertisement for myself," Jordan added. "I mean, it's gratifying to be told I'm pretty, but my self-esteem is totally tied to how people react to my online presentation."

"I know," agreed Aspen. "I am crushed when I see that my friends have more Instagram followers than me."

"I look at pages on fitness, exercise, and fashion, but I can't tell what's real," said Kendyl. "Does this exercise product really work? Is that model that curvy or is she a computer-generated bot? And then there's the whole issue of FOMO."

Izzie, who was stretched out next to Kendyl on our sofa, dramatically threw her hands into the air. "Oh my God, FOMO! The struggle is real. When I'm not online I feel as if I am missing out, but I sometimes wonder if I am missing out on real life."

Izzie went on, "After an evening online, I go to bed feeling unhappy with my day. I wonder, 'What did I do all day long?' Then I wake up and do the same things the next day."

"I follow celebrities on Insta," said Jada. "It warps my worldview. I find myself thinking that everyone but me is rich and famous."

Amalia sighed and added, "I've discovered there are no real answers for me on the internet. Maybe I can find out the year a president was born or if a restaurant is open, but the internet won't tell me how I feel, what I need, or who I am. Social media sites are made for the sender, not the receiver. The sender may feel good showing us her pictures of Jamaica or Hawaii, but the pictures won't help us feel happier."

"Facebook makes my stomach hurt," said Kendyl.

"It gives me hives," chimed in Olivia. All the girls nodded in sympathy.

Social media bombards girls with images of happy, popular girls with perfect bodies and keeps them caught in a twenty-four-hour whirlwind of potential self-hate and negative self-talk. Girl power is constantly used as a slogan to sell makeup and diets. YouTube stars or celebrities often model the smallest possible of souls in the most sexualized of packages. Watching an endless parade of selfies online, girls are likely to want to be rich, famous, and sexually appealing.

A 2007 American Psychological Association study found that girls were highly sexualized in virtually every form of media from toys to clothes to movies and the internet. They were presented as objects of desire rather than as real people with interests, goals, and personalities of their own. Online pornography is not only readily available, it is hard to avoid.

It's always been difficult for girls to stay true to their deepest goals and values and to act from a centered, authentic place, but when girls are online six hours a day, they have little opportunity to search for that deep central core we call the true self.

For example, we know there are two basic kinds of motivation. With intrinsic motivation, we feel rewarded when we meet our own goals and standards. That kind of motivation comes from a deep sense of who we are and what we want. Extrinsic motivation is when we act in the hope of acceptance and praise. When girls are online, they are constantly seeking external validation. Life becomes a search for likes and followers. This leaves girls vulnerable to whatever pops up next on their screen.

Many girls in 2019 are never truly alone. They are texting while they dress for school and in the middle of the night. In the 1960s, girls were free to walk or bike wherever they wanted and most spent time alone. In 1994, before personal computers and cell phones, girls still had time to journal, read, rearrange their rooms, paint, or simply reflect.

Quiet time creates reflective people. For example, in 1994, girls on high school swim teams might have worked out four hours a day and, over the course of several years, many became thoughtful, mature people. That time in the pool helped them sort their lives out and ponder the great questions. Now, even teens swimming underwater wear earbuds and listen to music or podcasts; they are focused on voices besides their own.

It takes commitment and reflection to find the true self. Especially in adolescence, girls need time alone to integrate the many rapidly changing aspects. Through introspection, girls develop into more mature, resilient people. Quiet alone time encourages the cultivation of the true self with its vibrancy, authenticity, and self-knowledge.

With less focus and more impulsivity, girls find it harder to develop a sense of self and an internal compass. If they maintain a constant focus on the number of likes on their selfies, their own true north will remain elusive.

Parents can support girls' search for their true selves in many ways. In one family we know, everyone keeps a journal and occasionally they share their writing with one another. Another mother and daughter treat themselves to a dinner out each month, just to snag a few hours of togetherness. Rasheeda lives in New York City, and she and her daughter love the Cloisters, a peaceful museum of medieval art that overlooks the Hudson River. As frequently as they can—in the midst of their highly scheduled lives—mother and daughter take the subway north for a few hours of reflection and conversation in a beautiful environment. Parents can build these types of activities into their daughters' lives, and they can also help girls access books, blogs, and magazines that can aid them in navigating early adolescence. What matters most is that they simply ask their daughters to talk about what they enjoy and value and then really listen.

Adolescence is a time for identity building, which is no small task in any time and place. Identity comes from introspection, deep talks with friends about one's place in the universe, and from time spent with grandparents, cousins, uncles, and aunts who help girls see themselves in the context of a family and community.

One of the sad paradoxes for adolescent girls today is that while they greatly value freedom and tolerance, they are captives of their devices and are imprisoned by their need for continual affirmation. Instead of searching for their true selves, they cultivate Instagram followers.

True freedom requires knowing oneself, a strong sense of intention, and careful choices about actions. In the era of social media, this kind of true freedom is rare. As Jada said, "I had the power to decide my own future, but I didn't know how to decide what I wanted."

Fortunately, some girls manage to turn away from the virtual world and search for their authentic identities. They discover and stay connected to their true selves, and in doing so they also set an example for other girls.

"I was hooked on Tumblr until I realized it perpetuated my depression," Emily explained. "Everyone on it was so cool and perfect. I could never compete with that. Then one day a girl in my biology class said, 'Why don't you just quit social media?' I know it's hard to believe, but I'd never thought of that!"

Emily didn't quit cold turkey, but she limited her social media use to thirty minutes a day. She told her friends that she looked at her Instagram just before dinner every night and then turned off her phone. She said that she couldn't respond to all their messages and that her lack of response would not be personal. She asked for their support, which her friends gave her. A year later, Emily was extremely grateful she had limited her time online. She felt calmer and more in control of her destiny.

"I read thirty-seven novels last year and I've been calling my great-aunt one night a week," she proudly announced to our focus group. "I'm thinking of getting a job after finals."

Emily is a strong girl who is in touch with her true self. She protected herself from continual pummeling from social media, which allowed her to slow down, think, and filter her decisions through her emerging sense of who she truly was. She was one of the happiest and most mature girls we met while conducting our research.

Of course, social media is not girls' only problem. Our culture remains sexist and misogynistic, and girls are well aware of this.

"Boys and even girls blame sadness, irritability, and frustration on PMS," Maddie said. "That really annoys me."

"When our school recruited a new principal, my English teacher told me that three 'girls' and one man interviewed for the job," Gracie added. "Guess who was hired—a man or a girl?"

Men still hold the most public power in our country. Women in America can't be powerful and competitive and still be perceived as likable, and they are never free from comments about their appearance and fashion choices.

In 2018, the World Health Organization and the John Hopkins Bloomberg School of Public Health looked at fifteen countries, including the United States, Belgium, Kenya, China, and India, and found among them a universal stereotype: girls are weak and boys are strong. They reported that girls internalize this stereotype by age ten. They learn it from parents, peers, and teachers. Because of this deep-seated belief, men possess more freedom and women tend to be more constrained. Globally, girls are sent the message that they are vulnerable and their bodies are a target. Girls are taught to be on guard with boys and boys are taught to be aggressors. This becomes a self-fulfilling prophecy.

However, all the current news is not bleak. In the 1950s, few women worked outside the home and their choices of careers were quite limited. In 1994, more women held professional roles, but men generally had a monopoly on management positions. Today more women than men are earning advanced degrees in diverse areas such as law, education, and medicine, and we have achieved a measure of professional parity. Yet women still don't earn equal pay for equal work and we tend to get stuck in middle management. Men dominate in politics and other high-profile professional environments including academia and corporate America.

Over the course of the last century, feminism itself has waxed and waned as a popular idea. In 1959, feminists were women who lived long ago, suffragettes such as Susan B. Anthony and Elizabeth Cady Stanton. However, in the late 1960s modern feminism burst forth with spokeswomen like Gloria Steinem, bell hooks, and Susan Griffin. By 1978, the University of Nebraska offered classes in women's studies, psychology of women, and sex roles and gender. Women were proud to be feminists and active in changing both women's and men's roles.

In 1994, it was not cool to call oneself a feminist. Thanks to Rush Limbaugh and his compadres, the '90s were the era of the "Feminazi." Our culture had spent decades portraying feminists as man-hating, ugly, and aggressive. Who wants to be a member of a group stereotyped in that way?

Now, according to the GenForward research of 2018, 22 percent of adolescent girls identify themselves as feminists and almost all girls say they are feminist in some ways. The women's marches that followed the inauguration of Donald Trump reactivated feelings of solidarity with other women. Most girls adamantly oppose harassment and rigid sex roles. The #MeToo campaign has inspired women and girls to stand up for and protect those who are harassed or sexually assaulted.

Most parents support their daughters' efforts to be strong, bold women. They are aware of the challenges children face today and they have more power to influence their daughters than they did in 1994. At the Women's Marches around the time of Trump's inauguration, many families marched together. Regardless of race, geographic location, or socioeconomic status, mothers and fathers want to help their daughters find and celebrate their true selves.

THREE

Developmental Considerations

CHARLOTTE (15)

Rain drummed on the office windows and rolled down the casings as Rob and Sue, looking weary, talked about their daughter. Charlotte was fifteen, but looked much older in her heavy makeup and tight dress. Her face had a hardness that I hate to see in anyone, especially in someone so young.

Sue thought that Charlotte's problems went back to her divorce, which had occurred when Charlotte was three. Charlotte hadn't missed her father, who was an abusive alcoholic, but she had missed Sue, who immediately began a full-time job at a Quick Shop. Sue looked at her nicotine-stained fingers and said, "After the divorce, I had less of everything—time, money, patience. I think that hurt Charlotte."

As Sue talked, Charlotte sat stiffly, her mouth a tight, thin line. Rob changed the subject. "Sue and I met at a singles group and dated for ten months. We got married when Charlotte was eight. She was our flower girl. Really a cute kid."

"Charlotte was okay till junior high, but then things started going wrong fast," Sue said. "She developed an attitude. She started smoking and dressing like a slut. She slipped out to drink with older kids."

"She's not the only one in trouble," Rob said. "Three of her friends have babies. Our town has one thousand people and three liquor stores. Kids have nothing to do but get into trouble."

Sue added, "We haven't been great supervisors. Rob commutes to manage a Safeway, and I run the Quick Shop six days a week."

Charlotte was in about every kind of trouble an adolescent girl could be in. She was flunking ninth grade. She smoked cigarettes, drank whiskey, and used pot. She had an older boyfriend. She barely spoke to her parents and had tantrums when they tried to keep her safe. A month ago, when they insisted on a drug and alcohol evaluation, Charlotte ran away from home.

For three weeks Rob and Sue worried that she'd been kidnapped or killed. Sue said, "You don't know what fear is until you have a daughter hitchhiking around the country."

Then Charlotte called from Seattle to say she wanted to come home. She sounded frightened and promised to do whatever her parents wanted. That's when they called me for a therapy appointment.

I asked Charlotte if she was willing to work with me for a while. Feigning exasperation, she shrugged elaborately. But over the next few months Charlotte and I figured a few things out. She really had been fine in elementary school. She had played baseball every summer until the town's insurance was canceled and Little League was discontinued. She liked hanging out at the Quick Shop, drinking root beer and reading magazines. She was happy when Rob became her dad. He took her camping and bought her a new bike. He made her mom laugh.

But adolescence changed everything. First it was the ordinary stuff: fights with girls and teasing by the boys. Her breasts developed early and boys were always rubbing against her, grabbing her from behind, and calling her names. She also was heavier than most of her classmates and she worried about her weight. She bought some diet pills and lost weight rapidly. Charlotte loved the light, airy feeling she had on those pills. She started smoking cigarettes to help herself lose even more weight. Charlotte stole her Virginia Slims from the Quick Shop.

Rob and Sue hated her smoking, but they smoked, too, and couldn't take the high moral ground on this issue. Sue and Rob didn't like her friends, her constant dieting, her music, her falling grades, or her mouthiness. Conversations at home became tense and angry. Charlotte stayed in her room or out of the house as much as she could.

The summer of her eighth-grade year she started "partying," a euphemism for getting loaded with friends. She met kids at a river south of town and drank beer and cheap wine around a bonfire until dawn. She told me, "Getting wasted erased my life."

Once Rob showed up looking for her, but she hid behind a cottonwood tree while her friends lied about her whereabouts. Several times Sue and Rob called the police to help find her. Charlotte was grounded, but she slipped out her window. Finally, Rob and Sue had what Charlotte described as an "emotional meltdown." They gave up and let her do what she wanted.

That is, they gave up until she began dating Mel. He was twenty-two and had a job that paid him just enough money to buy beer and lotto tickets. He was good-looking but sleazy, and Rob and Sue were adamant that their daughter couldn't date him.

Unfortunately, Charlotte no longer obeyed them. She wore seductive clothes, dyed her hair platinum blond, and did whatever she pleased. With guys she was quiet and docile, eager to please—exactly the kind of girlfriend Mel wanted. The harder Rob and Sue fought, the more appealing the forbidden fruit became, and eventually they lost this battle too.

When Charlotte talked about Mel, I was surprised by how realistic her perceptions were. She knew he was a loser and disapproved of his heavy drinking and gambling. She even admitted that sometimes she was bored with him. All they did was rent movies and drink at his place. Now and then they fished for catfish and carp, but as Charlotte said, "Those trips are really an excuse to stay out drinking all night."

Mel didn't even like to have sex that often. But Charlotte was fiercely loyal. Mel was the first guy she dated who wanted a relationship with her. As she put it, "With him, it wasn't wham, bam, thank you ma'am."

Mel had confided to her about his own difficult family situation. His father was an alcoholic living in another state. Once Mel came home from school to find all their furniture had been sold to buy booze. He had memories of Christmases without presents, of food baskets from churches delivered by his classmates, and of nice kids not being permitted to play with him.

Charlotte's eyes softened when she talked about Mel. She had a mission to save him and to make him happier than he'd ever been before. She conceded that, so far, Mel didn't seem that happy, but she thought that, in time, he might be.

Mel was the only person she trusted—she hated high-school boys, who "only wanted one thing." Most of the girls at her school were snobs. Her friends who had babies were okay, but they were busy now with their own problems and not able to be there for her. Rob and Sue argued frequently and "weren't as sweetie-sweet as they acted in therapy."

She particularly hated school and her teachers. She felt her math teacher deliberately humiliated her. Whenever he could, her Spanish teacher looked at her breasts. None of her classes had anything to do with real life. The kids who flattered the teachers got the good grades. The lunches were slop. When I asked her if there was anything she liked about school, Charlotte thought for a while. "I'd like biology, if the teacher weren't such a bitch."

One day Charlotte brought up sex. "Before Mel, I needed to be drunk to have sex. Otherwise, I remembered things from the past. When I was high, it didn't matter."

"Have you been raped?" I asked softly.

Charlotte pushed her platinum blond hair off her face and said in a flat voice, "I've had trouble you can't imagine."

She looked younger and more vulnerable as we sat quietly with her words. I didn't push for more information. I knew she would reveal more when she felt ready.

Charlotte faced problems that many girls in the 1990s encountered. She had an abusive, alcoholic father whom her mother had divorced when Charlotte was young. For many years, the family had been poor and overburdened. As a teenager, Charlotte was in all kinds of trouble. Charlotte had made many choices that sacrificed her true self and supported a false self. Her choices showed in her face. There was a deadness to her demeanor that came from giving away too much. Charlotte was evidence of a childhood lost. And what replaced childhood glittered but was not gold. I hoped therapy could help her find herself. It would be reclamation work.

LORI (12)

Lori, whom I had known since her birth, started junior high school at a large school known for its wealthy, competitive students. I visited her home to see how she was adjusting to junior high. We met in her newly redecorated bedroom. She had a white desk neatly arranged with paper, pens, and a dictionary; pink beanbag chairs; and a large glass cage for her gerbil, Molasses, "Mo" for short.

I was struck by how fresh and cheerful she was. She was dressed in green capris. Her short brown hair curled over silver star earrings. She bounced around her room showing me a book she liked, her swim team trophies, and Mo's tricks. Lori made me feel I was in another place and time, back in the 1950s in a home with plenty of money, happily married parents, and children who were not afraid or stressed. The cynical part of me wondered, *Where's the skeleton in the closet?* If I hadn't known this family for twenty years, I would have been even more suspicious about so much happiness.

Lori loved junior high. She had liked elementary school as well, but said that, by the end, she had outgrown it. Junior high was exciting, with its hallways full of kids, nine different teachers, a tableful of friends at lunch, and a swimming pool in the gym.

She was busy in and out of school. She swam and danced several nights a week and sang and acted whenever she had the chance. This year she was taking voice lessons at the university. Her mother was a stay-at-home mom who could run her to all these lessons, rehearsals, and swim meets. Her father was an attorney who could pay for these activities and who showed up for her meets and performances.

Her younger sister, Lisa, also swam and danced. Lori was social and bubbly, Lisa quieter and more introverted. While Lisa curled up with a book or played piano in the living room, Lori talked on the phone for hours. Lori kept most of her old friends and made many new friends at junior high. She said, "I'm popular enough. To be superpopular you have to look like a model and wear expensive clothes."

Lori said she was known for being independent and funny. She said, "I know who I am, and I don't always think like other people think." She was also unusual in that she was relaxed about her appearance. Unlike most of her friends, who awakened early so they would have time to get ready for school, Lori woke up ten minutes before it was time to leave and threw on anything she could find. She ate whatever she wanted and didn't worry about weight. She said, "Lots of my friends wish they could be like me about appearance."

I asked about alcohol and drugs.

"I think they're stupid. I would never consider them."

"What if you were pressured to use them at a party?"

"I'd say, 'You do what you want, I'll do what I want.'" She laughed. "And then I'd leave the party."

She knew some kids who drank, but none of her close friends did. I asked about sexual harassment. Lori scratched the top of her head. "Some of my friends have been hassled, but I haven't been. I know who to avoid. There's this certain hall that I don't walk down."

We talked about dating, a subject Lori had carefully considered. She didn't want to date until she was in high school and even then, not seriously. She believed that sex comes with marriage. I asked her how she felt about music and television shows that depict teenagers having casual sex.

"I turn that stuff off. I don't have time for TV anyway," Lori said. "When I listen to certain music, I don't pay attention to the lyrics."

I said, "It sounds like you screen out things that upset you."

Lori agreed. "Not everything, but things I can't change."

Lori lit up when we talked about dance. She was proud that her teacher had recently moved her into an advanced class. She liked swimming, too, and believed that all the exercise helped her manage stress.

Although she admitted that they could be embarrassing in public, she loved her parents. She felt her dad was too skinny and her mom was overly friendly. She said that just lately her mom had been getting on her nerves. She wanted more privacy than she used to. But still she loved Sunday nights when the family had Cokes, apples, and popcorn, and played cards or watched a movie.

I asked about career goals. She liked dance but suspected it was not a practical career. Lori was proud of her writing and thought she'd like a career in journalism. She had already had an article published in her school's newsletter, and she'd interviewed a reporter for a class project.

When we finished our talk, Lori showed me to the front door, her star earrings flashing. Lisa was practicing on the new grand piano as I left. Her mother sat beside her turning the pages of a Clementi sonatina. Her father read the newspaper nearby.

I thought about Lori as I drove home. She seemed to be holding on to her true self miraculously well. She was social but not overly awed by popularity. She chose to be with friends rather than have a mentor, but she still made straight As. She had kept all her prepuberty interests: singing, dancing, swimming, and acting. She was relaxed about her appearance and didn't worry about her weight. Even though she was slightly embarrassed by her parents, she still loved them and enjoyed spending time with them.

Lori was independent and funny. She made conscious choices about sex, drugs, and alcohol. In fact, she made conscious choices about everything. She looked within herself for guidance and answers. Lori already had sorted her experience into what she could and couldn't control, and she knew how to screen out what was beyond her control. She had a sense of who she was and an orientation toward the future. Though she certainly might change her mind about journalism, the fact that she had a goal demonstrated that her life was not all lived in the moment.

Lori was so well rounded and mentally healthy that I struggled to explain her. Ultimately, I settled on the idea that she was extraordinarily lucky. She had inherited a cheerful, energetic personality. She was pretty, smart, musical, and athletic. Her parents were loving and protective, but not overly protective or demanding. She lived in a safe and prosperous neighborhood surrounded by stable families, and she'd managed to escape being assaulted or traumatized.

She might have more trouble in the next few years than she anticipated. The high school social scene might be tougher, her emotions might become more turbulent, and the time might come when she thought family night is dumb. She was just moving into the time when adolescent girls really struggle. But she was much more likely than most girls to hold on to her true self. She had a strong inner focus. I wished I could wrap a magic cloak around her that would keep her safe. I thought of the last line of a poem that a mother named Netta Gillespie wrote about her child: "I hurl you into the universe and pray."

My horticulturist friend told me that the environment is the richest and most diverse at borders, where trees meet fields, desert meets mountains, or rivers cross prairies. Adolescence is a border between adulthood and childhood, and as such it has a richness and diversity unmatched by any other life stage. It's impossible to capture the complexity and intensity of adolescent girls. I think of one client at twelve, wanting to be a fashion model or a corporate attorney—whichever made more money. And another, a Vietnamese girl who shyly explained that she wanted to go to medical school. I think of Sara belting out songs from *Guys and Dolls* as I drove her to school, of the awkward movements and downcast eyes of a girl who worked in her parents' deli, or the self-assured way that a neighbor girl walked back from the mound after pitching a no-hitter.

Adolescents are travelers, far from home with no native land. They are neither children nor adults. They are jet-setters who fly from one country to another with amazing speed. Sometimes they are four years old, an hour later they are twenty-five. They don't really fit in anywhere. There's a yearning for place, a search for solid ground.

Adolescence is a time of intense preoccupation with the self, the self that is growing and changing daily. Everything feels new. I remember the impulse to hit my mother when she woke me one morning for school. Even as I felt that rage, I was appalled by my weirdness. I recall going weak-kneed when certain boys walked by me in the halls. These moments took my breath away and left me wondering who I was becoming. I was as surprised by my reactions as I would have been by a stranger's.

Sara, at twelve, needed to be reminded to brush her teeth, but she wanted to rent R-rated movies and get a job. One minute she was arguing with us about politics and the next she was begging for a stuffed animal. She wouldn't be seen with me in public, but she was upset if I missed her school programs. She no longer let us hug or kiss her. One night during this time of constant declarations of independence, Sara woke me in the night. She had a fever and wanted me to get a cold cloth and sit by her. I was pleased by this temporary reprieve from her ban on touching.

With adolescence, many kinds of development occur—physical, emotional, intellectual, academic, social, and spiritual—and they don't always occur in tandem. Tall, physically well-developed girls can possess the emotional skills of children. Abstract thinkers in their teens can have the social skills of first graders. These differences in developmental levels within the same girl confound adults. Should adults relate to the fifteen-year-old or the four-year-old part of the girl?

Generally, puberty is defined as a biological process while adolescence is defined as the social and personal experience of that process. But even puberty is influenced by culture. Girls are menstruating much earlier now than they did during the colonial era, and even earlier than in the 1950s. Some girls menstruate at age nine.

There are many theories about why puberty comes earlier—changes in nutrition may hasten girls' growth, hormones added to beef and chicken may trigger early puberty, and even electricity may play a role. Bodies are programmed to enter puberty after exposure to a certain amount of light, which comes much earlier in a woman's lifetime in an age of electricity.

Early development and the difficult culture increase the stress on adolescents. Girls who have recently learned to bake cookies and swan-dive aren't ready to handle offers for diet pills. Girls who are reading about Pippi Longstocking aren't prepared for the sexual harassment they'll encounter in school. Girls who love to practice piano and visit their grandmothers aren't ready for the shunning by cliques. And at the same time that girls must face events prematurely, they are encouraged by our culture to move away from parents and depend on friends for guidance. No wonder they suffer and make so many mistakes.

There is an enormous gap between what I call the surface structure of behaviors and the deep structure of forming an identity and finding our place in the universe. Surface structure is what is visible to the naked eye—awkwardness, energy, anger, moodiness, and restlessness.

Deep structure is the internal work—our individual struggle to create a self, to integrate the past and present, and to find a place in the larger culture. Surface behaviors convey little of the struggle within and in fact are often designed to obscure that struggle.

By definition, the deep-structure questions are not articulated clearly to adults. Rather, the surface questions are coded to speak to larger issues. "Can I dye my hair purple?" may mean, "Will you allow me to develop as a creative person?" "Can I watch R movies?" may mean, "Am I someone who can handle sexual experiences?" "Can I go to a different church?" may mean, "Do I have the freedom to explore my own spirituality?"

Deep-structure questions are processed in a serpentine manner with friends. Endlessly, girls discuss the smallest details of conversations and events—who wore what, who said what, did he smile at her, did she look mad when I did that? The surface is endlessly combed for information about the depths.

This deep structure–surface structure split is one reason girls experience so much failure in relationships. Girls misread one another's true meaning underlying all the surface talk. Communication is confused and confusing. Relationships between friends are so coded that misunderstandings abound. Parents who attend to the surface structure often miss the buried important point. Then girls don't feel heard.

Because the deep-structure work is so serious, the surface behavior is often tension releasing, a way of dispelling internal energy that must escape somehow. This marked difference in behaviors reminds me of my first few years as a therapist. I spent long days being serious, talking about problems. After work, I craved goofing off with my kids, telling stupid jokes, and watching comedies on television. The harder my day, the more I wanted comic relief. Teenage girls are doing therapy all day, too, only it's inside their own heads. They need the time off whenever they can get it.

When I worked with adolescent girls, I tried to understand what their surface behavior was telling me about their deep-structure issues. I tried to ascertain when their behavior was connected to their true selves and when it was the result of pressure to be a false self. Which thinking should I respect and nurture? Which should I challenge?

PHYSICAL SELVES

The adolescent girl's body is changing in size, shape, and hormonal structure. Just as pregnant women focus on their bodies, so must adolescent girls focus on their changing bodies. They feel, look, and move differently than they did when they were younger. These changes must be absorbed, the new body must become part of the self. The preoccupation with bodies at this age cannot be overstated. The body is a compelling mystery, a constant focus of attention. At thirteen, many girls spend more time in front of a mirror than they do on their studies.

Small flaws become obsessions. Bad hair can ruin a day. A broken fingernail can feel tragic.

Generally, girls have strong bodies when they enter puberty. But these bodies soften and spread out in ways that our culture calls fat. Just at the point that their bodies are becoming rounder, girls are told that thin is beautiful, even imperative. Girls hate the required gym classes in which other girls talk about their fat thighs and stomachs. One girl told me of showering next to an eighty-five-pound dancer who was on a radical diet. For the first time in her life she looked at her body and was displeased. One client talked about wishing she could cut off the roll of fat around her waist. Another thought her hips were "hideous."

Geena was a chubby clarinet player who liked to read and play chess. She was more interested in books than makeup and in horses than designer clothes. She walked to her first day of junior high with her pencils sharpened and her notebooks neatly labeled. She was ready to learn Spanish and algebra and to audition for the school orchestra. She came home sullen and shaken. The boy who had his locker next to hers had smashed into her with his locker door and sneered, "Move your fat ass."

That night she told her mother, "I hate how I look. I need to go on a diet."

Her mother thought, *Is that what this boy saw? When he looked at my musical, idealistic Geena, did he see only her weight?*

Girls in the 1990s felt an enormous pressure to be beautiful and were aware of constant evaluations of their appearance; that is still true for girls today. In an art exhibit on the theme of women and appearance, Wendy Bantam put it this way: "Every day in the life of a woman is a walking Miss America Contest." Sadly, girls lose if they are either too plain or too pretty. Girls who are plain are left out of social life and often internalize their peers' scorn. Our cultural stereotypes of the beautiful include negative ideas about their brains—think of the blonde jokes. Beautiful girls are seen primarily as sex objects. Their appearance overdetermines their identity. They know that boys like to be seen with them, but they doubt that they are liked for reasons other than their packaging. Being beautiful can be a Pyrrhic victory. The battle for popularity is won, but the war for respect as a whole person is lost.

The luckiest girls are neither too plain nor too beautiful. They will eventually date, and they'll be more likely to date boys who genuinely like them. They'll have an identity based on other factors, such as sense of humor, intelligence, or strength of character. Still, they don't feel lucky in junior high. A college girl told me, "In junior high I felt doomed because I was too tall. I could not conceive of happiness at that height." Another told of watching a cute blonde in her eighth-grade class flirt with boys. "The same boys who tripped over themselves to open doors for her would look away when I walked by."

Appearance was more important in the 1990s than in the 1950s and early 1960s. Girls who lived in smaller communities were judged more holistically—for their character, family background, behavior, and talents. However, when girls of the '90s lived in cities full of strangers, they were judged exclusively by their appearance. Often the only information teenagers had about one another was how they looked.

What is culturally accepted as beautiful is achieved only with great artifice. Even the stars cannot meet our cultural ideals without great cost. Jamie Lee Curtis, who worked months to get in shape for the movie *Perfect*, felt her body was not right for the part. Jane Fonda and Princess Diana both had eating disorders. Every time I speak in a high school or college class I'm struck by how intense and damaging and widespread these issues are. I ask, "How many of you know someone with an eating disorder?" Usually every hand goes up.

After my talks at schools in the 1990s, girls came up to ask about their friends, their sisters, or themselves. They all had horror stories of girls who were miserable because they didn't quite meet our cultural ideals. With early adolescence, girls surrendered their relaxed attitudes about their bodies and burdened themselves with self-criticism. Just at the point their hips were becoming rounder and they were gaining fat cells, they saw magazines and movies or heard remarks by peers that suggested that their bodies are all wrong. They allowed the culture to define who they should be. Charlotte, mentioned at the beginning of this chapter, thought of her body as something other people would examine and judge. How her body appeared to others—not how it felt to her—was what mattered.

A girl who remains true to herself will accept her body as hers and resist others' attempts to evaluate and define her by her appearance. She's much more likely to think of her body in terms of function than form. What does her body do for her? Lori, for example, was proud of her body's ability to dance and swim. Her self-esteem didn't revolve around her appearance. She eschewed diets and time spent in front of a mirror. Interestingly, even as her friends primped and dieted, they envied her casual attitudes about beauty. Lori cared more about being than seeming. She was lucky because, as de Beauvoir writes, "To lose confidence in one's body is to lose confidence in oneself."

EMOTIONAL SELVES

A friend once told me that the best way to understand teenagers was to think of them as constantly on LSD. That helped explain their goofiness, mood swings, and lack of logic or perspective. It was good advice. People on acid are intense, changeable, internal, often cryptic or uncommunicative, and, of course, dealing with a different reality. That was all true for adolescent girls.

The emotional system is immature in early adolescence. Emotions are extreme and changeable. Small events can trigger enormous reactions. A negative comment about appearance or a bad mark on a test can hurl a teenager into despair. Not only are their feelings chaotic, but girls often lose perspective. Girls have tried to kill themselves because they were grounded for a weekend or didn't get asked to the prom.

Despair and anger are the hardest emotions to deal with, but other emotions are equally intense. Just as sorrow is unmodulated, so is joy. A snowstorm or a new dress can produce bliss. There's still a childlike capacity to be swept away. One girl told me of wandering around in woods reading poetry and feeling in touch with the central core of the universe. She was elated by the sunlight dappling the leaves, the smells of wild plum blossoms, the blueness of the sky, and the songs of meadowlarks. The feeling of the moment was all that existed.

I taught girls to rate their stress as a way to modulate their emotions. I said, "If one is a broken shoestring and ten is a terminal brain tumor, rate things that upset you on this one-to-ten scale." Then I'd ask, "What would you rate your argument with your boyfriend today?" The girl would say, "A fifteen."

This instability of feelings leads to unpredictable behavior in adolescents. A typically energetic teen will be frenetic one moment and lethargic the next. A comment or a look from a parent can start a crying spell or World War III. A girl who is incredibly focused when it's time to plan a skit for prom night is totally disorganized about her social studies project due the same day.

It's hard for adults to keep up with the changes and intensity of adolescent emotions. When Sara was in junior high, I called her every day after school. Some days she was full of laughter and confidence. ("School rocks my world.") Other days she needed crisis intervention over the phone. ("It sucks to be me.")

Girls' emotional immaturity makes it hard for them to hold on to their true selves as they experience the incredible pressures of adolescence. They are whipped about by their emotions and misled by them. At a developmental time when even small events are overwhelming, big events such as date rape or a friend who tests positive for the HIV virus can be cataclysmic.

Girls deal with intense emotions in ways that are true or false to the self. A girl who operates out of her false self will be overwhelmed by her emotional experiences and do what she can to stop having these painful emotions. She may do this by denial of her feelings or by projecting her fear, sadness, and anger onto others. Charlotte did that by running away, by using alcohol and drugs, and by losing herself in a relationship in which she thought only of her boyfriend's feelings. When girls fail to acknowledge their own feelings, they further the development of a false self. Only by staying connected to their emotions and by slowly working through the turbulence of adolescence can young women emerge strong and whole.

Lori was remarkably stable emotionally. She might have had anger and despair, but she managed those emotions by crying, talking, and writing about her emotions. She could sort herself out and move on in a resilient manner. Most likely Lori emerged from adolescence somewhat tattered emotionally but intact. She probably possessed what Alice Miller called "vibrancy."

Thinking Selves

Most early adolescents are unable to think abstractly. The brightest are just moving into formal operational thought or the ability to think abstractly and flexibly. Their immature thinking makes it difficult to reason with them. They read deep meaning into casual remarks and overanalyze glances. They may not know how to tell what is important.

The concreteness of girls' thinking can be seen in their need to categorize others. In the 1990s, people were assigned to groups such as geeks, preps, and jocks. One girl's categories included "deeper than thou," a derogatory term for the poets and artists at her school. Another divided the world into Christian and non-Christian, and another into alternative, nonalternative, and wannabe alternative.

Teenage girls are extremists who see the world in black-and-white terms, missing shades of gray. Life is either marvelous or not worth living. School is either pure torment or is going fantastically. Other people are either great or horrible, and they themselves are wonderful or pathetic failures. One day a girl will refer to herself as "the goddess of social life" and the next day she'll regret that she's the "ultimate in nerdosity." This fluctuation in sense of self would suggest severe disturbance in an adult, but in teenage girls it's common.

Girls also overgeneralize in their thinking from one incident to all cases. One affront means, "I have no friends." One good grade means, "I am an academic diva." Offhand remarks can be taken as a prophecy, an indictment, or a diagnosis. One client of mine in the '90s decided to become a nurse because her uncle told her she would be a good one. When I was in eighth grade, my teacher returned my first poem with the word *trite* scribbled across the top of the page. I gave up my plans to be a writer for over twenty years.

This tendency to overgeneralize makes it difficult to reason with adolescent girls. Because they know of one example, they'll argue, "Everyone else gets to stay out till two," or "Everyone I know gets a new car for their sixteenth birthday." They'll believe that because the girl next door gets a ride to school, every girl in the universe gets a ride to school. They aren't being manipulative as much as they earnestly believe that one case represents the whole.

Teenage girls have what one psychologist called the "imaginary audience syndrome." They think they are being watched by others who are preoccupied with the smallest details of their lives. For example, my friend's daughter was upset that her mother wanted to take binoculars to her soccer game. She told her mom, "All the other kids will know you are watching my every move." Another friend told me how anxious her daughter was when she wore jeans and a sweatshirt to her daughter's school conference. A twelve-year-old told me how embarrassing it was to go to performances with her mother, who had a way of clapping her hands high in the air. Sometimes when her mother was particularly pleased, she loudly shouted "Bravo!" My client said, "I can't believe she does this. Everyone in the place knows she's a total dork."

Teenage girls engage in emotional reasoning, which is the belief that if you feel something is true, it must be true. If a teenager feels like a nerd, she must be a nerd. If she feels her parents are unfair, they are unfair. Girls possess limited ability to sort facts from feelings. Thinking is still magical in the sense that thinking something makes it so.

Young girls are egocentric in their thinking. That is, they are unable to focus on anyone's experience but their own. Parents often experience this egocentrism as selfishness. But it's not a character flaw, only a developmental stage. Parents in the 1990s complained that their daughters did only a few chores and yet claimed, "I do all the work around here." A mother reported that her daughter expected her to spend hours chauffeuring to save the daughter a few minutes of walking.

In the 1960s, many teenage girls thought they were invincible. They refused to wear seat belts or to deal with the possibilities of pregnancy. And in 1994, I still saw glimpses of that sense of invulnerability. For example, one of my clients who volunteered at a rehabilitation center came in with stories of injured patients. One day, after a particularly sad story about a boy her age, I blurted out, "Well, at least now you are wearing your seat belt." She gave me a surprised look and said, "Not really. I won't get in a wreck."

However, I saw this sense of invulnerability much less frequently. It had been shattered by trauma in the lives of girls or their friends. Most twelve-year-olds knew they could be hurt. They read the newspaper and watched television. Clients talked more often about death, had more violent dreams, more spooky fantasies, and more fears about the future.

It's important not to oversimplify this topic. Some children feel much safer than others. Becoming conscious of the dangerous world can happen overnight or be a gradual process. The same girl can be of two minds depending on the week. One week she'll lock doors and worry aloud about danger, the next she'll believe that she can fight off any attacker. But by 1994, adolescents no longer felt invulnerable in the ways they did in my childhood, or even ten years before 1994.

Girls deal with painful thoughts, discrepant information, and cognitive confusion in ways that are true or false to the self. The temptation is to shut down, to oversimplify, to avoid the hard work of examining and understanding the meaning of their experiences. Girls who operate from a false self often reduce the world to a more manageable place by distorting reality. Some girls join cults that make all their decisions for them. Some girls become anorexic and reduce all the complexity in life to just one issue: weight.

Some girls, like Charlotte, worked hard not to think about their lives in the 1990s. They ran from any kind of processing and sought out companions who were also on the run. They avoided parents who pushed them to consider their actions. Charlotte was heavily swayed by peers in her decision making. She was a sailboat with no centerboard, blowing whichever way the winds blew. She had no North Star to keep her focused on her own true needs.

Girls who stay connected to their true selves don't have an easy time of it. They are also confused and sometimes overwhelmed. But they have made some commitment to understanding their lives. They think about their experiences. They do not give up on trying to resolve contradictions and make connections between events. They may seek out a parent, teacher, or therapist to help them. They may read or write in a journal. They will make many mistakes and misinterpret much of reality, but girls with true selves make a commitment to examine and understand their experiences.

Lori was particularly good at looking within herself to make decisions. She thought through issues and decided what was best for her. After that, she was relatively immune to peer pressure. She was steering, not drifting, determined to behave in ways that made sense to her.

SOCIAL SELVES—FAMILY

Adolescence in America is the psychological equivalent of toddlerhood. Just as toddlers move away from their parents physically, so do adolescents move away from their parents emotionally. There are continuous negotiations between parents and children about distance. Children want to explore and parents want to keep them safe. Both toddlers and adolescents are outraged when their parents don't agree with them about the ideal balance of freedom and security.

Of course, since the 1950s, families have changed. Divorce, which was uncommon in my childhood, was a fact of life in the 1990s. One in every two marriages ended in divorce, and the most common family was a blended family. The average adult had been through at least one divorce, and half of all children spent some of their childhood in single-parent homes. There were many families in which the adults could not or did not protect their children. Adults who were struggling with their own problems such as depression, drug or alcohol addiction, or crippling poverty often had no energy to parent. There were families in which parents were abusive or neglectful. Many children were homeless or living in foster care or institutions.

Still, the majority of parents were motivated to do their best for their children. Unfortunately, adolescence is scripted in a way that builds in conflict between teenagers and their parents. Among my clients, conflict occurred when parents tried to protect daughters who were trying to be independent in ways that were dangerous. Teenagers felt under great social pressure to abandon their families, to be accepted by peer culture, and to be autonomous individuals.

Many clients no longer wanted to be touched by their parents. They grimaced and pulled away with a look of alarm when their parents approached. Partly that was a reaction to their new awareness of their bodies, partly it was a way of asserting their maturity. But it was also a statement: "I need space to be my own person."

At the same time, girls wanted to stay close to their parents. They even argued as a way to maintain a connection. Fights were ways of staying close and asserting distance at the same time. Baffled parents, especially mothers, reported that their daughters went out of their way to pick fights. "We can argue over whether the sky is blue," one mother said. Another said, "We fight ten times a day, over the most ridiculous stuff. It's like being nibbled to death by minnows."

Much of girls' behavior is not what parents think. The surface behavior is not all there is. The deep structure is on a quest for an autonomous self. The distancing and hostility are not personal. On the other hand, understanding why girls act the way they do doesn't take away all parental stress. It's hard when a daughter storms off in response to the question, "How was your day?" It's painful for parents to be criticized for the way they yawn or peel potatoes.

Because parents often are ignorant of how much the world has changed, further misunderstandings arise. Parents assume that their daughters live in a world similar to the one they experienced as adolescents. They are dead wrong. Their daughters live in a media-drenched world flooded with junk values. As girls turn from their parents, they turn to this world for guidance about how to be an adult. They cling to the new, reject the old.

Music is important to most girls. It catapults them out of the world of their family and into the world of their peers. Music expresses the intensity of their emotions in a way that words cannot. In music, love is a life-and-death matter and small events are dramatized and memorialized. Music fits the emotional experience of girls much more closely than ordinary adult speech. Unfortunately, much of the music girls hear offers them McSex. In much of teen music, girls are spoken of disrespectfully or treated as sexual machines.

A friend of mine in the 1990s told me about talking to her eleven-year-old daughter about sex. She was embarrassed, but wanted to give her daughter more information than she had received. She struggled through the mechanics of sex and then shared her values about healthy relationships. She confessed that she had had sex before marriage. The daughter listened as her mother shared her sexual values.

An hour later she went into her daughter's room. MTV was showing a nubile young woman clad in a leather bikini crawling all over a muscular young man. She mouthed song lyrics in praise of their sexual experience the night before. The young man had been too drunk to remember, so she was refreshing his memory with salacious details. My friend said, "I realized then that we were in different worlds with different languages. My daughter could no more understand my shame at being sexual before marriage than I could understand this girl in a leather bikini. It was a hard discovery."

Girls told me how radically their relationships with their parents changed when they hit puberty. Many said that they had once been "good little kids" but that with puberty they stopped being good. They lied, sneaked around, drank, smoked, yelled, and disobeyed. These girls realized the choices they made were self-destructive, but they were in terrible binds. They believed that only nerds stayed close to their parents.

Girls like Charlotte, who operated from a false self, were more likely to break emotionally from their families. They were vulnerable to peer pressure to reject all parental advice. They were more likely to cause great conflict in the family. Because they operated from false selves, they had no way of keeping peer culture in perspective. They gave up the relationships they most needed, the relationships with people who would protect them from girl-diminishing experiences.

Girls who held on to their true selves were more likely to keep their relationship with their families alive. Although they distanced themselves some, they did not totally abandon their families. Lori still loved and trusted her parents even though she had typical teenage reactions, such as wanting more time away from her parents and being embarrassed by their smallest flaws.

The role of parents had changed radically by the 1990s. Parents had helped their children fit into the culture. But by the time I wrote *Reviving Ophelia* many parents were fighting against the cultural influences that they knew would harm their daughters. This was true of both Lori's and Charlotte's parents. They wanted their daughters to have more time to grow and develop, time without sex, drugs, alcohol, and trauma. They fought to preserve their daughters' wholeness from girl-destructive environments. Most parents were not the agents of culture, but rather the enemies of the cultural indoctrination that their daughters faced with puberty. They battled to save their daughters' true selves.

SOCIAL SELVES—PEERS

In the 1990s, as girls pulled away from parents, peers were everything. Teens who hardly spoke to their parents talked all night with friends. Peers validated their decisions and supported their new independent selves. This was a time of deep searching for the self in relationships. There was a constant experimenting—What reaction will I get from others? Talking to friends was a way of checking the important question, "Am I okay?" The talk was endless, as any parent could attest. Cutting teens off from their friends was incredibly punishing. As one girl explained it, "Grounding teenagers drives them crazy."

While peers can be satisfying and growth-producing, they can also be growth-destroying, especially in early adolescence. Many girls can describe a universal American phenomenon—the scapegoating of girls by one another. Many girls become good haters of those who do not conform sufficiently to our culture's ideas about femininity.

Like any recent converts to an ideology, girls are at risk of becoming the biggest enforcers and proselytizers for the culture. Girls punish other girls for failing to achieve the same impossible goals that they themselves are failing to achieve. They rush to set standards in order to ward off the imposition of others' standards on them. The content of the standards is variable—designer jeans or leather jackets, smoking cigarettes or the heavy use of eye shadow. What's important is the message that not pleasing others is social suicide.

This scapegoating functions as the ultimate form of social control for girls who are not sufficiently attentive to social pressures. Scapegoats are shunned, teased, bullied, and harassed in a hundred different ways. Girls who are smart, assertive, confident, too pretty, or not pretty enough are likely to be scapegoated.

Girls do not learn to express anger directly. Unlike boys, they are not permitted to fight physically with their enemies. They express anger through cattiness and teasing. They punish by calling a girl to say that there's a party and she's not invited or by walking up to girls with insults about their clothes or bodies. They punish with nicknames and derogatory labels or by picking a certain girl—usually one who is relatively happy—and making her life miserable.

Of course, this shunning takes its toll. The pain often drives adolescent girls to despair. As one girl put it, "You can only go so long with people putting you down before you begin to believe it."

In junior high my classmate Patty was obese and slow-moving. She suffered the most. Her nickname was "Mammoth," and girls called her this to her face. Anything she did was scorned. One year her mother brought in lovely red popcorn balls for Halloween. Most girls wouldn't eat them, even though just looking at the bowl made their mouths water. They were afraid that if they ate popcorn balls made by "Mammoth's mother," they would be "germed."

My schoolmates frequently fell back on this "germs" method of shunning. Girls who were unpopular were considered to have germs, and anyone who touched them would be infected unless they immediately passed them along to another girl. Lots of between-class time was spent getting rid of germs from contact with undesirables. I never played, but I hated the days when I was labeled as the person with germs. I have since learned how common that game was in towns all over the country.

In 1994, drugs and alcohol were more available and more widely utilized than when I was a teen. A speaker in my college class told about his life in a small Nebraska town in the early 1960s. He said that in high school his buddies would buy a six-pack and cruise on a Saturday night after they dropped off their dates. After his talk, a young woman in the class said that she lived in his hometown in the 1990s. He asked how it was different. She said, "Kids buy cases, not six-packs, and the girls get drunk too."

By the 1990s, most teenagers were offered drugs by seventh grade. Marijuana wafted through the air at rock concerts and midnight movies. Gangs operated along the interstate and crack was sold in the suburbs.

Many girls complained about sexual harassment in school. While junior-high boys had always teased girls about sex, the level of the teasing was different. Girls were taunted about everything from oral sex to pubic hair, from periods to the imagined appearance of their genitals. The harassment that girls experienced in the 1990s was new in both quality and intensity. The remarks were more graphic, mean-spirited, and controlling.

In 1993, the American Association of University Women released a study titled, "Hostile Hallways," which documents what girls were experiencing. It reported that 70 percent of girls experienced harassment and 50 percent experienced unwanted sexual touching in their schools. One-third of all girls reported sexual rumors being spread about them, and one-fourth reported being molested. The study found that the classrooms and hallways of our schools were the most common sites for sexual harassment. Many girls were afraid to speak up for fear of worse harassment.

Often harassment extended beyond remarks to touching. It was usually from students, although girls also reported harassment from male teachers. Generally, girls did not tell school authorities about these incidents, but some refused to go to school. They told me they simply could not face what happened to them at school. Charlotte had trouble returning to school, where she was called a slut when she walked through the halls. Another client complained that boys slapped her behind and grabbed her breasts when she walked to her locker. Another wouldn't ride the school bus because boys teased her incessantly about sex.

Adolescents were exposed via music, television, movies, and pornography to models of sexuality that were brutal and callous. Girls were caught in the cross fire of the culture's mixed sexual messages. Sex was considered both a sacred act between two people united by God and the best way to sell suntan lotion.

Girls who maintain their true selves resist peer pressure to be a certain way. Lori, for example, knew she wouldn't drink or smoke just because other kids pressured her at a party. She also had her own position about sexuality and wouldn't be pressured to be sexually active before she was ready. She was unwilling to make the concessions necessary to be superpopular. She could see clearly that to be accepted by everyone she would have to give up too much of herself.

Charlotte, on the other hand, tried hard to win peer approval. She was sexually active with boys at her school. Her attempts to be popular with boys backfired. She made choices based not on her own true needs but on her sense of what other people, especially her boyfriend, Mel, wanted from her. Because she was so dependent on peer approval, she got into a great deal of trouble and was utterly lost to herself when I first met her.

Spiritual Selves

Many of the great idealists of history, such as Anne Frank and Joan of Arc, were adolescent girls. Adolescence is a time when girls actively search for meaning and order in the universe. Often this is the time of religious crisis and of exploring universal questions, such as, What happens after death? and What is the purpose of suffering? Some girls become deeply religious and will sacrifice everything for their beliefs. Others have a crisis in faith.

At thirteen I was a loyal Methodist. Then I read Mark Twain's story "Captain Stormfield's Visit to Heaven," in which he pokes fun at heaven as a place where people sit around and play harps all day. That story catapulted me into an examination of my faith. At fifteen I read Bertrand Russell's "Why I Am Not a Christian" and debated with my minister and my friends about the existence of God.

One of my clients formally accepted Christ as her personal savior on her thirteenth birthday. She committed herself to a Christian life and evaluated her behavior daily. She believed that her most important relationship was with God, and that her most important time was the time she spent in prayer. She became the spiritual leader of her family and chided her parents when they acted in un-Christian ways. She led her younger siblings in daily Bible study.

Adolescence is a time of great idealism—many girls this age become environmentalists or advocates for the poor or sick. One friend of Sara's in the '90s spent part of her allowance on sandwiches for homeless people. She carried food to their street corners and visited about their lives while they ate. Soon she knew most of the homeless people in town by name. Another friend monitored canned tuna to make sure it was caught in dolphin-free nets, and she protested fur sales at department stores.

Many girls become vegetarians in adolescence. They love animals and actively work for animal rights. This cause is popular with girls because they so easily identify with the powerlessness and lack of speech of animals. One girl I know wore a button that said, IF ANIMALS ARE TO TALK, WE MUST BE THEIR VOICES. Girls identify with gentle, defenseless creatures and they will work with great idealism and energy to save them.

The 1960s were a time of optimism and idealism. The civil rights movement was strong, the economy was good, and the world looked full of possibilities. Many girls say they wished they had lived in those times. It was much harder to be idealistic and optimistic in the 1990s. Girls who stayed true to themselves found some means of spiritual solace. They worked for the betterment of the world. Girls who acted from their false selves were often cynical about making the world a better place. They had given up hope. Only when they connected to something larger than their own egos would they find the energy to take on the culture and fight to save the planet.

Adolescence is an intense time of change. All kinds of development—physical, emotional, intellectual, academic, social, and spiritual—are happening at once. Adolescence is the most formative time in the lives of women and these choices have implications for the rest of our lives.

Of course, these generalizations about adolescence don't hold true for all girls. Some girls have had tough lives as children and don't experience their elementary school years as happy. Other girls who are stable and protected seem to slide through junior high. The intensity of the problems varies, as does the timing—from age nine to around age sixteen.

Another caveat: Much of what I know about junior-high girls I learned from high-school girls. I heard what happened in junior high after "the statute of limitations has run out." In junior high, many girls' thoughts, feelings, and experiences were too jumbled to be clearly articulated. Their trust level for adults was just too low. Girls were in the midst of a hurricane and there's not much communication with the outside world.

Girls like Lori, who are the happiest, manage against great odds to stay true to themselves. But all girls feel pain and confusion. None can easily master the painful and complicated problems of this time. All are aware of the suffering of friends, of the pressure to be beautiful, and of the dangers of being female. All are pressured to sacrifice their wholeness in order to be loved. Like Ophelia, all are in danger of drowning.

In 1994, girls appeared to be in a great deal of trouble. They came to therapy pregnant, enduring sexually transmitted diseases, alcohol and drug addiction, and academic failures. With their parents, they were sullen, disobedient, and constantly in conflict. Between 1994 and 2007, girls' mental health improved in virtually every way. Girls reported more happiness, confidence, and stability. Family relationships improved and schools made genuine efforts to encourage girls in math and science. Drug and alcohol use, depression, and disruptive and illegal behaviors dropped rapidly. Then with the invention of the iPhone, indices of girls' mental health plummeted.

Today's girls are more obedient and well-behaved. They tend to like their parents and express open physical and verbal affection for them. Still, we can't help but think that the girls in 1994 were luckier. Their problems were right on the surface for all of us to see and eventually discuss. They suffered more real-world trauma, but they also experienced more recovery. In many cases they became strengthened by their experiences. They learned resilience skills. And they were out exploring the world with their friends and developing some social competency. Most left home reasonably self-reliant.

Girls today sit alone in their rooms with Netflix and a smartphone. They remain dependent on parents longer and feel less confident about their life skills. Adolescent girls have fewer opportunities to solve problems and to take care of themselves. They are always either with their parents or a phone call away. Generally speaking, parents today feel close to their daughters, but often they do not understand them because they have no access to their online lives. They see their role as helping their daughters adapt to a rapidly changing culture, but they don't know how to fulfill that duty. None of us know what will happen next or how to prepare.

Adolescent development occurs more slowly in 2019 than it did in 1959 or 1994. Many girls remain financially dependent on their parents well into their twenties. Young women tend to enter the workforce later and to marry in their late twenties or early thirties, if at all. Parents often see their roles as protectors as extending well beyond their daughters' high school graduations.

Bailey, one of the people we interviewed for this edition, works as a camp counselor at a high-school girls' summer camp in the Northeast. This camp teaches girls to rock climb, navigate in the wilderness, and bungee jump off cliffs. It also empowers girls with self-knowledge and self-regard via meditation, achievement journals, and self-affirmations.

In her role as counselor, Bailey said she has seen that the girls at camp grow stronger and more confident every day. They also experience a real sense of community and team building with one another. Especially after they have mastered a major new challenge such as whitewater rafting, group spirits are buoyant.

Bailey described one glorious day when the girls succeeded in hiking to the top of a mountain. They were exhausted but elated. However, when they returned to the bus after the hike, they immediately pulled out their cell phones. They disengaged from the group and, as they read their messages, their moods darkened. Within seconds, the effervescent joy vanished and the girls lost their newfound confidence.

She recalled another afternoon that her campers had spent hiking and singing. They'd seen a black bear and splashed in a waterfall. Everyone was mellow when Bailey sent them to their rooms for their swimsuits. She told them, "Be back in five minutes."

The girls all checked their phones when they were alone and five minutes later their moods were wildly different. One girl had received texts from her parents that made her cry. Another had been caught up in a comment war and had been unfriended by an entire clique of girls from her school. Still another found out her online boyfriend "liked" a provocative photo of her best friend and wondered what that meant. Another girl was worried about the meaning of an emoji.

The girls loved the wilderness camp. At home, their lives were overscheduled and rushed. At camp, the schedule was leisurely and girls had ample time to talk and sleep. They were outside all day and gathered around a campfire under the stars at night. They worked in teams and supported one another's growth and skill building.

Bailey wished the camp could have a no-technology policy. However, she explained, that is complicated. Some parents wanted to be able to contact their daughters at any time and insisted the girls have access to their phones. Other parents supported the no-phones policy. Most of the girls said they wouldn't come to camp if they couldn't bring their phones.

Because of the internet, all aspects of development—physical, cognitive, emotional, relational, and maturational—have changed. When girls are online, they aren't working, reading books, studying, interacting with family members or neighbors, exercising, or reflecting on their lives. They also are not out in the world navigating life's many real challenges.

Girls today experience the same ups and downs in their emotional lives that they did in 1994. Their emotions are hard to modulate and their stress management skills are still developing. When Gracie couldn't find a shoe, she shouted to her mom, "Help! I'm having a crisis of epic proportions! I can't find my shoe and I'm late." Then when she found it, she laughed and called out, "Crisis averted."

A charming thirteen-year-old neighbor once said, "I've had twenty meltdowns this week and it's only Monday."

With hormonal changes, physical maturation, middle school, and the many challenges of turning thirteen, girls' lives are intense—even operatic—in their drama. The constant news from iPhones and iPads adds to this intensity.

According to *iGen*, girls study and read less than they did both in the 1960s and in 1994. As Kendyl told us in a focus group, "Girls get news from Twitter and Snapchat, which isn't ideal considering all the clickbait out there. I don't know anyone who gets their news from the newspaper or who watches news on TV." Jada joked that instead of reading, she consults "Google University." Of course, if girls' main teacher is social media, the quality of education is greatly compromised.

Another factor may be almost as important. The constant use of social media has been shown to greatly shorten attention span. Girls learn to think and act in nanosecond time. That induces both hyperactivity and impulsivity. These tendencies are exactly the opposite of what we hope to see with maturation—patience, persistence, and impulse control.

Teenage girls are in constant touch with their friends, but 96 percent of this contact is via devices. Between 2009 and 2015, the number of teens who spent time with friends daily dropped by 40 percent. Adolescents today are unlikely to go to shopping or to movies with friends, and they rarely spend time with their peers face-to-face. In fact, this generation of teens attends fewer parties than previous generations. And while this may help parents rest easy, when teenagers aren't together, they miss opportunities to develop social skills, discuss feelings and challenges, and teach others what they know. They don't learn how to share and resolve conflicts. Adolescence is the time to develop the relationship skills we all need to be mature adults. This simply can't happen via Twitter or Instagram.

Even as girls are not talking face-to-face, peers hold greater power than ever. They are signaling approval or disapproval twenty-four seven. Online relationships are poor substitutes for friends, family, and community. They are less stable, more reactive, and less empathic.

There have always been bullies, but girls experience more mean, obnoxious behavior online than they do in face-to-face interactions.

It's easier to communicate hate when you don't have to look anyone in the eyes. Girls also are more likely to be cruel to other girls and to teachers online. One girl in a focus group told me, "We have a teacher hate page where students write horrible stuff. I did it at first, then I decided I didn't want to anymore."

All this online bullying and trash talk increases girls' sense of victimization and decreases their self-confidence, sense of agency, and ability to empathize. A University of Minnesota review of seventy-two studies between 1979 and 2009 concluded that teens and young college students have 40 percent less empathy now than they did in 1979. Screen time also results in distrust and a sense of betrayal. In fact, the more time girls are on their screens, the more likely they are to feel depressed.

In 2019, the best support adults can offer teens is to help them be together face-to-face: in sports, theater, or other structured activities that involve real contact. Parents can encourage daughters to have slumber parties, dance parties, or cookouts, whatever activities encourage teens to work together and to talk to one another.

Peer counseling is an illustration of the importance of in-person contact. Through counseling or mentoring, teens aid each other in learning how to have deep discussions. Student activism can be another way to grow and mature by working with others toward a common goal.

The positive news is that girls blossom when they have opportunities for authentic connection: talking, reading, or engaging in creative pursuits. When they are connected to others or to their own deep selves, they report great happiness and they grow emotionally and socially. They develop empathy, a stronger sense of self, and confidence in their own capacities.

Our focus group and interview experiences demonstrate that girls enjoy deep conversations and opportunities to reflect on who they truly are. Given the chance to grow and learn, girls are eager to explore themselves and the world. All girls in early adolescence are egocentric and social media makes them more so, but when they engage with real people in meaningful ways, they quickly make gains in judgment and moral imagination. We adults can help by establishing ways for girls to experience genuine connection with the natural world, useful work, or friends of all ages.

FOUR

Then and Now, 1959–2019

CASSIE REMINDED ME of myself as a girl. With her long brown hair, blue eyes, and gawky, flat-chested body, she looked like she could have been my relative. We both loved to walk in the woods and cried when we read poetry. She wanted to visit the Holocaust Museum and join the Peace Corps. She preferred books to clothes and didn't care a fig for money. She loved her parents even though they were now divorcing and had little energy to care for her. At school, she was shy, studious, and a good listener.

But I was fifteen in 1963 and Cassie was fifteen in 1993. When I was her age, I'd never been kissed. She was in therapy because she'd been sexually assaulted. With her hands folded in her lap and her head bowed, she whispered the story.

She'd been invited to a party by a girl in her algebra class whose parents were out of town. The girl was supposed to stay with a friend, but instead she organized a party. The kids could use her parents' hot tub and had easy access to their liquor cabinet. Cassie accepted the invitation, but planned to leave if things got out of control. She told her mother the truth about her plans, except she didn't mention that the parents were gone. Her mother was preoccupied by her divorce proceedings and didn't ask for more details.

At first, the party was okay, with lots of loud music and sick jokes. Cassie was glad to be there. A guy from her lunch break asked her to dance, and a cheerleader she barely knew asked her to go to the movies. But, by eleven, the house was packed with crashers and everyone was drinking. Some kids were throwing up, others were having sex. One boy knocked a lamp off a desk and another kicked a hole through a wall. Cassie wanted to go home.

She slipped away to the upstairs bedroom for her coat. She didn't notice that a guy followed her into the room. He knew her name and asked for a kiss. She shook her head no and searched for her coat in the pile on the bed. He crept up behind her and put his hands under her shirt. She told him to quit and tried to push him away. Then things happened very fast. He grabbed her and called her a bitch. She struggled to break free, but he pinned her down and covered her mouth. She tried to fight but he was muscular and too drunk to feel pain when she flailed at him. Nobody downstairs heard anything over the music. In ten minutes it was over.

Cassie called her mother and asked her to come get her. She shivered outside until her mother arrived. Cassie told her what had happened and they cried together. They called her father and the police, then drove to a nearby hospital. Cassie was examined and she met with a crisis counselor.

Two weeks later Cassie was in my office, in part because of the rape and in part because of the flak she'd taken at school. The guy who sexually assaulted her had been suspended from the track team pending his trial. His friends were furious at Cassie for getting him in trouble. Other kids thought she led him on, that she had asked for it by being at that party.

Cassie awakened me to an essential truth: in 1993, girls' experiences were different from those of myself and my friends in the 1960s. To work with girls in the 1990s I had to explore a new world. I had to let go of my conceptions of how their world was and look at their situations with fresh eyes. I had to learn from them before I could help.

During my adolescence, I lived in a town of four hundred people where my mother practiced medicine and my father sold seed corn and raised hogs. I spent my days riding my bike, swimming, reading, playing piano, and drinking limeades at the drugstore with my friends. I raised all kinds of animals—baby coyotes that we bought from bounty hunters, turtles we picked up on the highway, birds washed from trees in heavy spring rains, mice pulled from their nests by dogs, and snakes and rabbits we caught in the fields on the edge of town.

I had eleven aunts and uncles and thirty cousins who showed up for long visits. The women cooked and watched babies; the men played horseshoes and fished. We all played cards in the evenings. My grandfather recited limericks and demonstrated card tricks. Conversation was the main entertainment. We cousins compared stories about our towns and families. The older cousins impressed the younger ones with their worldly wisdom. Children sat and listened as grown-ups told stories and talked politics. My fondest memory is of falling asleep to laughter and talk in the next room.

The word *media* was not in our language. I saw television for the first time when I was six, and I hid behind the couch because the cowboys' guns scared me. I was eight before we had a black-and-white television on which we watched one grainy station that showed a test pattern for much of the day.

As a young teenager I watched *The Mickey Mouse Club, American Bandstand,* and *The Ed Sullivan Show*. I wasn't allowed to watch *Perry Mason* or *Gunsmoke* because my parents thought these shows were too violent. We had one movie theater with a new movie every other week.

The owner of the theater was a family man who selected our town's movies carefully. His wife sold us salty popcorn, Tootsie Rolls, and Cokes. Kids went to the movies on Saturday afternoons and spent most of their time spying on other kids or giggling with their friends.

Forty-five rpm records were big in the early 1960s. I listened to mushy songs by the Everly Brothers, Roy Orbison, and Elvis. My favorite song was Elvis's "Surrender," a song whose lyrics gave me goose bumps and filled me with longing for something I couldn't name. My parents forbade me to listen to Bobby Darin's hit "Multiplication" because it was too suggestive. I learned to twist, a dance that was considered daring.

Money and conspicuous consumption were downplayed in my community. Some people were wealthier than others, but it was bad taste to flaunt a high income. We all shopped at the Theobald's grocery and the Rexall and ordered our clothes from Sears and JCPenney catalogs. A rancher's widow with asthma had the only home air-conditioning unit in the county. The only places to spend money foolishly were the Dairy King and the pool hall.

After school I worked for my mother at her clinic. I sterilized syringes and rubber gloves and counted pills. The money I earned went into a college account. By junior high, most gifts I received (good china, luggage, a dictionary, and hand-embroidered pillowcases) were for my hope chest.

The surgeon general had yet to issue his report on smoking, and cigarettes were everywhere. At the Methodist Youth Fellowship, we saw films about the deterioration of people who drank or used marijuana. Women in particular were portrayed as degraded and destroyed by contact with alcohol. After these films, we signed pledges that we would never drink or smoke marijuana. I didn't break mine until I was in college.

As Tolstoy knew so well, in all times and places there have been happy and unhappy families. In the 1950s, the unhappiness was mostly private. Divorce was uncommon and regarded as shameful. I had no friends whose parents were divorced. All kinds of pain were kept secret. Physical and sexual abuse occurred but were not reported. Children and women who lived in abusive families suffered silently. For those whose lives were going badly, there was nowhere to turn. My friend Sue's father hanged himself in his basement. She missed a week of school, and when she returned, we treated her as if nothing had happened. The first time Sue and I spoke of her father's death was at our twenty-fifth class reunion.

There was cruelty. Alcoholics and addicts were shamed rather than helped. Mentally and physically challenged people were teased. The Green River Ordinance, which kept undesirables—meaning strangers, peddlers, and in particular people of color—out of town, was enforced.

Most of the mothers were homemakers who served brownies and milk to their children after school. They may have been miserable with their lives of service to men, children, and community, but most children didn't know this.

Most of the fathers farmed or owned stores downtown and walked home for lunch. Babysitters were a rarity. Everyone went to the same chili feeds and county fairs. Adults were around to keep an eye on things. Once I picked some lilacs from an old lady's bush. She called my parents before I could make it home with my bouquet.

Grown-ups agreed about rules and enforced them. Teenagers weren't exposed to an alternative value system and they rebelled in milder ways—with ducktails, tight skirts, and rock and roll. Adults joked about how much trouble teenagers were, but most parents felt proud of their children. They didn't have the strained faces and the anxious conversations that parents of teenagers had in the 1990s.

Men held most of the public power. The governor, the state senators, the congressmen, the mayor, and city council members were men, and men ran the stores downtown. My mother was the first "lady doctor" in our town, and she suffered some because of this. She wasn't considered quite as feminine as other women and she wasn't considered quite as good a doctor as the male doctor in the next town.

Language was unselfconsciously noninclusive—leaders were "he," hurricanes and secretaries "she," humanity was "mankind." Men made history, wrote books, won wars, conducted symphonies, and created eternal works of art. The books we read in school were written by men and about men. They were shared with us by women teachers who didn't comment on their own exclusion.

Kent, Sam, and I were the top students. The teachers praised them for being brilliant and creative, while I was praised for being a hard worker. Kent and Sam were encouraged to go to out-of-state colleges to study law or medicine, while I was encouraged to study at the state university to become a teacher.

A pervasive, low-key misogyny inhabited our world. Mothers-in-law, women drivers, and ugly women were sources of derisive humor. Men needed to "wear the pants in the family." Uppity women were quickly chastened and so were their husbands for allowing themselves to be "henpecked." Women's talk was regarded as inferior to the important talk of men. Girls were admonished that "it's not smart to be smart" and that we should "let boys chase us till we catch them."

By junior high the all-girl activities were different from the all-boy activities. Boys played sports while we walked around the gym with books on our heads so that we would develop good posture. Boy Scouts camped and fished while Girl Scouts sold cookies and learned to sew, bake, and care for children.

One summer, I devoured the Cherry Ames student nurse books. In every book, Cherry would meet a new young doctor and have an innocent romance in a glorious setting. Thank goodness I also read Nancy Drew and the Dana Girls books. Those amateur sleuths were competent and confident, brave and adventurous. They gave me role models that were lively and active. They had boyfriends, but they were always ditching them to go solve a mystery.

In the 1950s and 1960s, boys preferred dating girls whom they could best in every way. Achievement in girls was valued as long as it didn't interfere with social attractiveness. Too much education or ambition was considered unattractive. When I received the Bausch & Lomb science award at a high-school assembly, I almost expired of embarrassment.

Sexuality was seen as a powerful force regulated by God himself. There were rules and euphemisms for everything. "Don't touch your privates except to wash." "Never let a guy go all the way or he won't respect you in the morning." Sex was my most confusing problem. I wasn't sure how many orifices women had. I knew that something girls did with boys led to babies, but I was unable to picture just what that was. I misunderstood dirty jokes and had no idea that songs were filled with sexual innuendo. Well into junior high I thought that the word *adultery* meant trying to act like an adult.

One of my girlfriends had an older cousin who hid romance magazines under her bed. One day when she was away at a baton-twirling competition, we sneaked up to her room to read them. Beautiful young women were overwhelmed by lust and overpowered by handsome heroes. The details were vague. The couple fell into bed and the woman's blouse was unbuttoned. Her heart would flutter and she would turn pale. The author described a storm outside or petals falling from flowers in a nearby vase. We left the house still mystified about what really happened.

There was a scary side of sexuality. One friend's dad told her, "Don't get pregnant, but if you do, come to me and I'll load up my gun." One of my second cousins had to marry because she was pregnant. She whispered to me that her boyfriend had blackmailed her into having sex. She was a homecoming queen candidate and he said he'd go to homecoming with her only if she gave in. He claimed that he was suffering from "blue balls," a painful and unhealthy condition that only sex would remedy.

Lois and Carol taught me my most important lessons. Lois was a pudgy, self-effacing fourteen-year-old whose greatest accomplishment was eight years of perfect attendance at our Sunday school. One Sunday morning she wasn't there, and when I remarked on that fact, the teacher changed the subject. For a time, no one would tell me what had happened to Lois. Eventually, I was so anxious that my mother told me the story. Lois was pregnant from having sex with a middle-aged man who worked at her father's store. They had married and were living in a trailer south of town. She was expelled from school and would not be coming to church anymore, at least not until after the baby was born. I never saw her again.

Carol was a wiry, freckled farm girl from a big family. She boarded with our neighbors to attend high school in town. In the evenings, after she had the chores done, Carol came over to play with me. One night we were standing in our front yard when a carload of boys came by and asked her to go for a ride. She hesitated, then agreed. A month later Carol was sent back pregnant to her farm. I worried about her because she'd told me her father used belts and coat hangers on the children. My father told me to learn from Carol's mistake and avoid riding with boys. I took him literally and it was years before I felt comfortable riding in cars with any boys except my cousins.

In my town the rules for boys were clear. They were supposed to like sex and go for it whenever they could. They could expect sex with loose girls, but not with good girls, at least not until they'd dated them a long time. The biggest problem for boys was getting the experience they needed to prove they were men.

The rules for girls were more complicated. We were told that sex would ruin our lives and our reputations. We were encouraged to be sexy, but not sexual. Great scorn was reserved for "cockteasers" and "cold fish." It was tough to find the right balance between seductive and prim.

The rules for both sexes pitted them against their Saturday-night dates. Guys tried to get what they could and girls tried to stop them. That made for a lot of sweaty wrestling matches and ruined prom nights. The biggest danger from rule breaking was pregnancy. This was before birth control pills and legal abortion. Syphilis and gonorrhea were the most common sexually transmitted diseases, and both were treatable with the new miracle drug, penicillin.

Sexual openness and tolerance were not community values. Pregnant teachers had to leave school as soon as they "showed." None of my girlfriends admitted to being sexually active. There was community-wide denial about incest and rape. The official story was kept G-rated.

There was a great deal of hypocrisy. A wealthy man in my town was known for being a pincher. We girls called him "the lobster" among ourselves and knew to avoid him. But because his family was prominent, no one ever told him to stop his behavior.

In my town, male homosexuals were mercilessly scorned. The one known homosexual was the son of a Protestant minister. He made the enormous mistake of asking another boy for a kiss, and forever after lived a nightmarish life of isolation and teasing. I didn't hear the word *lesbian* until I was in college.

Outsiders—such as socialists, Native Americans, or blacks—were ostracized in small communities. Restaurant signs that read "We have the right to refuse service to anyone" were used to exclude nonwhites. Adults told racist jokes and held racist beliefs about ethnic groups they had never even encountered. My father warned me never to dance with or talk to "Negroes" when I went to college or people would think I was low-class. Terms like "Jewing people down" and "Indian giver" were part of everyday language.

Crime was garbage cans and privies being overturned on Halloween. No one locked their doors. Our town sheriff mostly looked for lost pets and speeders. I could go anywhere before or after dark without my parents' worrying. My most traumatic experience was reading *The Diary of Anne Frank* and realizing that somewhere people could be incredibly evil.

As I recall my childhood, I'm cautioned by Mark Twain's line, "The older I get, the more clearly I remember things that never happened." Remembering is more like taking a Rorschach test than calling up a computer file. It's highly selective and revealing of one's deep character. Of course, others had different experiences, but I recall small-town life as slower and safer. Everyone knew everyone. Sometimes that made the world seem cozy and sometimes that made the world seem small and oppressive.

My client Cassie attended a high school with twenty-three hundred students. She didn't know her teachers' children or her neighbors' cousins. When she met people, she didn't try to establish their place in a complicated community network. When she shopped for jeans, she didn't expect the clerk to ask after her family.

Cassie visited her extended family infrequently, particularly after her parents' divorce. Her relatives were scattered all over the map. Most of the adults in her neighborhood worked. In the evening, people no longer sat on their front porches. Instead they preferred the privacy of backyard patios, which kept their private lives invisible. Air-conditioning contributed to each family's isolation. On hot summer days and nights people went inside to stay cool. Cassie knew the media celebrities better than she knew anyone on her block.

Cassie fought with her parents in more aggressive ways than did the teens of my youth. She yelled, swore, accused them of trying to control her and threatened to run away. Her parents tolerated this open anger much more readily than earlier generations would have. I was confused about whether my generation of girls was more repressed or just happier. Sometimes I think this new openness was progress but, particularly when I talked to beleaguered mothers, I wondered.

Cassie had been surrounded by media since birth. Her family owned a VCR, a stereo system, two color televisions, and six radios. Cassie woke to a radio, played the car stereo on the way to school, watched videos at school, and returned home to a choice of stereo, radio, television, or movies. She could choose between forty channels twenty-four hours a day. She played music while she studied.

Cassie and her friends had been inundated with advertising since birth and were sophisticated about brand names and commercials. While most of her friends couldn't identify the Nebraska state flower, the goldenrod, in a ditch along the highway, they could shout out the brand of a can of soda from a hundred yards away. They could sing commercial jingles endlessly.

Cassie had been exposed to years of sophisticated advertising in which she heard that happiness came from consuming the right products. She could catch the small lies and she knew that adults often told children lies to make money. She did not consider that a sin—she called it marketing. But I wasn't sure that she caught the big lie, which was that consumer goods were essential to happiness.

Cassie had more access to books than I had. I was limited to a town library the size of a Quick Shop and a weekly bookmobile. She had a six-branch public library system, a school library as big as a gymnasium, and subscriptions to several popular magazines. But she read less than I did. Particularly the classics that I loved, *Jane Eyre*, *Moby-Dick*, and *Return of the Native* bored her with their loopy, ornamental prose. She had more choices about how to spend her time.

Girls' magazines in the 1990s were much the same as the ones I had purchased as a teen. Their content was about makeup, acne products, fashion, weight loss, and attracting boys. Some headlines could be the same: "True Colors Quiz," "Get the Look That Attracts Boys," or "The Ten Commandments of Hair." Others were updated to pay lip service to the 1990s: "Two Coeds in Gray Chill Out at Oxford University," "Should I Get Tested for AIDS?," or "Rev Up Your Looks When Stress Has You Down."

Cassie listened to the Dead Milkmen, 10,000 Maniacs, Nirvana, and They Might Be Giants. She danced to Madonna's song "Erotica," with its sadomasochistic lyrics. Sexist lyrics and the marketing of products with young women's naked bodies were part of the wallpaper of her life. Cassie's favorite movies were *The Crying Game* and *My Own Private Idaho*. Neither of these movies would have made it past the theater owner of my hometown.

By the 1990s, our culture had changed from one in which it was hard to get information about sexuality to one in which it was impossible to escape information about sexuality. Inhibition and shame had quit the scene. In the 1950s, a married couple on TV had to be shown sleeping in twin beds because a double bed was too suggestive. In the 1990s, everything—incest, menstruation, crotch itch, or vaginal odors—was discussed and portrayed on TV.

The plots of romance movies were different. In the 1950s, people argued, fell in love, then kissed. By the '70s, people argued, fell in love, and then had sex. By the '90s, people met, had sex, argued, and then, maybe, fell in love. Hollywood lovers didn't discuss birth control, past sexual encounters, or how a sexual experience might affect the involved parties; they just did it. The Hollywood model of sexual behavior couldn't have been more harmful and misleading if it had tried.

Cassie had seen *Playboy* and *Penthouse* on the racks at the local CVS and Quick Shop. Our city had XXX-rated movie theaters and adult bookstores. She'd watched the adult channels in hotel rooms while bouncing on "magic fingers" beds. Advertisements that disturbed me with their sexual content didn't bother her. When I told her that I first heard the word *orgasm* when I was twenty, she looked at me with disbelief.

Cassie's world was more tolerant and open about sex than was mine. Her friends produced a campy play entitled *Vampire Lesbians of Sodom*. For a joke she displayed Kiss of Mint condoms in a candy dish in her room. Her world was a kinder, gentler place for girls who had babies. One-fifth of all babies in 1994 were born to single mothers. Some of her schoolmates brought their babies to her school's in-house child care center.

In some ways, Cassie was more informed about sex than I was. She had read books on puberty and sexuality and watched films on childbirth at school. She had seen explicit movies and listened to hours of explicit music. But Cassie still hadn't heard answers to the questions she was most interested in. She hadn't had much help sorting out when to have sex, how to say no, or what a good sexual experience should entail.

Cassie was as tongue-tied with boys as I was, and she was even more confused about proper behavior. The values she had learned at home and at church were at odds with the values broadcast by the media and proffered by her peers. She had been raised to love and value herself in a society where an enormous pornography industry reduced women to body parts. She'd been taught by movies and television that sophisticated people are sexually free and spontaneous, and at the same time she'd been warned that casual sex could kill. She'd been raped.

Cassie knew girls who had sex with boys they hardly knew. She knew a girl whose reason for having sex was "to get it over with." Another classmate had sex because her two best girlfriends had had sex and she didn't want to feel left out. More sexual harassment happened in the halls of her school than it did in the halls of mine. Girls were referred to as bitches, whores, and sluts.

Cassie had been desensitized to violence. She'd watched made-for-TV movies about incest and sexual assaults and seen thousands of murders on the small screen.

Cassie couldn't walk alone after dark. Her family locked doors and bicycles. She carried Mace in her purse and a whistle on her car keys. When she was late, her parents were immediately alarmed. Of course, there were girls who were traumatized in the 1950s and there were girls who led protected lives in the 1990s, but the proportions had changed significantly. We felt it in our bones.

When I compared my youth to Cassie's in the first edition of *Reviving Ophelia*, I was not claiming that our childhoods were representative of the childhoods of all other females in America. In some ways, Cassie and I both had unusual childhoods. I grew up in a rural, isolated area with much less exposure to television than the average child of the times. Cassie lived in a city that was safer than most and she came from a family with plenty of money for vacations and music lessons. Even taking into account her rape, Cassie's situation was by no means a worst-case scenario. Her parents weren't psychotic, abusive, or drug addicted.

Also, I was not claiming that I had lived in the good old days and that Cassie lived in the wicked present. I didn't want to glorify the 1950s, which were not a golden age. They were the years of Joe McCarthy and Jim Crow. There was a great deal of sexual, religious, and racial intolerance. Many families had shameful secrets, and if revealed, they led to public disgrace rather than community help. I left my town as soon as I could, and as an adult, I am much happier living in a larger, less structured environment. Many of my friends came from small towns, and particularly the smart women among them had horror stories of not fitting in.

What I *was* claiming was that our stories had something to say about the way the world had stayed the same and the way it had changed for adolescent girls. We had in common that our bodies changed and those changes caused us anxiety. With puberty, we both struggled to relate to girls and boys in new ways. We attempted to be attractive and to understand our own sexual urges. We were awkward around boys and hurt by girls. As we worked to grow up and define ourselves as adults, we both distanced ourselves from our parents and felt some loneliness as a result. As we searched for our identities, we grew confused and sad. Both of us had times when we were moody, secretive, inarticulate, and introspective.

But while some of our experiences were similar, many were radically different. Cassie's community was a global one, mine was a small town. Things that shocked adolescent girls in the 1950s made them yawn in 1994. The world had changed from one in which people blushed at the term "chicken breast" to one in which a movie such as *Pretty Woman* was family fare. We'd gone from a world with no locks on the doors to one of bolt locks and handguns. The issues that I struggled with as a college student—when I should have sex, should I drink or smoke—had to be considered in early adolescence.

Neither the 1950s nor the 1990s offered young adolescents environments that totally met their needs. My childhood was structured and safe, but the costs of that security were limited tolerance of diversity, rigid rules about proper behavior, and lack of privacy. As one man from a small town said, "I don't need to worry about running my own business because there are so many other people who are minding it for me." Although my community provided many surrogate parents and clear rules about right and wrong, this structure was often used to enforce rigid social and class codes and to keep people in their place.

Cassie lived in a town that was less rigid about roles and more supportive of autonomy, but she had little protected space. Cassie had more options than I did. But in some ways she was less free. On a summer night, she couldn't walk alone looking at the Milky Way. The ideal community would somehow be able to combine the sense of belonging that small towns offer with the freedom to be oneself that small towns sometimes inhibit. Utopia for teenage girls would be a place in which they were safe and free, able to grow and develop in an atmosphere of tolerance and diversity, and protected by adults who have their best interest at heart.

It's exceedingly difficult to write about three generations without making generalizations, and what is this book without reflections about the changing culture's effects on girls across the decades? In this update, I rely on research from Pew Research Council and the book *iGen*, as well as anecdotal information from friends, neighbors, and interviews. Yet even as I draw conclusions based on what I read and see, I want to caution my readers that there are always exceptions to general trends.

The 1960s, 1990s, and 2010s are different in hundreds of ways—some of great significance, others relatively trivial. For example, today the middle-aged man who has sex with an eighth grader would be imprisoned for sexual assault of a minor. Lois, the fourteen-year-old whom I mentioned earlier, wouldn't be forced to drop out of school today and marry the older man she had had sex with; she would be in therapy.

Yet the generations are also strikingly similar. Across the last sixty years, girls have been appearance and fashion conscious. They have worried about their popularity and their place in social hierarchies. They have idolized popular bands and favorite celebrities. They have kept secrets from their parents and, at the same time, they have greatly needed their guidance. They have been perplexed by how to handle relationships with the opposite sex. For six decades, adolescent girls have manifested an unlikely combination of egocentrism and idealistism.

We have done our best in this edition to avoid better-or-worse comparisons and nostalgia. Every decade possesses its positives and negatives. For example, in 1959 segregation was still legal. The Voting Rights Act wasn't passed until 1965. In 1994, smoking in public spaces was still permitted. Likewise, in the 1960s, few laws protected children from domestic physical or sexual abuse. By 2019, we have much more reporting of abuse and better laws and enforcement to protect family members from violence.

In 2019, there is more economic insecurity and inequality than in earlier decades. In the 1960s, only one parent needed to work to support a family, own a house, and buy a car. By 1994, both parents generally worked but many couples could afford high-quality lives. By 2019, even in households with two working adults, housing, quality medical care, and college tuition are often beyond reach.

In 1965, 84 percent of people in the United States were non-Hispanic white. In 1994, America was becoming more diverse. Today, only 53 percent of Americans are non-Hispanic whites. Girls today are likely to have friends of different races and ethnic origins. They are less inclined to stereotype or to possess negative attitudes toward people of color.

When I compare the 1990s to today, I am most struck by how technology has changed virtually every aspect of our lives. When families traveled in the 1990s, teenagers read books or sang along with music on the car radio. They also had family conversations, were bored as they looked out the windows, and grudgingly played word games with their younger siblings. Thanks to tablets and earbuds, teens roadtripping today need not interact with their families or with the world passing outside their windows.

In my generation, many girls worked weekends and during the summer. We all tested for our driver's licenses the day we turned sixteen. I celebrated that birthday by driving with my friends for a short vacation in the Rockies. Most of Sara's generation also received their driver's licenses at sixteen, but they were less likely to work. Today one-fourth of students graduate from high school without a driver's license and are unlikely to hold jobs in high school.

Driving a car used to be a significant marker of independence and freedom. Without wheels, girls are also more likely to be homebodies. As Jean Twenge discovered, in terms of dating, drinking, and unsupervised time, eighteen-year-olds in 2019 act like fifteen-year-olds in 2009, and fifteen-year-olds today are similar to thirteen-year-olds of the past.

If I were to come up with a word for each of the three generations we are discussing, I would call my generation *confident*, and Sara's 1994 generation *rebellious*. In 2019, girls are *cautious*.

Girls today have many reasons to feel vulnerable. Economic conditions are harsh, climate change is an overwhelming threat, and school shootings are commonplace. Teens describe threatening incidents at their schools or in their communities. One girl told us about a boy who had been stabbed while trying to stop a sexual assault at a party. Yet statistics reveal that America is much safer today than it was in 1994. Today's teens are murdered and robbed less frequently and have fewer car accidents and alcohol-related deaths. Yet in light of the information they see every day, most teenagers—and adults—are surprised by that statistic.

In general, this generation is more gender fluid than previous ones. Girls have more permission to be boyish in dress and manner and, in fact, they are likely to be teased now if too girly. Nameberry.com, an online naming site, has an entire category of gender-neutral names. New baby names for girls—Harley, Eliot, and Sutton—reflect this new gender fluidity. It's as if the parents are declaring, "I want this baby to be free to be whoever it wants to be."

Girls still must come to terms with their own sexuality but, in this gender-fluid era, girls have more permission to explore their sexual identities. They can be asexual, bi, pansexual, lesbian, or trans. Then they can change their minds and try some other identity.

Sexual identity is much discussed. In one focus group, high-school senior Jordan reported, "Everyone I know is questioning her sexuality and I know one person who doesn't want to identify as either gender."

"Our generation accepts all 'alphabet people" (LGBTQA), Aspen agreed. "We have a gender-fluid senior prom. Girls wear tuxedos if they want and boys can wear dresses. My friends believe in total equality and support gay marriage."

Gay marriage was unthinkable when I was a girl and illegal in 1994. By 2016, 65 percent of Americans supported gay marriage. However, gay kids are still bullied in many schools. Many girls keep quiet about their sexual orientation in middle school, but come out in high school, when they are more likely to find acceptance.

Transgender was almost unheard of in 1965 and rare in 1994. By now, most of the girls we interviewed knew at least one transgender high-school student. Psychologist Margaret Nichols wrote in *Psychotherapy Networker* about the gender spectrum. She found that many teens today don't like rigid definitions of gender. They play around with gender roles and are more accepting of gender fluidity. However, the trends in acceptance and advocacy can be overstated. Nichols reports that transgender teens continue to exhibit higher rates of suicide than their peers.

Many girls today self-identify as transgender. We hear from girls who are desperate to be acknowledged as trans by their parents and friends, and we listen to parents who are concerned their daughters are moving too quickly toward a major life change. A number of therapists work primarily with individuals considering transitioning and their families, and there are guides available on this topic (see Recommended

Reading). We are not authorities in this very complex area but, from our vantage point, we can make several observations.

Identifying as transgender initiates a voyage of discovery for a girl and her family. It's impossible to generalize about all girls grappling with these questions. What we do know is that parents are most helpful to their children when they listen with an open mind and encourage deep thinking and the honest expression of emotion. Withholding judgment allows for a more honest exchange of ideas and creates trust and respect.

When girls first self-identify, it's important to pay more attention to the process than to the outcome. A thoughtful process involves time, education, therapy, and a strong support network. Parents can help their daughters find peers, mentors, and discussion groups. In the meantime, we support calling girls by the name(s) they choose. Especially with younger teens, this identity may change over time; however, it's a mark of respect to affirm all adolescents' desire to claim their own identities. We recognize that this journey can be anxiety inducing for parents. We encourage them to find their own support communities as they help their daughters explore their evolving gender identities.

Religion and ethnicity influence views on gender issues. Evangelical and conservative churches often teach that anything but heterosexuality is a sin. On the other hand, some churches advocate for LGBTQ people and offer them a spiritual home.

"People told me I was too pretty to be gay and boys got mad that I wouldn't date them," Marta told us in a focus group. "It helped I was a strong Christian. My church support group helped me navigate all the criticism and helped me come out as a proud and confident lesbian."

Of course, red and blue states differ in their attitudes towards the LGBTQ community. As Olivia from a small Nebraska town said bitterly, "Small towns, small minds."

Girls whose parents are homophobic are anxious and often closeted well into high school. One girl told us that she knew she was a lesbian but kept quiet. She said that one time at a movie her mother mocked the gay character and spoke harshly of that "lifestyle." The girl said nothing, but went home and sobbed into her pillow.

Other parents are fairly relaxed about their children's sexual orientation. When Aspen told her parents she was bisexual, her dad choked on the water he was drinking. But then he laughed and said, "Well, okay, but no boyfriends or girlfriends until you are older."

Marta's parents were stunned when she came out to them at fourteen. She said, "They didn't have a clue. To them, I looked and acted straight." But after several weeks of discussion her mom told her: "Your sexual orientation isn't an issue for us. We just want you to find a partner who loves and respects you."

Since the early 1960s the most significant changes have arisen in the ways we relate to one another. I grew up in a quiet, slow world. I related to other people in more or less the same ways my ancestors had. Sara's generation still lived in a world where many communities existed. Parents formed extended "families" with close friends, neighbors, and groups such as choirs, baseball teams, or colleagues. By today most connection comes from the digital world, although people still yearn for face-to-face communities.

Over the last fifty years people have become increasingly lonely. In the 1950s, most people felt more crowded than lonely, and many were surrounded by lifelong friends and family members. In the 1970s, on average, people reported that they had three close friends. That number has fallen steadily and many Americans now report having no close friends.

By today most girls thoroughly understand the mechanics of sex, and they have been exposed to a great deal of online sexuality. But they are just as uncertain about love, sex, and relationships as we were in 1950 and Sara's generation was in the 1990s. Now some girls are part of hookup culture, but these same girls need help having a conversation with a potential date. Talking is what is scary.

The fundamental ways in which children are socialized and communicate with one another are different. We are creating a new kind of human. For the first time in human history, teenage girls no longer relate primarily through face-to-face interactions. Their community is a virtual community built by social media sites and emojis.

Meanwhile, we already know enough to know that the virtual community is a poor substitute for a real one. The desires for connection and group bonding are basic hominid needs, at least two million years old. Since the beginning of our species, we humans have shared our food, told stories, and huddled together to feel warm and safe.

No one knows where our changing behaviors will lead us, but I suspect that, unless we reclaim our nonvirtual lives and rebuild some semblance of the communities of the past, we will lose much of what is rewarding about our humanity.

FIVE

Families:
The Root Systems

FRANCHESCA (14)

Betty and Lloyd came to therapy to discuss their daughter, who was born on a Lakota Sioux reservation in western Nebraska. When Franchesca was three months old, Catholic Social Services placed her with Betty and Lloyd. Betty showed me a picture of Franchesca in an infant swing. "We loved her from the moment we saw her. She had shiny hair and eyes the color of black olives."

Lloyd said, "There was some feeling against the adoption in Betty's family. They didn't call it prejudice, but they worried about bad genes and wondered if Francie would fit in."

Betty apologized for her family. "They were small-town people. It took us a while to teach them to say 'Native American' instead of 'Indian,' but once they saw Francie they loved her."

Lloyd clasped his hands over his ample stomach and looked sober. "Everyone's done their best really. We don't blame them for what's happened."

"What's happened exactly?" I asked.

Lloyd and Betty explained that Franchesca had a typical childhood. Lloyd was a pharmacist who ran his own store. Betty stayed home with Franchesca until first grade, then she worked part-time with Lloyd. Franchesca fell off her bike in second grade and broke her leg. She had a slight speech impediment that was corrected with speech therapy in third grade. They lived in a quiet neighborhood with lots of kids. Franchesca had birthday parties, summer vacations, Girl Scouts, and pottery lessons.

Lloyd added, "In elementary school her grades were good and she was popular with her classmates. She had a sweet disposition—always smiling."

Betty agreed. "We never treated her differently because she was adopted or Sioux. At the time, we felt that was the right thing to do. Now I wonder if we didn't gloss over things that needed to be discussed."

Lloyd looked surprised. "What do you mean?"

"Francie got teased at school about being a Native American. When we knew about it, we stopped it, but I wonder if we always knew. We told her that being adopted didn't matter, that we were just like other families. But we weren't really. She was brown and we were white."

I thought about how adoptions were handled before the 1980s. Adoptions tended to be closed. Social service agencies reassured parents that adopted children would be just like their own. This was truer for the parents than for the children. Parents tended to bond immediately, but children almost always felt that adoption made them different.

In particular, teenagers, who are focused on identity issues, struggle with the meaning of adoption. Often, they are silent about their struggles because they don't want to be disloyal. When adoption crosses racial lines, the issues become even more formidable. In our country, we have so few good discussions about ethnic differences that even to acknowledge differences makes most of us feel guilty. Instead, differences tend to be ignored and feelings about them become shameful, individual secrets.

"In seventh grade, Francie started her periods and was cranky all the time," Betty continued. "I thought it was hormonal. Before, she'd always told us everything, but in seventh grade she hid in her room. I talked to my sister and we agreed that teenagers go through stages like this. In fact, her girls were giving her fits at the time. So we let it slide. But then her grades dropped and that worried us."

She sighed. "We called the counselor, and he said lots of kids have trouble their first year of junior high. We made her study two hours a night and her grades picked up a little. She wasn't seeing her old friends, but we let that slide too."

"We let too much stuff slide," Lloyd said.

"This year has been horrible," Betty confessed. "Lloyd is the main disciplinarian. He's not that strict really, only the ordinary rules—let us know where she's going, no alcohol, and passing grades—but you'd think he was beating her. She hardly speaks to him, and it's breaking his heart. She'll talk to me a little more, but not much. She won't go to church with us."

Lloyd twisted in his seat. "She's running with a rough crowd and drinking some," he said. "We've smelled it on her. She's lying and sneaking around."

"Last week we let her go to a ball game with friends and she didn't come home. We were worried sick," Betty said. "Lloyd drove around until sunrise. The next day when she came home, she wouldn't tell us where she'd been."

"I'd like to meet Franchesca," I said.

Lloyd responded, "She doesn't want to come, but we'll make her."

"Just one time," I said. "I usually let teenagers decide whether to return."

The next week Franchesca sat stiffly in my office. She was dressed in green jeans and a Worlds of Fun T-shirt. Her long black hair was pulled back into a ponytail and her eyes were filled with tears. At first, she was quiet, almost sullen. She looked over my head at the various diplomas on the walls and answered my questions by nodding. I searched for an issue on which we could connect—school, friends, books, or her parents. She barely acknowledged my questions. I asked her about adoption and noticed that her breathing changed.

Franchesca raised her eyes and looked me over. She inhaled deeply and said, "I'm living with nice people, but they are not my family." She paused to see how I was taking this. "Every morning when I wake up I wonder what my real mother and father are doing. Are they getting ready for work? Are they looking in the mirror and seeing faces that look like mine? What are their jobs? Do they talk about me and wonder if I am happy?"

Big tears dropped onto her shirt and I handed her the Kleenex box.

She wiped her cheeks and chin and continued. "I can't stop feeling that I'm in the wrong family. I know it would kill Mom and Dad to hear me say this, but I can't make it go away."

I asked Franchesca what she knew about her real mother.

"She gave me up when I was three months old. Maybe she was poor or unmarried. I'm sure she never meant to hurt me. I feel in my heart that she loved me."

Outside, flakes of snow floated by. We watched the snow.

"How does it feel to be Native American?"

"For a long time, I pretended that it didn't matter, but all of a sudden it's the most important thing in the world." Franchesca sighed. "I've been teased since I was little about being a Native American and my tribe doesn't even know I exist." Franchesca talked of the years of teasing, the names—Redskin and Squaw—and the remarks about Indian drunks, welfare cheats, and Indian giving. She ended by saying, "The worst is that line, 'The only good Indian is a dead Indian.'"

I asked what Franchesca knew about Native Americans.

"I saw *The Last of the Mohicans* and *Dances with Wolves*. Before that, the movies about Native Americans made me sick. Have you ever seen *The Lone Ranger*? Do you remember his pal Tonto? Do you know that Tonto in Spanish means 'fool'?"

She paused. "Sometimes I see Native Americans among the homeless downtown. I don't even know if they are Sioux. My mother might be one of them."

I asked, "Would you like to know more about your people?"

Franchesca looked out at the snow. "In a way no and in a way yes. It will make me madder and sadder, but I feel like I can't know myself until I know."

I wrote down the name of a Native American writer, Zitkala-Sa. "Maybe you could check out some of her books."

"Do you think I am being disloyal?"

I thought how to answer. "Your interest in your past is as natural as that snowfall." Franchesca rewarded me with a smile—her first that hour.

Franchesca loved the books of Zitkala-Sa, who was a Sioux of the Yankton band, born in 1896. She wrote of being ripped from her family on the reservation and being sent to an Indian school. After reading about Zitkala-Sa's experiences, Franchesca asked Betty and Lloyd to take her to visit Genoa, a now abandoned Native American school.

The trip went well. They walked around the three-story brick building and peeked through its dusty windows at the old sewing machines and work benches. Later they ate roast beef sandwiches in the main street café and talked about other places to visit. In the following months, they traveled to powwows and to a conference for Plains tribes entitled "Healing the Sacred Hoop."

Over the next few months, Franchesca visited the Native American Center and volunteered to work part-time. She was assigned the job of making coffee and serving cookies to the senior citizens. She joked with them and listened to their stories. From them, she learned many things about the Sioux nation and reservation life.

Some of our sessions were family sessions. We tried to distinguish between adoption, race, and adolescent issues. Franchesca thought her father was too strict and her mother too intrusive. She felt that Lloyd and Betty still saw her as a little girl, and Lloyd struck her as rigid and inflexible. Betty got on Francie's nerves. "For no reason, I just want to yell at her."

Lloyd compromised with curfews, but remained firm about knowing where Francie was. Betty agreed to stay out of Francie's room. After these talks, Francie began to joke with Lloyd again. After school, she sat in the kitchen and told Betty about her day.

We stopped pretending that the family had no feelings about adoption. Everyone had feelings. Lloyd worried that Franchesca might be more vulnerable to alcoholism. Betty was fearful that someday Franchesca might find her real mother and abandon them. Franchesca felt she lived between a brown world and a white one and wasn't totally accepted by either. She loved Lloyd and Betty, but she could not look to them for clues about her identity.

Franchesca told Betty and Lloyd that she wanted information about her biological mother. They were ambivalent but agreed to allow her to look into her health and tribal background. Franchesca was glad to have some information, but she wanted more. She told Betty and Lloyd, "Someday I will have to find her."

In our individual sessions Franchesca grappled with many issues. She was uncertain who to befriend. "My old friends are shallow," she explained, "but my new friends are getting into trouble."

I suggested she consider making one or two close friends and not worry about belonging to a crowd. I reminded her that the people at the Native American Center were her friends.

Franchesca began to pray to the Great Spirit for guidance. She had two worlds to combine, two histories to integrate. She made conscious choices about what she would keep for herself from both worlds. She would live with Betty and Lloyd, but she would visit the reservation and learn more about the Sioux. She would return to her parents' church, but she would worship the Great Father as well.

As she worked on her issues, Franchesca became an advocate for the Native American students at her mostly white junior high. She decided to challenge all racist remarks. She pushed for more Native American literature and history in the school district curriculum.

At our last meeting, Franchesca was dressed in blue jeans and a woven blouse. Betty and Lloyd sat proudly on either side of her, Lloyd in his white pharmacist jacket and Betty in a polyester pants suit. Lloyd said, "I've learned to speak a few words of Lakota." Betty added, "This research has opened a new world for us." Franchesca said, "I belong to two families, one white and one brown. But there is room in the sacred hoop for all my relatives."

Franchesca is an example of how complicated family life could be in the 1990s. At fourteen she was dealing with race and adoption issues as well as issues around alcohol, sex, religion, and school. She was searching for an identity and distancing herself from her parents by rebelling and keeping secrets. Yet she loved her parents and needed their support. From the outside, she looked mildly delinquent, but her behavior was really a signal about the struggle within to find herself.

Franchesca and her family were "up to their ears in alligators," as Lloyd put it. Fortunately, the family sought help. They turned out to be an affectionate family with about the right mix of structure and flexibility. The parents had rules and expectations and the energy to enforce them, but they also had the ability to grow and change as their daughter changed. When they realized that Franchesca needed contact with her people, they developed an interest in Native American customs. They developed some appreciation for diversity, even of religious beliefs. With time and effort on everyone's part, life settled down. Franchesca was on her way to developing her own identity and yet she remained connected to her parents. She explored who she was, but not in ways that were self-destructive.

In the 1990s at the Whitney Biennial Art Show in New York City, I stood before a tableau entitled "Family Romance." Four figures—a mother, father, son, and daughter—stood naked in a row. They were baby-doll shapes of spongy tan material and real hair. They were all the same height and the same level of sexual development. I interpreted this work as a comment on life in the 1990s. To me it broadcast, "There is no childhood anymore and no adulthood either. Kids aren't safe and adults don't know what they are doing."

When we think of families in the 1990s, most of us still envision the traditional family, with a working father and a mother who stayed home with the children, at least until they went to school. In reality, only 14 percent of families were configured this way. Family demographics had changed radically since the 1970s, when less than 13 percent of all families were headed by single parents. In 1990, 30 percent of all families were headed by single parents. (Mothers were the parents in 90 percent of single-parent homes.)

Our culture had yet to acknowledge the reality of these figures. In the 1990s, a family could be a lesbian or gay couple and their biological or adopted children, a fourteen-year-old and her baby in a city apartment, a gay man and his son, two adults recently married and their teenagers from other relationships, a grandmother with twin toddlers of a daughter who has died of AIDS, a foster mother and a meth baby, a multigenerational family from a traditional culture, or unrelated people who were together because they loved one another. Whatever the composition of families, they were under siege. Parents were more likely to be overworked, overcommitted, tired, and poor. They were less likely to have outside support.

Money was a significant problem. We had become an increasingly stratified society with some children living in a luxurious world of designer clothes, private schools, and camps, while other children walked dangerous streets to inadequate schools.

Supervision was also a challenge in the 1990s. The small, tight-knit communities that helped families rear children were increasingly extinct. Instead, television was the babysitter in many homes.

The great respect that Americans had for independence created certain difficulties in families. A philosopher friend said to me back then, "Aren't you proud of your daughter? She's turning out so differently from you and your husband. What better definition could you have of successful parenting?" When I bemoaned the distance between Sara and me, another friend said, "Would you want it any other way?"

Our nation began with a Declaration and a War of Independence. We admire feisty individualists, and our heroes are explorers, pioneers, and iconoclasts. We respect Harriet Beecher Stowe, Sojourner Truth, Rosa Parks, Amelia Earhart, and Ruth Bader Ginsburg.

The freedom that we value in our culture we also value in our families. Americans believe adolescence is the time when children emotionally separate from their parents, and this assumption can become a self-fulfilling prophecy. Daughters in the 1990s behaved as they were expected to behave, and ironically, if they were expected to rebel, they rebelled. They distanced themselves from their parents, criticized parental behavior, rejected parental information, and kept secrets.

This distancing created a great deal of tension in families. Parents set limits to keep their daughters safe, while daughters talked about their rights and resented what they viewed as their parents' efforts to keep them young. Parents were fearful and angry when their daughters took enormous risks to prove they were independent. For most families, the heavy battles began in junior high.

Parents who grew up in a different time with a different set of values were unhappy with what their daughters were learning. They felt like they were trying harder than their parents tried, and yet their daughters were more troubled. The things that worked when they were teenagers were no longer working. They saw their daughters' drinking, early sexualization, and rebelliousness as evidence of parental inadequacy. They diagnosed their own families as dysfunctional.

I postulated then that we had a dysfunctional culture. Almost all parents wanted their daughters to develop into healthy, interesting people. They were hindered in their efforts to help their daughters by the dangerous culture in which we lived, by the messages that our culture sent young women, and by our ethic that to grow up one must break from parents—even loving parents.

In the 1990s, our family lived in a neighborhood filled with three-story houses and lovely oak and maple trees. Most of the parents had worked hard at parenting, yet their teenagers were driving them crazy. As an attorney said to me at a block party, "Parenthood is the one area of my life where I can feel incompetent, out of control, and like a total failure all of the time."

At a New Year's Eve party, I asked another couple how their teenage daughters were. The husband said without a smile, "I wish they'd never been born."

Another thing that separated girls from their parents was their own unhappiness. In junior high, many girls had lost their childhood gaiety and zest. Because of their developmental level, girls held parents responsible for this. They were still young enough that they expected their parents to protect them and keep them happy. When they crashed into larger forces and found themselves miserable, they blamed their parents, not the culture.

In the '90s, parents were not the primary influence on adolescent girls. Instead, girls were heavily swayed by their friends, whose ideas came from the mass media. The average teen watched 21 hours of TV each week, compared to 5.8 hours spent on homework and 1.8 hours reading. The adolescent community had become an electronic community of rock music, television, videos, and movies. The rites of passage into this community were risky. Adulthood, as presented by the media, implied drinking, spending money, and being sexually active.

The mass media had the goal of making money from teenagers, while parents wanted to raise happy, well-adjusted adults. These two goals were not compatible. Most parents resisted their daughters' media-induced values. Girls found themselves in conflict with their parents and with their own common sense.

For example, Jana was the petite only child of older, professional parents. Until junior high, she had loved and felt loved by them. But in junior high she faced the choice of being the good daughter her parents expected or being popular and having a boyfriend.

"All through junior high, I'd do anything to fit in. I tried out friends like flavors of ice cream, but eventually I settled in with the popular crowd," she told me. "I went to a Catholic school where the nuns told us that we would go to hell if we swore. But to be cool I had to swear. So I had the choice of eternal damnation or being unpopular."

We had laughed together at her rueful tone. "In junior high this guy in math class liked me and I liked him. But he wasn't popular, so I didn't go out with him."

Once her dad caught her sneaking out late at night to meet her friends. Jana said, "He sat on the couch and cried. He lectured me about rape and all that stuff." Another time she came home drunk on "purple passion." As our interview ended she whispered to me, "My parents have no idea all the trouble I've been in. They'd be totally shocked."

Adolescents and their families challenged mental health professionals. We needed to strike a balance between respecting parents' responsibility to protect their children and supporting adolescents' need to develop as individuals and move into a broader world.

Eleanor Maccoby and John Martin studied what kinds of families produce what kinds of children. They focused on two broad dimensions. The first was affection. At one end of a continuum were parents who were accepting, responsive, and child-centered; at the other end were parents who were rejecting, unresponsive, and self-centered. The second dimension examined control strategies. At one end of the continuum were parents who were undemanding and low in control, and at the other end are parents who are demanding and high in control.

These two dimensions interacted to produce different outcomes for teenagers. Low-control and low-acceptance parents produced teens with a variety of problems, including delinquency and chemical dependency. Parents who were high in control and low in acceptance (authoritarian parents) produced children who were socially inadequate and lacking in confidence. Parents who were low in control and high in acceptance (indulgent parents) had teenagers who were impulsive, irresponsible, and lacking of confidence. Parents who were high in both control and acceptance (strict but loving parents) had teenagers who were independent, socially responsible, and confident. According to this research, the ideal family was one in which the message children received from parents was: "We love you, but we have expectations."

LUCY (15)

As a teenager, Lucy was recovering from leukemia. She, like many young people who had been ill, was close to her parents in ways that were adaptive when she was fighting the disease. Now that she had recovered, this closeness was keeping her from developing her own sense of self.

Lucy was chubby, with the soft, pale skin of the chronically sick. Her radiation and chemotherapies had caused her hair to fall out, and by the time I met her in therapy, she had just started to grow stubby new hair. When she went to school or shopping, she covered her head with a knitted purple cap, but that first day in my office I could see her scalp.

Lucy sat placidly between her parents as they explained her medical history. Two years ago, she had been diagnosed with leukemia and she had been through a series of hospitalizations. The doctors were optimistic about her long-term prognosis.

I asked how all this medical turmoil had affected the family. Sylvia said, "We did what we needed to do to save Lucy's life. I never left her side when she was in the hospital. Frank came every night after work." She looked at her husband. "Frank's a policeman. He was passed over for promotion this year. I'm sure his captain thought he had his hands full. But there will be other years. I am sick to death of hospitals, but Lucy is alive; I'm not complaining."

Frank spoke carefully. "Our boy had the toughest time. He stayed with my sister. Lucy came first."

"Mark's been a brat since I came home," Lucy interrupted.

I asked Lucy about the hospital time. "It wasn't so bad except when I was sick from the chemo. Mom read to me; we played games. I know the answers to all the Trivial Pursuit questions."

It had been hard for her to return to school. Everyone was nice to her—almost too nice, like she was a visitor from another planet. But she was left out of so many things. Her old friends had boyfriends and were involved in new activities. When she was in the hospital, they visited with flowers and magazines, but now that she was better, they didn't seem to know what to do with her.

Frank said, "Lucy's personality has changed. She's quieter. She used to clown around. Now she is more serious. In some ways she seems older; she's suffered more and seen other children suffer. In other ways she's younger; she's missed a lot."

Lucy had missed eighth-grade graduation, the beginning of high school, parties, dating, sports, school activities, and even puberty (the leukemia had delayed her periods and physical development). She had lots of catching up to do. She'd been so vulnerable that her parents were understandably protective. They didn't want her to become tired, to eat junk food, to forget to take her medicines, or to take unnecessary risks. Her immune system had been weak and she could be in trouble with the slightest injury. Lucy, unlike most teens, didn't grimace at her parents' worries. She associated them with staying alive.

The first time I saw Lucy alone, she was shy and tongue-tied. She sat looking out the window, her forehead wrinkled with worry. She was good at quoting what her mother or the doctors thought she should think or do. Lucy volunteered that when she watched television she marveled at the energy of the characters. "They move around so much and sound so perky. I get tired and jealous just watching them."

I began by asking her what she thought was fun. She drew a blank. I suggested that by the next session perhaps she would know. Lucy agreed to sit alone for ten minutes a day and think about what she enjoyed.

Lucy came in the next time rather discouraged. She had religiously followed my instructions and the main thing she had discovered was that she had no thoughts of her own. "All I think is what I'm supposed to."

I said that realizing this was the beginning of the process of finding her private thoughts. We talked about how Lucy was different from her parents and brother. At first this was difficult, but as we talked she became interested and animated for the first time since we'd met. Her differences were small: "I like candy and Mom doesn't. I like rock music and Mark likes country." But later they became more important. "Mom suffers without complaining, while I like to tell others. I cry when I'm upset and Mark gets mad. I like people around when I'm worried and Dad likes to be alone." We discussed these differences without judging and Lucy seemed pleased that she could be different from her family and still be close to them.

The next week Lucy came in with a jubilant smile on her face. "I know what I like," she said. "Last Thursday my family went to a Cub Scout meeting and I stayed home. I thought, 'How should I spend this evening?' I realized that what I wanted to do was watch an old movie on television. *Casablanca* was on and I loved it."

Lucy said proudly, "No one told me to do this or cares whether I like movies or not. I just did it for myself."

I congratulated Lucy on her insight. Even though the content of her self-discovery was small, the process was critical. Lucy had managed to discover something about herself and to respect that discovery.

After this first thought, Lucy slowly built a more independent personality. She wrote about her time in the hospital. At first, she wrote her polite feelings—she was grateful to the doctors and nurses, grateful to her parents for sticking so close. Later she was able to write about her fear of death, her anger at being a cancer patient, her rage at the painful treatments, and her sadness about the children who didn't make it.

Lucy worked her way back into the world of friends and school. She joined the Spanish Club at her school. She invited an old friend to spend the night with her. Sylvia worried these activities would tire Lucy. Her worrying, which had been so adaptive during the fight against leukemia, was less adaptive now that Lucy was recovering. After five sessions, Lucy reported that she and her mother had argued over a late-night phone call. I laughed in relief.

The family therapy became a post-traumatic stress debriefing. Lucy's leukemia had affected everyone's life. Sylvia told of coming home from the hospital after a night when Lucy had thrown up every fifteen minutes from the chemotherapy. She walked into Lucy's empty bedroom, lay down on her canopy bed, still decorated with unicorns. She'd picked up Lucy's My Little Pony and cried till she felt her body had no more tears.

Frank talked about how hard it was to work. He'd be ticketing speeders and thinking of Lucy in her hospital bed. "Sometimes a speeder would be rude or argumentative," Frank said. "I'd just want to punch him in the mouth."

Mark was mad at Lucy for getting sick. "I thought she did it to get attention. Sometimes I thought she was faking it, and other times I was sure she would die. She got lots of presents and Mom and Dad did whatever she wanted. I wanted to get sick too."

After eight months, Lucy was ready to stop therapy. Her voice had become firmer and more animated. Her hair had grown into a sleek brown cap. She had begun an exercise program and her body had slimmed down and firmed up. Her periods had started. She'd reconnected with some old friends and made some new ones. She was losing the serious personality of the sick. She had learned that she could disagree with her parents and no one dropped dead. She could say what she thought and develop into the person she wanted to become.

LEAH (18)

Leah had been born into a country with different assumptions about families than those of the United States. In Vietnam, adolescents were nested in extended families whom they would be with forever and, because Vietnam was impoverished, Leah had missed the information explosion of the Western world.

I interviewed Leah at her high school during her junior year. She was dressed casually in a Garfield sweatshirt and jeans, but she was carefully groomed with long ice-blue nails and an elaborate hairstyle. Only her crooked teeth betrayed the poverty she must have experienced in Vietnam.

Leah was born in 1975. She was the daughter of an American Marine and a Vietnamese woman who had lost her husband to the war and was struggling to support her four children. The Marine left the country without knowing that Leah's mother was pregnant, and Leah never met her father. He gave his home address to Leah's mother and she wistfully wrote it out for me. She read the words aloud like a mantra, but added, "I would never bother him. Perhaps my father is married and would be embarrassed by me."

Leah grew up in Vietnam, the beloved baby of the family. Her mother worked long hours to support her children. She said, "I sat by the window and cried as I waited for my mother to come home from work. When she arrived home, I followed her everywhere and begged to sit on her lap."

She described her childhood as happy. The family lived in one house, and when her brothers married, they brought their wives home to live. Leah never had to work and had all the toys she wanted. "My brothers and sisters protected me and competed to hold me."

When I asked her if she fought with her mother, she said, "Why would I fight with my mother? She gave me the gift of life."

I asked her if she ever disobeyed her mother's rules and she said no. She explained, "She is my mother and I owe her obedience, but it's more than that. She knows what is good for me. Her rules will help me."

Three years prior to our interview, because of Leah's parentage, she and her mother were able to come to America. They would miss her siblings but, as Leah explained, "Vietnam is a communist country. There is no freedom and no money. I couldn't even go to school beyond ninth grade."

At first, she and her mother lived in a small apartment with no furniture and wore clothes from Goodwill. The Refugee Center helped Leah's mother find work at a local cannery, and they had an adequate income and even sent money back to Vietnam.

At night, after her mother went to bed, Leah wrote letters to her brothers and sisters. Holidays, especially the Vietnamese New Year, were lonely for her. Still, she was happy to be in America. Her high school was much better than the schools in Vietnam. She had made friends with some of the Vietnamese students. "The teachers are kinder and we have computers."

I asked her to describe a typical day in her life.

"I wake early so I can cook breakfast for my mother. It makes me sad to see her work, so I try to help her," she explained. "Then I walk to school. After school I clean the house and fix dinner. In the evening I study and help my mother learn English."

When I inquired about hobbies, Leah said, "I like to listen to Vietnamese music, especially sad music. I write poems about my country."

Leah considered herself too young to date. "I would never have sex before marriage," she told me. "That would bring great shame on my family."

When she reached her twenties, Leah planned to date Vietnamese men who promised that her mother would always be able to live with her. She showed me a class ring and a silver bracelet. "Mother bought me this. I begged her not to, but she wanted me to look like an American teenager. I could never leave my mother. My mother has given me everything and kept nothing for herself. I am all she has now."

She and her friends spoke mostly Vietnamese, and American teenagers left them alone. She had yet to see an American movie. When we discussed American teenagers, Leah hesitated, clearly concerned not to appear rude. Then she said, "I don't like how American children leave home when they are eighteen. They abandon their parents, and they get in a lot of trouble. I don't think that's right."

Leah liked the freedom and the prosperity of America. "It's easier to earn a living here," she said. "I can hardly wait to finish school and get a job so I can support my mother."

In Leah's home culture, autonomy and independence were not virtues. Vietnamese families were expected to be harmonious and loyal. The good of the family was more important than the individual satisfaction of its members. Children were expected to live at home all their lives (sons with their parents and daughters with their husbands' parents). No one anticipated that children would rebel or disagree with their parents, and children rarely did disagree. Authority was not questioned, which may have been tolerable when the authority was wise and benevolent, but could be tragic when authority was malevolent or misguided.

These beliefs in obedience and loyalty allowed Leah to have a less turbulent adolescence. She didn't need to distance herself from her family or reject family beliefs in order to grow up.

I struggled with the questions this interview raised for me. Why was a girl raised in a traditional and, by American standards, controlling culture so content? Why was she so loving and respectful of adults? And why did she seem so content and confident?

I realized that many of Leah's choices had been made for her. Her life was held in place by her cultural and familial traditions. The diversity of mainstream American culture in the 1990s put pressure on teens to make complicated choices, but most adolescents didn't yet have the cognitive equipment necessary to do this. Young adolescents did not deal well with ambiguity. If the parents were affectionate and child-centered, teenagers were comforted by clarity and reassured by rules. Teens like Leah were protected from some of the experiences of their peers. She had challenges that she could be expected to meet— challenges that had to do with school, housework, and family loyalty.

ABBY (18) AND ELIZABETH (14)

One of my favorite families was the Boyds. Bill was a warmhearted man who played the ukulele and had formed our state's chapter of Men Against Sexual Violence. Nan was an organic gardener who brought extraordinary dishes to political potluck dinners. Once she brought a casserole made of nettles, once a salad of morel mushrooms and wild onions, and another time a mulberry cheesecake.

Bill and Nan were community organizers and political activists who drove a beat-up pickup and spent their money on good causes. I saw them at marches for human rights or the environment, at peace workshops, and at tree plantings. They had lots of company—foreign exchange students, friends of friends driving through our state, relatives, and political allies. Every summer they took their daughters on month-long camping vacations.

Bill could make anyone laugh. He could cut the tension in a room of angry people with a joke or a song. He gave everyone nicknames they wanted to keep forever. Nan's vegetables took over the neighborhood in late July. She traveled door to door begging neighbors to take her zucchini and bell peppers. Once their cat Panther had a litter of six black kittens whom they named after their friends in order to entice them to adopt. Not surprisingly, it worked.

Abby was blond and willowy, the most serious member of the family. In elementary school she won the statewide spelling bee. Elizabeth was shorter and red-haired. As a girl, she was the leader of a pack of adventurous pranksters we called the Crazy Kids. Abby and Elizabeth were involved in everything—politics, drama, music, sports, camps, and their church. The family had parties for the first snowfall, the first day of spring, a straight-A report card, or May Day. Their parents were loving and low-key. Problems were handled by discussion. The parents trusted Abby and Elizabeth to make their own choices. They had the freedom to grow into whomever they wanted to be.

Both girls had trouble with adolescence. Abby got depressed in eighth grade. She missed weeks of school because of allergies and stomach ailments. Her grades fell and she dropped out of activities. She skipped the family parties and no longer marched beside her parents at demonstrations.

Much to her parents' consternation, Abby dropped her neighborhood friends and joined a group of drug users. She became secretive about her whereabouts and locked her bedroom door. Her parents wondered if she'd been drinking or smoking. Once she came home red-eyed and confused, and Bill and Nan took her to an emergency room for a drug test. It was negative, and they never tried that again. It was too traumatic for everyone.

During Abby's adolescent years, Bill would suggest a bike ride and Abby would give him a withering look. Nan would bake a gooseberry pie and Abbie would call it "hippie food" and refuse to eat it. She quit coming to meals with the family. When they tried to talk to her about the changes, she clammed up or attacked them for being unreasonable.

Nan and Bill couldn't understand what was going wrong. Nan had some family history of depression, but she had never worried about it. When she was young, Abby had seemed calm and stable. They took her to a therapist, but Abby wouldn't talk. She claimed she could work her life out on her own.

Two years later Elizabeth was in trouble. She dropped the Crazy Kids and stayed in her room, which she turned into a dark cave. She listened to music and read science fiction. Elizabeth also hated school and managed to flunk three courses in eighth grade. Her only friend was Colin, who shared her interest in science fiction.

Although Elizabeth managed to pull her grades up—by high school she was again an honor roll student—she remained distant from the other students. She and Colin became a couple and formed a small world of their own. She argued with Bill and Nan, who encouraged her to see her other friends. Unlike Abby, she never used drugs, but she was the angrier daughter. She hurled insults at her parents and told them nothing about her life.

When Elizabeth first had trouble, Nan and Bill again found a therapist. This one talked to Elizabeth alone and then assured Nan and Bill that they were doing everything right. She said, "I've never seen quite so much trouble in such a healthy family." Nan told me later that she wasn't sure whether to feel good or bad about that remark.

The therapy may have helped some, but both girls blamed Bill and Nan for the difficulties they were having, as if somehow perfect parents would have protected them from the chaotic world they were entering. In spite of her intelligence, Abby barely graduated from high school and never attended college. Elizabeth got pregnant her junior year and decided to keep the baby.

At first, I was baffled by this family's trouble. I wondered if there were problems I didn't know about, or if the girls had been assaulted by a relative or family friend. Reading the research on families with different control strategies and levels of affection helped me understand this family.

The Boyds were an affectionate family but had minimal controls. They wanted their daughters to experience the world in all its messiness and glory. Their daughters turned out much as the research would have predicted. They had low self-esteem and problems with impulsivity. Clearly in their early adolescent years they would have benefited from more structure.

The Boyds believed in autonomy, tolerance, and curiosity. They raised daughters who were open to experience, eager to try new things, socially aware, and independent. Because girls like this in the 1990s were so open and aware, when they reached junior high they were hit full force by the gales of the hurricane. When all that force hit, they were temporarily overwhelmed. It was too much to handle too fast. Often, they handled it in the way Abby and Elizabeth did, by withdrawal and depression. They screened out the world to give themselves time to process all the complexity.

Abby and Elizabeth were now in their early twenties. They were both "in recovery" from their adolescent experiences. Abby worked at a food co-op as a produce manager and was active in Ecology Now. She hated drugs, even caffeine, and allowed herself only herbal teas. She loved the community of like-minded people who worked at the co-op. She and Nan shopped together for herbs and vegetables to plant in the spring. Together they concocted natural-food recipes for the co-op deli. She and Bill biked across Iowa together.

Elizabeth was a good mother to her lovely redheaded daughter. She and Colin matured during her pregnancy and decided to make a commitment to stay together and raise the baby. They lived with their daughter on a rented farm outside of town. Neighbor kids followed Elizabeth around as she fed the goats and chickens on her farm. When her daughter was older, she intended to go back to school and study biology.

ROSEMARY (14)

Gary ran a silk-screening business and Carol gave violin lessons to children after school. They had three children: Rosemary, in eighth grade, and twin boys three years younger, who were stars of their neighborhood soccer team.

Carol and Gary were new age parents. Gary wore beads and had a ponytail. Carol collected crystals and spent time in the brain wave room at the new age bookstore. They had raised Rosemary to be her own person. They hadn't tried to mold her in any way, but rather believed in letting her character unfurl. Gary said, "Our biggest fear was damaging her spirit."

They tried to model equality in their relationship and to raise their children free of gender-role constraints. Rosemary mowed the lawn, and the twins did the dishes and set the table. Gary taught Rosemary to pitch and draw. Carol taught her to read tarot cards and to throw the I Ching.

This was a child-centered home, very democratic, with an emphasis on freedom and responsibility rather than conformity and control. The parents didn't believe in setting many limits for the children. Rather they felt they would learn their own limits through trial and error. They both liked to describe themselves as friends of their kids. They taught Rosemary to stand up for herself and shared many stories of her assertiveness with adults and peers. Carol and Gary spared no expense to offer their children enrichment opportunities. Rosemary took art lessons from the best teacher in town and attended baseball camp every summer. The boys had ball teams, YMCA camps, and yoga classes.

At our first appointment Carol and Gary seemed vulnerable and shaken.

"I want my daughter back," Carol announced. She talked about how happy and confident Rosemary had been in elementary school. She'd been a good student and student council president in her sixth-grade year. She was interested in everything and everybody. They had trouble slowing her down enough to get rest and food. She once said to her art teacher, "I'm your best student, aren't I?"

With puberty she changed. She hated the way her wiry body "turned to dough." She was still assertive with her parents, even mouthy and aggressive much of the time, but with peers she was quiet and conforming. She worried about pleasing everyone and was devastated by small rejections. Many days she came home in tears because she sat alone at lunch or because someone criticized her looks.

She stopped making good grades because she felt grades didn't matter. Popularity was all that counted. She obsessed about her weight and her looks. She exercised, dieted, and spent hours in front of the mirror.

Suddenly she cared more about being liked by athletes than about being an athlete. She became what her parents called "boy crazy." They found notes she'd written filled with sexual innuendos. She talked about boys all the time and called them on the phone. She was asked to parties by ninth-grade boys who were experimenting with sex and alcohol.

"We're in over our heads with Rosemary," Gary admitted. "She's doing stuff now that we thought she'd do in college. We're not sure that we can protect her."

"I wish we could find a nice safe place and put her there for about six years until she matures," Carol added. We all laughed.

"We're both from small towns," Carol continued. "When we were Rosie's age, we didn't have these kind of temptations. We don't know what to do."

Carol handed me a CD they'd found in her room. "Look at what she's listening to: 'Reckon You Should Shut the Fuck Up and Play Some Music,' 'Crackhouse,' and 'You Suck' by the Yeastie Girls." Gary said, "We had a family rule that anyone who swore put a quarter in the jar, and when it filled we'd all go out to eat. After listening to that CD, we realized that we were in a new ballpark."

Gary stared at his hands. "We taught her to be assertive and take care of herself, but it seems like she uses all her assertiveness against us. She keeps things stirred up all the time. She has a real flair for the dramatic and her timing's impeccable. She'll blow up during my meditation time or when I have a customer on the phone."

All the preceding year they had worried about Rosemary. Then the Saturday night before our session she had stayed with a boy in a hotel room after a concert. She lied and claimed to be at a sleepover with girlfriends.

I agreed to visit with Rosemary. She was petite, with dark hair and dramatic eyes. She wore designer jeans and Nikes to the session and carried a paperback copy of *The Anarchist's Cookbook*. She immediately told me that she wanted my help in getting her parents to lighten up.

I just listened. I knew that any advice would sound parental, and hence unacceptable. I asked about her concerns. She was worried about her weight and her physical flaws. She felt she needed to lose ten pounds; her left profile was "hideous" and her skin too splotchy. She had tried dieting but hated it. She felt crabby and depressed and eventually would cave in and eat.

Rosemary felt her friends were lookist and so was she. She was frightened of not being pretty enough. She said, "Wherever I go, I look around and there's always someone prettier than me. That drives me nuts."

We talked about how sexualized and unnatural models looked and about the ways women were depicted on MTV and in the movies. A part of Rosemary hated the pressure, but another part was obsessed with looking right. A part of her scorned lookism, yet she couldn't help evaluating everyone on the basis of appearance.

We talked about how her life had changed since elementary school. Rosemary smiled when she talked about baseball and drawing with her dad. She had loved her parents and felt close to them then, but now she didn't. "They don't understand what I'm going through. They always give me stupid advice. They don't want their little baby girl to grow up."

Rosemary felt close to her friends, but she admitted that friendships were difficult. She worried about betrayal and rejections. The social scene changed from day to day. She felt uneasy standing up for herself with boys. She did things she didn't agree with to fit into the popular crowd.

We talked about her friends' experiences more than her own. She had friends who were dumped after they had sex with their boyfriends. Other friends were raped or had abortions. Generally, she felt that she wouldn't get in the same kind of trouble, but she admitted she had experienced a few close calls.

When we talked about guys, she was surprisingly insightful. She had wanted a boyfriend so badly that she had done anything to win favor. She said, "I don't feel good about myself unless a guy likes me. I do whatever it takes."

Our work proceeded erratically. It was hard to do therapy with an anarchist. Like her parents, I wanted to keep her safe while she grew up, and like them, I had to be careful or I might say the wrong thing. If she folded her arms over her chest and looked out my window, I knew it was over for that session.

Rosemary saw the world in rigid categories. She overgeneralized, simplified, or denied what she couldn't understand. Her feelings were chaotic and often out of control, and her need for peer approval, particularly male approval, placed her in dangerous situations. She had a hard time saying no to boys who pushed for sex. Furthermore, she was determined to figure everything out for herself. She literally flinched on those rare occasions when I offered suggestions.

I thought of the many ironies in this family. These new age spiritual parents had a daughter whose main concern was weight. The parents' laissez-faire approach didn't work well in a time of AIDS and addictions. Carol and Gary had been careful to raise Rosemary in a gender-nonconforming environment, and she became ultrafeminine so that she could attract and hold boys. They taught her to be assertive, but she used those skills only with grown-ups. Most ironic of all, Rosemary, who had grown up in a home with a meditation room, needed centering.

All these clients' families were loving, but the parents varied in their expectations and discipline. Leah came from a family that was high in control. Franchesca and Lucy came from families that were moderate in control, and Rosemary, Abby, and Elizabeth were from families that were low in control.

Leah's family believed that the best defense against bad ideas was censorship. Development was carefully channeled so that it fit the family's values. Sheltered from the storms, Leah experienced challenges at a rate she could handle. But this protection had a cost. She sacrificed some freedom and control.

Lucy and Franchesca had families who were reasonably protective and yet allowed their daughters freedom to grow in their own directions. Not surprisingly, their daughters were less stressed than Abby, Elizabeth, and Rosemary and less well behaved than Leah.

Abby and Elizabeth's family as well as Rosemary's family believed that the best defense against bad ideas was better ideas. They were more liberal, democratic, and prone to negotiating. They valued experience more than structure, autonomy more than obedience. These families had many strengths—respect for individual differences and commitment to the developing potential of their daughters. But the daughters weren't ready for existential choices, and often they made bad decisions. In early adolescence, these girls looked miserable and out of control. Later, however, they became self-reliant, confident adults.

In a perfect universe, all girls would be loved. Adolescent girls would be protected by their families and yet allowed to blossom and flower as individuals. Families would provide moral clarity without sacrificing too much personal freedom. But in reality, this perfection is impossible. Families have choices. With less structure comes more risk to girls in the short-term and more potential for individual growth over time. With more structure comes less short-term risk but more risk of later conformity and blandness. Families of adolescent girls struggle to find a balance between security and freedom, conformity to family values and autonomy. Finding this balance involves numerous judgment calls. The issues are complex and mistakes can be costly. Parents can be overwhelmed by the intensity of the issues. The perfect balance, like the golden mean, exists only in the abstract.

Parent-teen dynamics are quite different today than they were in 1994. Somewhat surprisingly, teen rebellion is no longer a cultural expectation. Teens require less supervision because they are not acting up. In 2019, divorce is less common that it was in 1994. In fact, divorce rates are at a forty-year low. Families are more democratic, and parental relationships tend to be more equitable. Dads are more engaged with their daughters, and moms have more power at home and in the workforce.

In the early 1960s, most parents felt that the United States was a good society and were eager to teach their children how to live in it. By 1994, parents found themselves fighting against the broader toxic culture on behalf of their often-rebellious teenagers. By now, parents and teens agree that our culture is tricky to navigate. No one wants girls out there early or alone. What parents worry about the most is how to prepare their daughters for the future.

The dimensions that seemed so significant in 1994 seem less relevant today. Families are, in general, more congenial and relaxed. However, technology is one area in which clear agreements and limits are critical. Parents need to limit their own smartphone and computer use. (According to the Center for a Digital Future, the average adult is online over six hours a day and checks email every seven minutes.) Families can negotiate time to unplug. Policies are better than punishments. Proactive planning is easier than reactive damage control.

Teens still thrive most in families with high affection and control, but there aren't many of these families around today. Most families today are high affection and low control. Open communication, time spent talking or working together, and an emphasis on perspective-building skills and resiliency are the keys to healthy, balanced children and adolescents. Rebecca, a first-generation American citizen discussed next, embodies many of these positive traits.

Another change today is that many more parents were born in other countries. America is multicultural, populated with many families who are keeping many traditions from their home countries even as they adapt to their new culture. Girls raised in these families often possess some "typical" American traits, while at the same time hewing to their native traditions.

REBECCA (16)

"My parents' flight landed in New York during a blizzard. They had traveled for nearly two days from the refugee camp in Kenya. My mom was pregnant with me but she didn't even know. She was sixteen."

There was something captivating about Rebecca. She was a beautiful girl, with dark skin and waist-length braids. She also projected an energy that was both calming and cheerful. I could only assume that she was swimming in friends.

Rebecca was born mere months after her mother and father, Sudanese refugees, were resettled by the US government into a small apartment in Lincoln, Nebraska. Sameah and John arrived in 2002 as part of a wave of the "Lost Boys of Sudan." (That moniker is a misnomer, as many girls and young women emigrated as well.)

Unable to speak English with her doctor and nurses, Sameah delivered her baby girl on the first day of spring. Devout Christians, she and John named their daughter Rebecca, a biblical name and also one they hoped would help her assimilate into her new culture.

In quick succession, Sameah and John had four more children. Then, when Rebecca was a first grader, John was killed in a car accident during an ice storm. Unable to read or write, with five children to support, Sameah had to quickly find work. Rebecca began caring for her siblings while her mother worked twelve-hour shifts at a chicken processing plant.

"I've been responsible since my dad died," Rebecca explained. "I have always been reliable and strict, like a mom. I don't let my brothers and sisters watch as much TV as they want, and I make sure they eat healthy food."

"I've observed that about you," I replied. "To be honest, sometimes I've worried about you. You haven't had a 'typical' American childhood. No swimming in summers, no bike riding, no sleepaway camps.

As long as I've known you, you've been caring for your siblings. Did you ever resent that?"

"I actually like it." Rebecca shrugged and smiled. "I didn't need to have friends over, I already had friends around me, all the time. My brothers and sisters are my best friends."

"How was middle school for you?"

"The main thing I remember is that I got my first period during the first week of sixth grade . . . that was terrible timing! I'd have to stay home some days because my cramps were so painful. At school, most of my friends were Americans, mostly black kids. We didn't have too much drama.

"Right before I started middle school my mom remarried. We all loved Jacob. He was like an uncle to us before he became our stepfather. But it was still a lot to deal with. Suddenly I was at a new school and my mom was pregnant again."

"Did you continue your caretaking role with your newer siblings?" I asked.

"Yes and no. Because Jacob had a good job, my mom was able to take some time off for maternity leave. I was still mainly in charge of the older kids. One thing was frustrating—middle-school clubs met in the late afternoons. I couldn't join any because I had to leave my school to walk to pick up the littles at their elementary school. I still wish I could have been in swing choir."

Rebecca burst out laughing. "I would have rocked swing choir."

Still giggling, she continued, "I was really scared about going to high school. The building was huge. I was nervous the first day, but then I started taking music classes and I found 'my people.' Now I'm in three different choirs at school. I love my choir friends . . . we're just goofy all the time."

Rebecca unearthed an iPhone with a cracked screen and showed me an Instagram profile—@choirgrrrls—that she'd created with her classmates. I was pleased that most of the photos featured her surrounded by a circle of silly, theatrical friends.

"What is your relationship with your mom like now that you're a teenager?" I asked.

"My mom is my best friend. She is strict but we never fight about anything. She's always supportive and positive. Honestly, I don't think she ever has a bad day; if she does, she hides it from us kids. She and I work at the same place, in food service on the University of Nebraska campus. She cooks, and I restock the salad bar and stare at cute college boys. We love working together."

"What are some words you would use to describe your mother?" I asked.

"Beautiful. Positive. Joyful. She spreads kindness to anyone who feels down. We really do have a friend relationship as much as a mother/daughter relationship.

"I hear friends complaining about their mothers, but I can't relate," Rebecca continued. "My mom doesn't ask me about where I'm going because she trusts me. She doesn't bug me about my grades because she knows I'm doing my best at school. One time she did have a problem with me wearing leggings, but it wasn't a big deal."

"You're wearing leggings today," I noted.

Rebecca winked. "See?"

"Rebecca, how do you identify yourself? Do you feel Sudanese? American? African American?"

"I feel like a Nebraska girl. I know some things about Sudanese culture, but I don't know the language, so when aunties and uncles come over, I can't talk to them," she admitted. "None of my friends ask me about my Sudanese background; I guess they see me as African American. My mom hopes we'll be 'half-and-half'—able to speak her language, but also able to fit in here."

"Embarrassing question alert: Are you dating anyone?" I asked.

"I'm not allowed to date during high school, probably because my mom got pregnant so young," Rebecca replied. "She said I can't date until college. I couldn't care less. I'm not into flirting or 'talking to' boys, I just want to be friends. I use Insta and Snapchat to see what my friends are doing. I just sit here and enjoy the gossip about boys and girls and dating, but I don't want any of that in *my* life!"

"You're a focused student and you work twenty hours a week," I said. "What do you do for fun?"

"I like to sing at home with my brothers and sisters. I can't stay away from them. I love being around kids!" Rebecca dug out her phone again to show me a video of her youngest siblings rapping and dancing to a Cardi B. song. Wielding the camera off-screen, she gleefully led them through the chorus.

"They're adorable," I said.

"Right? What's more fun than that?" She continued, "I want to be a children's doctor so I can be around children all the time. Omaha has a children's hospital and I want to work there, but I still want to live in Lincoln to be close to my family. They are my everything."

In spite of her relative poverty and limited access to enrichment outside of public school, Rebecca is a lucky girl. She has a loving family and plenty of responsibility and challenges. She feels useful and valued and she's confident that she can accomplish whatever she wants in her future.

Today, many girls have highly involved parents who are extremely protective, the textbook definition of helicopter parents. They stay in constant contact with their daughters via phone and text. With GPS tracking apps, parents can always know where kids are. Teenage girls can call their parents anytime for help. This gives them a sense of security, but it costs them a sense of efficacy.

The irony is that while parents often drive their daughters to school and have frequent contact with them, they don't actually know what their daughters are seeing or doing online. One mother told me, "I feel as if I am hanging on to my daughter with my fingernails."

"My husband and I feel as if we are in a foreign territory with our daughter," she continued. "We don't have any maps or speak her language. We have no idea how to help her with all the complexity she is dealing with."

When contemporary girls leave home, they know less about coping and resilience than did their counterparts in 1994. "Adulting" is now a verb, and many teens don't want to do it. They are more risk averse, and many doubt their own basic competency. They sense quite rightly that they have skill deficits. They aren't as likely to be victims of crimes as were girls in the 1990s, but they feel more vulnerable because they have had limited experience of coping while on their own.

Children don't thrive when they are shielded from all stress. Stress is critical for development. We grow as a result of meeting challenges. The great trick is finding the right kinds and amounts of stress. Ideally, children experience enough stress to grow into emotionally sturdy people with plenty of skills and good coping mechanisms, but not so much that they are overwhelmed and unable to cope.

One of the main jobs for parents is to help children grow into independent adults who are resilient in the face of our rapidly changing culture. That's easier said than done. When do we protect our daughters and when do we encourage them to push on and master their fears? Many girls do not tolerate much distress, and parents are anxious about inflicting it on them. Never mind that stress is an ordinary and necessary aspect of human life.

Especially if girls have a history of panic attacks, suicide attempts, or self-harm, parents have a difficult time stepping back. However, overprotection is as dangerous as "underprotection." Teenagers who are too protected have a rough time entering the world of work or college. Without any inner direction and support, they are at risk to binge drink, use drugs, fail classes, or sleep through job interviews.

Perhaps the kindest gift parents can give their children is preparation for life. That means teaching them critical-thinking and human-relations skills, encouraging them to be out in the world mastering difficult challenges, and having conversations with them about how relationships, politics, and society work.

Children treated as if they are frail become frail. Expecting strength leads to strength. But timing is everything. What is an appropriate challenge must be evaluated on a day-by-day basis. Parents and daughters can decide the milestones that girls want to meet. For example, at what age can a daughter stay home alone, do the grocery shopping, cook a family meal, or manage her own social calendar? At what age can she be the one who watches younger children or works part-time? Girls can also set goals for themselves. For example, they might decide on their own when they want to navigate their city using public transportation.

Of course, not all families have constantly available parents. Especially parents who are struggling financially often work long hours and can be unavailable to their children. Focus group member Jordan was able to see her mother when she drove her to school, but her mother worked double shifts and often didn't see her until the next morning. But Jordan, like many girls whose mothers work long hours, was more self-reliant and competent than her protected peers.

Some parents are deployed for military service. Immigrant parents are sometimes separated from their children by our government. Still other parents are mentally or physically ill, in prison, alcohol or drug addicted, or simply unable to be supportive parents. However, no matter their circumstances, all parents are faced with the dual challenges of loving their children and setting limits, helping them grow and yet allowing them space for independent development. By today, limits tend to revolve around time and technology, both of which are significantly harder to manage.

SIX

Mothers

MY MOTHER WAS a general practitioner in small Kansas and Nebraska towns. This was when most people died at home and much of what a doctor did was sit with the patient and family. She once told me, "Just before old people die, they get addled. They leave this reality and go some other place. The men become farmers again, driving their horses home through a blizzard. They'll call out, 'Giddy up, go on. It's not far.' They'll see a light in the window and their breathing will relax. They'll see their wives watching for them and laugh in relief. 'I'm coming,' they will shout. They'll flail at their bedclothes, whipping their team on through the snow. 'Giddy up, now. We're almost home.'"

"What do women say?" I asked.

"Women call out for their mothers."

When I was ten, my mother often didn't make it home until late at night. She wore a tailored dark suit, red lipstick, and black high heels. Her hair was short and curly and her eyes were always tired. When she walked in with her doctor bag and trench coat, I ran to her side and stayed there till bedtime. I watched her eat warmed-over stew, look through her mail, and change into her housecoat and slippers. I rubbed her sore feet and asked about her day.

I accompanied her on house calls and on her trips to the hospital sixteen miles from our town. She told me stories about her childhood on a ranch. She'd killed rattlesnakes, found fossils in the creek bed, buried herself in a haystack during a hailstorm, and played on a championship high-school basketball team. She'd gathered cow chips for fuel during the Depression. I begged for more: "Tell me about when you ate watermelons right from the patch; tell me about the Gypsies who came through; tell me about the twins who died from drinking the water in the chicken coop; or about the time the stunt pilot crashed at the county fair."

In junior high I grew irritated with her. She had a big stomach, thin hair, and wasn't as pretty as my friends' mothers. I wanted her to stay home, bake tuna fish casseroles, and teach me to sew. I wanted the phone to stop ringing for her.

For my high-school graduation gift in 1965 she took me to San Francisco. We went to a coffeehouse in North Beach where Beat poets read. I was sure that everyone was staring at my mother, and even though I liked the poetry, I insisted we leave early.

As an adult, I traveled with my family to her house for holiday dinners. She fixed my favorite foods—vegetable soup, and pecan pie. She gave my children too many sweets and presents. At midnight when I tried to go to bed, she offered to fry me a steak or go for a walk—anything to keep me talking for another hour. When it was time to go, she walked me to the car and held on to the door handle. "When are you coming back?" she asked.

The last month of her life, I sat by her in the hospital. She liked me to read and tell her stories. I brushed her hair and teeth for her and fed her grapes one at a time. One night when she was out of her head from all the medicines, she imagined she was fixing spaghetti for twelve.

"Hand me those tomatoes. Chop that onion quick. They'll be here soon." Another night she was delivering babies. "Push, push now," she said. "Wrap that baby up." When I slept beside her, she could sleep.

My relationship with my mother, like all relationships with mothers, was extraordinarily complex, filled with love, longing, a need for closeness and distance, separation and fusion. I respected her and mocked her, felt ashamed and proud of her, laughed with her and felt irritated by her smallest flaws. I felt crabby after twenty-four hours in her house, and yet nothing made me happier than making her happy.

The day after her funeral I started writing *Reviving Ophelia*. Because of my experiences with my mother, I had great empathy for mothers. In the mother-bashing era of the 1990s, I was determined to write a book that helped girls and their mothers feel closer. I wanted the book to be a voice of support for mothers.

Western civilization has a history of unrealistic expectations about mothers. They are held responsible for their children's happiness and for the social and emotional well-being of their families. Mothers are either idealized like the Virgin Mary or bashed in fairy tales and modern American novels. We all think of our mothers with what Freud called primary process thought, the thinking style of young children. We have trouble growing up enough to see our mothers as people.

Western civilization has a double standard about parenting. Relationships with fathers are portrayed as productive and growth-oriented, while relationships with mothers are depicted as regressive and dependent. Fathers are praised for their involvement with children. Mothers, on the other hand, are criticized unless their involvement is precisely the right kind and amount. Distant mothers are scorned, but mothers who are too close are accused of smothering and overprotecting.

Nowhere are the messages to mothers so contradictory as with their adolescent daughters. Mothers are expected to protect their daughters from the culture even as they help them fit into it. They are to encourage their daughters to grow into adults and yet keep them from being hurt. They are to be devoted to their daughters and yet encourage them to leave. Mothers are asked to love completely and yet know exactly when to distance emotionally and physically.

Daughters are as confused as mothers by our culture's expectations. Girls are encouraged to separate from their mothers and to devalue their relationships to them. They are expected to respect their mothers but not to be like them. In our culture, loving one's mother is linked with dependency, passivity, and regression, while rejecting one's mother implies individuation, activity, and independence. Distancing from one's mother is viewed as a necessary step toward adult development.

When Sara was fifteen she made a joke that was funny in a painful way. I liked to take her swimming, walking, or out to lunch. Tongue in cheek, we labeled those outings mother-daughter bonding experiences. Then one day she began calling them mother-daughter "bondage" experiences. We both had tears in our eyes from laughing. To this day, we call our outings "mother-daughter bondage."

Growing up requires adolescent girls to reject the person with whom they are most closely identified. Daughters are socialized to have a tremendous fear of becoming like their mothers. There is no greater insult for most women than to say, "You are just like your mother." And yet to hate one's mother is to hate oneself.

The experience of American girls is so different from that of Leah, mentioned in the last chapter, who was reared in a culture that respected the mother-daughter bond. In Western culture, mother-daughter tensions spring from the daughter's attempt to become an adult, to be an individual different from and not dependent on her mother. Because of mixed messages within the culture, conflict between mothers and daughters is inevitable. To have a self, daughters must reject parts of their mothers. Always mothers and daughters must struggle with distance—too close and there is engulfment, too distant and there's abandonment.

These age-old tensions were exacerbated by the problems of the 1990s. My office was filled with mother-daughter pairs who were struggling to define their relationships in positive ways. Part of the problem was that mothers didn't understand the world that their daughters lived in. Their experiences were different. For example, most mothers were teased by boys in junior high about their bodies and their sexuality. When they heard their daughters complaining about what happened to them at school, they thought it was similar to what they had experienced, but it was not. The "teasing" was more graphic, mean-spirited, and unremitting. It was no longer teasing, but rather sexual harassment, and it kept many girls from wanting to go to school.

Mothers were often unprepared for how their daughters behaved. Some daughters swore at them, called them bitches, or told them to shut up. This shocked them because they had never sworn at their own mothers. Daughters in the 1990s often were sexually active at a much younger age. The mothers had struggled with sexual issues in committed relationships, but their daughters' casual attitudes toward sex really floored them. Mothers had kept secrets from their mothers, but they had no idea how different their daughters' secrets were.

Most mothers in the 1990s did their best to raise healthy daughters, but they were often unsure how to operate. For example, a neighbor had raised her daughter to fight for her rights and to resist anyone's efforts to control her. Then, at eleven, her daughter was often in trouble at school. She started fights with teachers she thought were unfair, and she hit kids who picked on other kids. While her scrappiness was admirable from a feminist perspective, it was getting her in trouble. Other children had realized that she was a fighter and they set her up for skirmishes. The mother wondered if she had done the right thing.

A friend actively encouraged her daughters to keep up with sports, to eschew makeup, to eat hearty meals, and to speak up in class when they knew the answers. During adolescence, her daughters were teased and rejected by more feminine girl friends.

My cousin's common sense told her that her daughter shouldn't have a two-hundred-dollar low-cut dress for her eighth-grade graduation. But all her daughter's friends had such dresses. Her daughter begged her to buy it because she was afraid that she would feel like a geek at her graduation party.

This same cousin had strong beliefs about alcohol and teenagers. She said no to parties where alcohol was served. But her daughter insisted that all the popular kids went to the parties and that she'd be left out of her crowd. My cousin was torn between her fear of alcohol and her desire for her daughter to be accepted at her school.

Mothers wanted their daughters to date but were terrified of date rape, teenage pregnancy, AIDS, and other diseases. They wanted their daughters to be independent, but they were aware of how dangerous the world was for women. They wanted their daughters to be relaxed about their appearance but knew that girls suffered socially if they weren't attractive.

Daughters struggled to individuate, but also needed their mothers' guidance and love. They resisted their mothers' protection even as they moved into dangerous waters. And they were angry when their mothers warned them of dangers that they understood even better than their mothers.

Most girls in the 1990s were close to their mothers when they were young, and many returned to that closeness as adults. But few girls managed to stay close to their mothers during junior high and high school. Girls at their most vulnerable time rejected the help of the one person who wanted most to understand their needs. Mother and daughter constantly jostled each other in their efforts to find the right amount of closeness. Jessica and Brenda had been so close that, with adolescence, Jessica rejected everything her mother offered. Sorrel and Fay had a good relationship with mutual respect and empathy. Whitney and Evelyn were in a deeply conflicted relationship. Whitney was more mature than her mother.

JESSICA (15) AND BRENDA

Jessica and Brenda were a study in contrasts. Brenda was a social worker in her late thirties. She was casually dressed and pudgy with wild, blond-gray flyaway hair. She talked earnestly and rapidly, using her hands to punctuate her expressive speech. She had words for every feeling and a sophisticated theory about every problem that she and Jessica were having. Around her blue eyes were deep laugh lines. Beside her sat Jessica, as still and distant as an ice sculpture. She was thin with long dark hair and a pale complexion, and she was dressed in a black silk shirt and pants.

Brenda said, "I'm at my wit's end with Jessie. She won't go to school and the authorities are on my case. Since I'm a social worker, this really embarrasses me. But I can't physically force her to go."

She sighed. "I can't make her do anything. All she does is sleep, watch MTV, and read magazines. She's not doing chores or going out with friends. She's throwing her life away."

I asked Jessica how she spent her time. She looked away and Brenda answered. "She likes the television in my bedroom. All day while I'm at work she lies on my bed and generally messes things up. I bought her a television, but she still goes into my room. She claims my bed is more comfortable."

Jessica sniffed dramatically and Brenda continued. "I wasn't married when Jessie was born. She missed having a father. That's affected her self-image."

Jessica scowled when her mother talked about her, but she refused to speak for herself.

"Jessie and I used to do everything together. She was a wonderful, enthusiastic girl. I'm amazed by what's happening." She sighed. "I can't do anything right with her. If I ask her a question, she thinks it's stupid. If I'm quiet, she accuses me of glaring. If I talk to her, I'm lecturing. I have to brace myself to deal with her. She yells at me constantly."

Brenda patted her daughter's leg. "I know she has low self-esteem, but I can't figure out how to help her. What more can I do?"

I asked Jessica to leave the room. For someone so apparently disgusted by the conversation, she seemed surprisingly reluctant to go. For the next thirty minutes Brenda gave me a history of Jessica's life. Then Jessica knocked on the door. "I'm sick. I need to go home."

I handed Jessica an appointment card. "I'll see you alone on Tuesday."

I was glad this mother-daughter pair had come to counseling. Brenda, perhaps because she was a social worker, was reluctant to judge her daughter. She was so afraid of rejecting Jessica that she wasn't being firm. She had parenting confused with abuse, and she was trying so hard to be good to her daughter that she was denying Jessica a chance to grow up. Brenda was in danger of "understanding" Jessica all the way into juvenile court.

On Tuesday Jessica came dressed in black jeans and a black turtleneck. She sat silently on the couch, waiting for me to begin. I wrestled with my own feelings of pessimism about what the hour would bring. Already, after three minutes with her, I felt I was dragging a barge across a desert.

"How do you feel about being here?"

"Okay."

"Do you really feel okay?"

"I don't see any need for it, but morning television isn't that thrilling anyway."

"How are you different from your mom?"

Jessica arched one black eyebrow. "What do you mean?"

"Do you have different values, ideas about life?"

She smirked. "I totally disagree with her about everything. I hate school, she likes school. I hate to work and she loves it. I like MTV and she hates it. I wear black and she never does. She wants me to live up to my potential and I think she's full of shit."

I considered saying that her life goal seemed to be to frustrate her mother, but instead I asked, "What have you wanted to do?"

Her eyes widened. "Modeling. Mom hates the idea. She thinks it is sexist and shallow."

I suggested that she look into modeling for herself. She could do some research on the profession: What should she be studying now to prepare herself? Where would she get training? Are there jobs locally? How much does it pay?

After Jessica left, I thought about the family. Brenda had devoted her life to Jessica's happiness, and with adolescence all their closeness became a problem. Jessica tried to get distance by rebelling, but Brenda was too understanding. She forgave her and continued to be loving. So Jessica would be even more difficult and Brenda would be even more understanding. By the time we met, Jessica felt so engulfed that she would do anything to separate herself from Brenda. She was defining herself almost exclusively as "not Brenda."

I saw Brenda later that day and warned her, "Whatever you do, don't express any interest in Jessica's research on modeling. Don't offer to help or tell her that you're glad she's doing something productive."

I asked Brenda about her life. "My life is Jessie and my work. I haven't had time for anything else. I hoped that when she was a teenager I'd have more time, but it hasn't worked out that way. I need to be around constantly. I wake her up every morning, go home at lunch to fix her something to eat. Otherwise she won't eat, and you can see how thin she is. At night I keep her company. The poor kid doesn't have anyone else."

"You need a life of your own."

She nodded. "I know you're right, but . . ."

I said, "Let's plan some fun for you."

I continued to work separately with Brenda and Jessica. They were terribly connected to each other and resistant to outsiders. Our therapy reminded me of the old joke—Question: "How many therapists does it take to change a light bulb?" Answer: "One, but only if the light bulb wants to change."

With Brenda, I pushed for some life apart from her daughter. Could she occasionally go for lunch with a friend or go for a walk in the evening with a neighbor? Did she like to read, listen to music, or work with her hands? She decided to work on a school bond issue and once a week she left Jessica alone and went to a meeting. The first time she did this, Jessica called and said she was sick. But the second time Jessica made it through the evening in fine shape. When Brenda returned, she'd actually made them some popcorn and lemonade.

At first Brenda's concerns were all about Jessica. Would she be sick, lonely, or get into trouble? She felt guilty and anxious leaving her daughter in the evenings. Later she admitted that she had her own concerns: she was uneasy socially after all these years of no practice and she worried that a man might ask her out.

She said dramatically, "I am not ever going to date."

"That's one way that you and Jessica are alike," I said. "Neither of you wants to deal with the opposite sex."

With Jessica, I asked questions that I hoped would help her define herself as separate from her mother. She considered her mother's views stupid, but she knew exactly what they were. We had our most success with the modeling research, which Jessica pursued throughout our time together. She sent off for information about clinics and schools. She read the autobiography of a famous model and a book with tips on becoming a professional model. She experimented with her hair and makeup. One day she came to our session dressed in royal blue. I looked surprised and she said, "Black is just not me."

After three weeks away, Jessica returned to school and decided to join the photography club. All my work with Jessica was funneled through her desire to be a model. I encouraged her to exercise by noting that models with muscles were popular. As she exercised, she became less depressed and more energetic.

I suggested that models needed self-confidence to cope with all the competition. Jessica agreed and worked on this. She kept a record of three things she was proud of each day. She recorded: "I'm proud I fed the cats, went to school, and didn't yell at Mom." "I'm proud I washed my hair, turned in my homework, and smiled at a girl in my gym class."

Later she bought a counter at a drug store and clicked it every time she did the smallest thing that pleased her. This put Jessica on a positive search for what she liked about herself. Also she, not her mother or anyone else, determined what was valuable about her. Her feelings of self-worth were coming from within. Soon Jessica was able to click fifty or sixty times a day. We defined victories as times when she made an effort to accomplish her long-term goals. Jessica began reporting regular victories. She signed up for an aerobics class at the YWCA. She talked to a friend who was also interested in modeling, and they agreed to exchange information about local competitions and shows. She developed a portfolio of pictures of herself.

I encouraged Jessica to write down her thoughts and feelings and to sort out which values of her mother's she wanted to keep or reject. Gradually Jessica had thoughts that were not simply reactions to Brenda. She discovered the joy of developing her own ideas rather than rebelling against Brenda's.

One day Jessica said, "I hate it when Mom doesn't respect my choices. That's worse than her not loving me." That led to a discussion of how important her mother's regard for her really was. She desperately wanted her mother to acknowledge that she was growing up into her own person.

This case was one in which I needed to set aside my own judgments and stay humble. I shared much of Brenda's antipathy toward modeling, and I generally worked in my counseling sessions to minimize emphasis on physical appearance and help my clients foster their other qualities. But I needed to trust Jessica to do what was right for her. Ultimately, Jessica's interest in modeling helped her reenter the world and develop a self.

At our last joint session, Jessica was dressed in a fitted green shirt and neon-yellow tights. Her eyes were lively and she talked easily. She had an opportunity to model clothes for a local store. Her grades were just average, but she was proud of her Bs in business math and merchandising.

"I'm not nuts about modeling, but I'm happy that Jess is happy," Brenda admitted. "She doesn't have to choose something I would choose. I am trying to acknowledge that Jess is growing up and becoming her own person. I want that for her."

"You need your own life, too," Jessica said. Brenda nodded. "I'm working on that."

I quoted the old saying: "Velvet chains are the hardest to break."

SORREL (16) AND FAY

Fay and Sorrel sat in my office late one winter afternoon. A week earlier Sorrel had told Fay that she was a lesbian, and Fay urged her to seek help in understanding what this meant to her life. Mother and daughter both wore jeans, dark sweaters, and old hiking boots. I asked Sorrel how she felt about being a lesbian.

"I have known I was different for a long time, but I couldn't say exactly how. When I was in sixth grade, I imagined kissing cheerleaders and pretty teachers. But I didn't know any lesbians and I'd heard the word only as an insult. So even though I was attracted to girls, I refused to label myself lesbian."

She looked at her mother, and Fay nodded encouragement to continue. Sorrel exhaled deeply. "I found some old books written by psychologists about homosexuality, but they didn't help at all. I wanted stories about girls like me that were okay. There was nothing like that. I was happy when Ellen DeGeneres announced she was a lesbian. She was talented and pretty, someone I wouldn't mind knowing."

Fay said, "Sorrel has always been unique."

"Well, my dad left us when I was two. I carry a grudge against men," Sorrel said. "I made life hell for Mom when she married Howard."

"We don't see Sorrel's dad," Fay explained. "I married Howard rather impulsively."

"Howard was a jerk," interrupted Fay. "He tried to control me and make me into a little lady."

Fay agreed. "Howard wanted her to wear dresses and she refused. He insisted that we teach Sorrel who was boss, and we fought about that. I never have tried to control Sorrel. I have loved her uniqueness and wanted her to be exactly who she is."

"Mom and Howard divorced when I was eleven," Sorrel said. "I don't plan on ever living with a man again."

Fay continued. "Even as an elementary student, Sorrel was different. She spent a lot of time alone reading or sketching. She collected rocks and leaves."

Sorrel interrupted. "I liked things that humans hadn't touched."

I asked how other children treated Sorrel. Sorrel answered, "I didn't have many friends unless you count imaginary ones. I preferred boys to girls. Girls were catty and superficial."

"I couldn't protect her," Fay said. "At least I had the sense to not try and change her. I knew she was fine the way she was. I tried to make our home a safe haven for her."

Sorrel said, "Junior high was the pits. I felt like I was on a different planet from the other kids. I was the untouchable of my school."

She looked at Fay and said softly, "Mom doesn't like to hear this, but I thought some about killing myself. I didn't fit anywhere. I didn't dare admit even to myself why I was different."

Fay winced at the mention of suicide, but she held her peace and let Sorrel continue with her story.

"I survived by living in my own world. The real world was too hostile so I made new ones. I drew lots of fantasy pictures."

Fay beamed. "Sorrel had her own vision of the world."

"Drawing saved me," Sorrel agreed.

I asked Sorrel how I could help.

"I need to meet other lesbians. I need to know that I'm not the only one. I want to read more about girls like me."

We talked about the local Women's Resource Center and a nearby women's bookstore. I told her about the gay/lesbian support group for teenagers.

Fay reminded us that Sorrel was different in many ways besides her sexual orientation. She was more self-sufficient than other girls. She was sensitive, intuitive, and acutely tuned into the world around her, sometimes so acutely that Fay worried that her perceptiveness and responsiveness would destroy her.

Sorrel said, "I want to compliment Mom on her support. She's stood by me through all my weirdness."

Fay smiled. "I have tried to teach her that intelligent resistance is a good thing. Sorrel has wonderful things to offer the world, and I've tried to protect her gifts. As a girl, I was fearful. I wanted to fit in and be popular. I lost a lot by being such a conformist. As an adult, I have spent years sorting out the mess I became in high school. I was determined to help Sorrel resist."

Sorrel didn't fit into our cultural categories for young women in the 1990s. She belonged to a fairly invisible population: lesbian adolescents. Particularly in junior high, she had suffered for the sin of being different. Luckily, Fay possessed an uncommon ability to give her daughter unconditional love. She accepted Sorrel as she was and valued her daughter when others didn't. She resisted the temptation to urge Sorrel to conform and fit in. She made their own home a safe house.

WHITNEY (16) AND EVELYN

Whitney and Evelyn resembled each other with their blond hair and round freckled faces, but stylistically they were different. Whitney was relaxed and wholesome-looking in jeans and a turtleneck sweater, while Evelyn was dressed in an elegant suit with matching shoes. Clearly Evelyn had been a knockout when she was younger, and she still spent a great deal of time cultivating the perfect look. That day years ago in my office she held herself stiffly and seemed uncomfortable. Whitney was open and flexible while Evelyn was quiet and cautious. She grimaced when I asked why they were in my office.

"Sam insisted. He's fed up with our fighting. He's worried about both of us, but particularly Whitney."

Whitney said, "I wanted to come. I asked Mom a year ago if we could see a therapist, but she said it cost too much."

Evelyn said, "I don't think it will help, but I'm willing to try. I promised Sam."

First, I talked with Evelyn, who told me that she had had trouble with Whitney since the day she was born. She had a difficult labor and suffered a major postpartum depression. Immediately after Whitney's birth, she made Sam promise no more children. Evelyn had been a shy, well-behaved girl, and Whitney was boisterous and outgoing. From the moment of her birth, Whitney had stolen the show.

Evelyn clearly resented Sam's relationship with Whitney. "He thinks she walks on water. He doesn't see her sneakiness and self-centeredness. She's got him snowed."

I asked about Evelyn's relationship with Sam. She said it was good when he was around. Sam ran an international business and spent lots of time abroad. Evelyn felt they would get along fine if it weren't for Whitney. They fought about her constantly. Evelyn felt he spoiled her, and Sam felt Evelyn was cold and uncaring.

As Evelyn talked, I was impressed by how lonely she was. If she had any affection for her daughter, I could not discern it. She had no close friends and seemed utterly dependent on Sam for companionship and support. And Sam was a scarce commodity. She was devoted to him and resented that his devotion was divided between her and Whitney.

Evelyn said, "Sam doesn't know Whitney like I do. She drinks and she's had sex. I wasn't raised that way. I was a virgin when I married."

I asked about her relationship with Whitney. Evelyn said, "She's mouthy. I never, ever yelled at my mother. I don't want her to touch me or talk to me. I'm counting the days until she moves out."

In fact, Whitney was pretty well behaved. She worked part-time at a sporting goods store and she was an honor roll student. She was on student council and active in the Young Republicans. She was sexually involved with her boyfriend of a year, but she'd been honest with her parents about this. She'd made her own arrangements for birth control pills.

I suspected that Evelyn's antipathy came from deep within herself—perhaps from her own unsatisfied needs for love or her disappointment that Whitney was not a replica of herself. Evelyn wasn't able to change with the times and appreciate that Whitney lived in a different world from the one she inhabited as a girl. She seemed stuck on the idea that things should stay the same.

When I met with Whitney alone, she was surprisingly positive about her mother. She clearly respected her mother's talents as a homemaker, an expert on grooming, and a seamstress. She yearned for more connection and less competition between them, but she was baffled about how to make that happen. She said, "I can't be someone I'm not just to please her."

Whitney felt closer to her father, who she knew loved her. But he was gone so much, and when he was home he had to be careful not to side with Whitney. "Mom notices who Dad hugs first," she noted. "She tells him stories so he'll be angry with me.

"Mom calls me a slut because I've had sex," Whitney continued. "Nothing I do is right for her. She gives me the silent treatment, and sometimes I can't even figure out what she's mad about."

She began to cry as we talked. "I need my mom. Things happen that I wish I could tell her, but I'm afraid to."

I asked for an example. "Right now, I'm being bugged by these guys in the parking lot after school. They gawk at me and call me names, and one of them tried to get into my car last week. If I told Mom, she'd say it was my own fault, that I deserve what I get."

Whitney had other problems too. She was working too many hours and worried about balancing her time. She loved her boyfriend, but they fought almost daily and Whitney wanted to talk about improving that relationship. She didn't bring these things up with her mother because she was certain she'd be blamed for her troubles.

At the end of that first session we all met together. Evelyn said, "The basic problem is I don't respect Whitney's morals."

Whitney said, "No. We need to communicate more. I need you to understand me."

Evelyn was white-lipped as she talked. "I'll never approve of what you're doing. That's not the way things were done in my family."

I thought to myself, *But Whitney is not you and the world isn't the same.* I searched for a way to end the session on a positive note. This was an unusual case because the mother had broken her bonds with the daughter. Evelyn seemed more fragile than Whitney and more rigid in her thinking. Until Evelyn felt better about herself, she couldn't care for Whitney. Evelyn needed more friends and interests, a life besides waiting for Sam to come home. I asked if Sam could come with them next time, and I complimented Evelyn on her honesty. I would have to nurture her before she would nurture her daughter.

When I look back on the 1990s, I am sad for the mothers who worked so hard to get along with their daughters and also for the daughters who felt betrayed and angry without knowing why. It was a terrible era for this critical relationship. Fortunately, most of the mothers and daughters I knew then get along better now. But scars and tension remain from that troubled time.

These daughters of the 1990s who are mothers of teenaged girls today are often pleasantly surprised and deeply relieved by how loving their daughters are. Based on their own behavior as teens, they didn't expect easy, cooperative teenage daughters. These mothers are not anguished like their own mothers were. Their daughters somehow have the culture's permission to love them.

The surprising news in 2019 is that mothers and daughters have generally moved into harmonious relationships. Mothers are more aware of the dysfunctional culture that girls must cope with, and daughters tend to trust and respect their moms. They want to individuate, but they don't need to do it by being mean to their mothers. Of course, there are still conflicts but, in most families, there are fewer. And, within the family and in the culture at large, there is less mom blaming and mom bashing.

Because of their developmental level, teenage girls are self-centered, but as life in America has grown more difficult, girls appreciate the efforts their mothers put in creating a positive family environment for them. The girls we interviewed openly acknowledged their gratitude. Open admission of love for mothers was rare in 1994.

Still, we found consistently that girls lived online lives that their mothers often knew nothing about. Girls have always kept secrets, but today, more of girls' lives are hidden from their parents.

Because of the centrality of the mother/daughter relationship, we interviewed both mothers and daughters about their relationships with each other. Unquestionably, we still observed "typical" mother/daughter issues. My friend Pat told me that when her daughter marched down the main street with the high-school marching band, Laurel waved and smiled at everyone but her. Pat said that there were years when she and her husband felt invisible to Laurel, but that their relationships were better now. Their daughter had "aged out" of her irritability.

Laureen had trouble with her rebellious daughter Addison, who got a lip piercing when she was away at soccer camp. Laureen admitted that she hated coming home from work for the entire year that Addison was in eighth grade because there was so much shouting and conflict. However, at the beginning of ninth grade, Laureen suggested they negotiate a truce and formulate new rules together. That greatly improved the situation.

In the girls' focus groups, we were struck by the relatively low level of mother/daughter discord.

Olivia complained mildly, "My mom was annoyed when I quit marching band."

"My mom pushes me to take more advanced classes and to find a job," said Aspen. "I told her I can't do both."

"My mom isn't my best friend, but she's not my nemesis either," Jordan said. "We like the same things. Luckily she's not too embarrassing."

"My mom *is* my best friend," Kendyl acknowledged. "She's always there for me. We never had that weird mom/daughter tension. As I get older, I appreciate her even more."

Addie told us a story about her junior year, when she broke her jaw and couldn't eat solid food for several weeks. Her mother pureed her meals and encouraged Addie to sip smoothies through a straw. As Addie put it, "She coaxed and hugged me into surviving." Addie cried as she told this story, which she concluded with, "I will always love my mother."

Today's mothers' main worries about their daughters revolve around academics, time spent on social media, and overscheduling. In our focus groups, they reported close, mostly positive relationships, especially with their older daughters; middle-school girls were more likely to be argumentative and critical.

None of the mothers in our focus groups knew much about their daughters' online lives and they seemed unaware of many of the problems we were hearing about from the girls we interviewed. Mothers loved discussing their daughters and often left our meetings saying that they learned a great deal and wished they could have more of these kinds of conversations.

"My daughter is pretty open with me," said Kim. "In middle school she had some friend upheavals, and I tried really hard not to tell her what to do. I bit my tongue and just asked questions. When I was in junior high, I didn't talk about my troubles with my mom. I feel grateful that my daughter talks to me."

"Because I was adopted, my daughter Caitlan was the first genetically related person I had ever known," Suzette explained. "When I realized that she loved me, it broke my heart. She has been my soul child.

"Beginning in fifth grade, Caitlan went through a difficult time. All her classmates were obsessed with *Twilight*, the girls started getting boobs, and her friends who were boys turned into hormone monsters," Suzette continued. "I remember her observing her peers; she didn't quite know where she fit in. She called me from the school bathroom almost every day. She skipped some Mondays because she just didn't want to go. I tried to be tender with that. By now I am proud of Caitlan's self-awareness and emotional maturity. Recently she said, 'I'm starting to realize that I don't identify myself as a basketball player, a Catholic, or even a girl . . . these are pieces of me but who I am is much deeper.'"

We asked mothers if they felt they had enough time to communicate their values and points of view on the world.

"We talk sometimes when we're in the car," said Donna. "We don't sit down and have formal conversations."

"I try to make myself available," said Kim. "My daughter walks to school or takes the bus, so we don't have car conversations, but we talk while we're cooking meals and doing dishes. I leave her little notes in the morning before I go to work."

Suzette nodded and chimed in, "Mealtimes are sacred in my house. At dinner, we have a rule about no devices. That helps us converse."

"We don't have many family dinners, we're all just too swamped with activities," Anna said. "We do try to make time for a weekend brunch. But honestly, none of us are big talkers. Most evenings, if we're home at the same time, we eat while we watch *Black-ish* reruns."

All the mothers agreed that the middle-school years were the worst and that, by high school, their daughters were happier and easier to get along with. Donna told the group that her daughter once texted her, "I hate you, you stupid bitch." Donna lost control and texted back, "Shut up, you little shit." Everyone laughed at that story and chimed in with similar experiences.

"My tenth-grade daughter has a small, tight-knit group of friends, but when they have problems, she doesn't have a fallback group," said Consuela. "I thank my lucky stars that she has no interest in boys yet. She told me that when girls say they are dating someone, that means they post pictures together on Instagram. It's just about the presentation on social media."

"That's so true," nodded Jeanine. "My daughter rarely leaves the house. She sees her friends at school and is on the phone with them all the time."

We poured more tea and coffee and asked passed around a plate of gluten-free snickerdoodles.

"Let's talk about social media," I suggested. The mothers all looked defeated as we moved on to that topic.

"As a high-school teacher, I constantly confiscate phones," Amy said. "Our school outlawed them after administrators noticed that kids weren't talking to one another at lunch.

She sighed and continued, "Students are terrified that I might look at their phones. They are unbelievably attached to them. Their identity is 100 percent wrapped up in their phones."

Many of the mothers said that they bought their daughters phones to know when to pick them up from events, but they all agreed that soon they lost control of their daughters' social media use. Donna had a rule that, at any time, she could look at her daughter's phone and read her texts.

"Have you ever looked?" Sara asked.

"No way," she admitted. "It would freak her out."

"We signed a contract with our daughter," Kim said. "We can look at her phone any time, she can't take sexy selfies, and she can't take her phone to bed; it charges overnight in the kitchen. But we've never taken advantage of our agreement and looked at her phone."

"When our daughter acts up, my husband and I can't use grounding as a punishment, because she doesn't really go anywhere," said Jeanine. "She sits on the couch in front of the TV with her laptop and phone. If we need to punish her, taking away screen time is the only thing that gets through to her."

"I worry about my daughter's need for immediate gratification," said Anna. "When I had a decision to make, I'd discuss it with friends and take some time to think it through. For her, everything is just one click away.

"My daughter is an extrovert," she continued. "She invites her friends over on Saturdays, but they spend their time texting other friends or recording makeup tutorials for YouTube. I guess that's a creative outlet . . . right?"

"I was far more social than my daughter," said Consuela. "I lived for the weekends and threw parties all the time. I always imagined that my home would be the hangout spot for Alicia and her friends; I'd keep the fridge stocked with soda and snacks and be the 'cool' mom. That has totally *not* happened. I encourage Alicia to see her friends, but she doesn't even like to talk on a phone, let alone go to parties or invite people to our house."

As our time wound down, we steered the conversation to sex and dating. None of the mothers had experienced much success talking to their daughters about these topics.

"I've tried to have conversations about safe sex and values around intimacy, but my daughter literally bolts out of the room," Susan said with a laugh. "Clearly, she doesn't want to talk about it."

The mothers all agreed that while their daughters dress in sexy clothes and are exposed to sexual imagery, they don't like conversations about sex or dating.

"My daughter told me that dating doesn't even exist anymore," Kim shrugged. "Teenagers either text or hook up. There's no in-between."

"How does she feel about that?" Anna asked.

Kim answered ruefully, "She won't say." The mothers all laughed.

Consuela said that when Alicia was thirteen, her period started and didn't end for a year. Her body changed and suddenly she was a seventh-grade Marilyn Monroe. Boys were after her constantly and her phone chimed with so many text notifications that Consuela threatened to throw it out the car window.

Still, when Alicia turned sixteen, she told Consuela she'd never been kissed. Consuela sighed as she explained, "I think it's because of the virtual world teenagers live in now."

"My daughter's a senior," said Donna, "and maybe one-fifth of her friends are dating."

We inquired about the daughters' depression and anxiety. For the most part, the mothers mentioned stress caused by academic and financial issues. However, a few acknowledged that their girls were grappling with anxiety, depression, or self-harm.

"My generation didn't have twenty-four seven information about global crises, terrorist attacks, and threats to the environment," said

Kim. "My daughter and her friends hear about trauma every day. They are afraid of school shooters. Life is much more complicated for them.

"Our parents knew that if we went to college, we'd get a job," Kim went on. "My daughter feels like she has to do everything right so she can graduate from a good college without too much debt and find a job with a living wage. When I attended college, I viewed it as a time to explore my options and learn who I was. My daughter sees it as a means to financial security."

Several mothers nodded in agreement.

"My oldest girl has had quite a bit of anxiety," said Jeanine. "It started when she decided she needed to be in the top three percent of her high-school class. She wanted to attend a private college and would require a big scholarship. She took one class that wasn't weighted, so her A didn't count as much as other people's. That made her so anxious she couldn't sleep."

"My husband and I worry about suicide because our daughter runs with high-achieving girls who have the 'It's never enough' syndrome," said Donna. "She and her friends study late and don't know how to relax. We know of one extremely successful girl who killed herself because she didn't get accepted to the right college. That girl's story keeps *me* up at night."

"Many of my students seem to suffer from chronic low-grade depression," said Amy. "They don't seem to care about much and they don't interact with teachers or other kids. I think they'd benefit from Outward Bound or volunteering at a soup kitchen. They have such limited perspectives on the world."

Switching gears, Amy mentioned this generation's gender fluidity.

"One place I do think today's teenagers have good perspective and empathy is around sexuality and the LGBTQ community," she said. "I see much more openness to all kinds of sexual preferences or orientations, and to different definitions of gender identity. Most of my students have friends who are gay."

"I was introduced to the word 'pansexual' by my niece," Anna said. "I had to google it."

Our focus group mothers theorized about this new gender fluidity. Kim felt that teens wanted as much freedom and ability to maneuver as possible. Donna believed that girls influenced one another and that, in some circles, being gay, bi, and trans was considered cool. Amy noted that LGBT students at her daughter's high school were still ostracized by some of their peers. Most of the mothers were grateful that our culture was moving toward understanding and acceptance.

Blushing, Jeanine said, "My daughter and I went to see *Call Me By Your Name*. It has some realistic gay sex scenes, and there we were, mother and daughter, watching them side by side. That would not have happened in earlier generations. My mom would have fainted; she still lowers her voice to a whisper if she says the word 'homosexual'!"

"If our kids are doing most of their socializing online, gender doesn't matter anyway," Amy observed. "Eventually they'll be with someone in person, but almost all of the prep work is online, so it's more personality-driven now."

As the sun began to set and several cell phones began buzzing with reminders and texts, we asked the mothers to identify their goals for their daughters.

"I want what my mother wanted for me," said Jeanine. "At the end of the day, she needs to trust her inner voice. Whatever makes her happy will make me happy."

"I don't want Alicia to organize her life around making money. I want her to help people," Consuela said.

"We've spent a lot of time discussing what her future will be. I'd love to see her get lost in a passion which has yet to be determined," said

Anna. "She's figuring out who her true self is. I hope that she comes to understand her true, multifaceted selves and listens to her own wisdom."

Our focus group mothers came from different backgrounds, ethnic groups, and income levels, but they all wanted essentially the same things for their daughters. They wanted their girls to grow into healthy, productive, and authentic adults. These goals haven't changed in decades.

Danika and Sequoia exemplify some of the most positive aspects of current mother/daughter relationships. They are exceptional in their direct communication and teamwork in making their small family work well. Still, both share the fears that plague many contemporary families.

DANIKA AND SEQUOIA (14)

"I picked her name out eight years before she was born," Danika began. "My mom died in a car accident. She was a Wiccan, so all the women in my family got together and had a little ceremony at the family farm. That day I declared that if I ever had a child, her name would be Sequoia Druscilla. It means pillar of strength."

Danika reached over to tousle her daughter's enviable riot of curls and continued. "My mom was a single mom, so the thought of being a single mom did not scare me at all. When I got pregnant after a few dates with Quoia's father, everyone assumed I'd have an abortion, including me. But I called my best friend and she said, 'You know, you *can* have this baby.'

"I just needed to hear that, because in my heart, I knew I wanted this little Sequoia."

I glanced over at Quoia, expecting a typical teenager eye-roll, but she smiled encouragingly at her mother as she nibbled on carrots and homemade sweet potato hummus. One of the family's two rescue dogs had draped itself across her lap and she scratched its belly between bites.

"Sequoia was an easy baby," Danika said. She pinched her daughter's cheek and said in mock amazement, "What happened?"

We all laughed as she continued. "I lived with my aunt and uncle on their farm for the first year, so I did have some help. I wasn't working, so I was able to sleep when the baby slept. But eventually, we truly were on our own, just the two of us. And it's been that way ever since."

"What was Sequoia like in elementary school?" I asked.

"I was definitely more cheerful," Sequoia chimed in. "There was more random giggling. When we cleaned the house, we would take dance breaks and run to the dining room to dance together."

"I miss little things like that," Danika added. "She was very cheery and bouncy. Now, she's definitely developed a little more self-consciousness. I'll still spy her dancing out of the corner of my eye but she doesn't dance with me. I'm just glad I can still see the glimmer of the goofy, giggly girl."

"I don't want to make assumptions, but I'm guessing you've weathered some financial challenges," I said.

Mother and daughter nodded in unison. "Money is always an issue. We've always talked about it," said Danika, who currently works as a paralegal. "I told her when she went into kindergarten, 'If you want to go to college, you're going to need scholarships.' She may have absorbed that a little too well . . . It's something that affects her, that she feels stress about. I've been up front about what we can afford to do, and what we can't. I'll explain, 'Here is where this paycheck is going, and we might have to wait a minute if you want or need something.'"

"How have you managed your financial reality with all the expenses that go hand in hand with parenthood?" I asked.

"I sent her to an elementary school that has a lot of ethnic and economic diversity. I didn't want her to worry about wearing clothes from the thrift store. That was important to me. I feel like I do a good job of making sure that all of her needs are met, and most of her wants. I hope she doesn't feel underserved, or poor. I've tried to walk that line of, 'I want you to be comfortable in your life, but we have to do it on a budget.'"

Sequoia smiled and jumped in. "We're a team, that's just who we are. I've always understood about money, but what am I going to do about it? Obviously, I want a million dollars, but I've never really wanted or needed *things*. I don't feel poor."

"Have you dated as you've been raising Quoia?" I asked Danika.

"Once I had Sequoia, I kept those relationships separate," she replied. "I knew no one was gonna love this girl like I love this girl. Also, my mom dated a lot when I was young and that wasn't good for me. There's nothing worse than being uncomfortable in your own home."

She turned and gazed at her daughter. "Besides, I never feel lonely. I don't think life would be better if I had a partner."

I shifted to Sequoia. "Now that you're in middle school what, if anything, has changed?"

"I'm more sarcastic and pessimistic," Quoia admitted.

"My struggle is being the mom, the authority figure, but also realizing that she's going to make her own choices," added Danika.

"Our communication style has changed, too. I'm recognizing that she is her own person. She's a young woman. It's been a long time since I had to share space with another woman. It's a delicate balance of letting her grow into the woman she is and also being her mom."

"I snap at you more," Quoia said softly.

"Yeah, sure, but I think we handle it well," Danika replied.

"Socially, things started feeling different for me in sixth grade," Quoia said. "I definitely felt more stress about schoolwork. In middle school, none of my friends shared any classes with me, so I was kind of lonely until I met new friends. Trying to fit in was a struggle. I knew I wasn't going to be a cool kid. It's also where I first met some rich kids; they're so shallow and annoying."

"Currently I'm most focused on how she internalizes stress about how she's doing in school, because she's really hard on herself," Danika said. "She has straight As, but she is as stressed out about grades as I've ever seen her. She didn't do well on a math test and just melted down. I like that she cares about her grades, but I worry about how she processes these emotions and how much she lets it get to her. We've started talking a lot about stress management.

"With all of that said, I feel really lucky that we haven't had any educational or behavioral issues. She's a balanced kid."

"How do you deal with the 'big conversations'?" I asked. "Do you sit down deliberately and have serious talks or do conversations arise naturally?"

"I tend to comment on things as they come up, like if I notice something on TV, I'll say, 'Yeah, that's not how sex actually works.'" Danika laughed and paused to pop a radish in her mouth.

"Sequoia reads and watches a lot of news, so I try and take time to talk to her about it—especially news related to teenagers. My theory has always been, 'When the kid asks the question, they're ready for the knowledge.'"

Belying her laid-back temperament, Danika added, "Every time that girl walks out the door I'm scared. I hear about school shootings, kidnappings, and so on. We don't talk about that much, just a little about what she should do if someone tries to abduct her. And I've told her that nobody has the right to hurt her, ever. She has a right to defend herself and make herself heard."

"That's true," Sequoia nodded. "One of the things my mom said to me was that you never deserve to be hurt. You could walk through a fraternity stark naked, and you wouldn't deserve to be hurt."

"What will high school be like next year?" I asked.

"I'm filling out the [international baccalaureate] application now," Sequoia replied. "I'm stressed about school already, so that will probably get worse. Taking the time to read helps me relax. Or I'll randomly start singing in the house. Little things make me happy."

"This is new terrain for us," Danika said, before turning in her chair to address Sequoia. "I want to help you realize you're getting stressed *before* you're breaking down, *before* you're crying. More importantly, I want you to realize that you are not your grades. You are a fantastic, wonderful person. Grades are not a measure of your quality as a person."

"What are your aspirations?" I asked Sequoia.

"Currently, I want to be a doctor. I'd like to go to Stanford. I like taking in new information and I like to talk about science. I think it's cool."

"I just want her to have a happy life," Danika said. Even if there's a lot of stress in your life, you can be a happy person. I mean, I know that things happen . . . life happens. But being a happy person is something that happens aside from the details of your life. You can decide to be happy.

"That is all I want for Quoia. I want her to be successful and I want her to be happy. I am completely indifferent to whether she becomes a doctor or not."

"I like arguing. Maybe I should be a lawyer," Sequoia muses.

"When Sequoia was five or six, she wanted to be a librarian and a belly dancer." Danika grinned. "That's how I'll always see her."

It was deeply heartening to witness the love and respect between mothers and daughters. Of course, those relationships are often intense and never perfect, but most mother-daughter relationships are no longer adversarial. This change is of great benefit to daughters. In many cases, girls now aspire to be like their mothers. That's progress.

SEVEN

Fathers

MY FATHER GREW up in the Ozarks during the Depression. He was a good-looking, slow-talking southerner. He left the South for World War Two, and his military service took him to Hawaii, Japan, and, later, Korea. In San Francisco he met and married my mother, who was in the navy. When I was young, he attended college on the GI Bill and later he traveled abroad and to Mexico, but until he died in 1973, he remained 1930s southern in his beliefs about race.

I was his first child and he insisted I be named Mary after the Blessed Virgin and Elizabeth after the English queen. He would wake in the night to check on my breathing. When he came home from work, he played Benny Goodman records and, by the time I was six months old, I would hear that record and start moving in my crib. He would pick me up and dance me around our small living room.

When I was five, he taught me to fish. We walked to a pond filled with bluegill and sun perch and sat all afternoon talking and filling a gunnysack with keepers. Later, he taught me to drive a blue 1950 Mercury on the back roads of our rural county. Smoking Chesterfields and drinking Dr. Pepper, he sat beside me, his black curly hair blowing in the breeze. He was an anxious teacher, always grabbing the wheel and shouting, "Steer, steer, goddammit."

When I was twelve, I told him I loved the smell of new books. I said I loved to hold them to my face and breathe in their aroma. He looked alarmed and said, "Don't tell anyone that. They'll think you are a pervert."

When he and my mother drove me down to the state university, he was full of advice. "Don't date anybody but freshmen and don't get serious with them. Don't get in with a crowd that smokes or drinks. Stay away from foreigners. Don't get behind in your studies." When he left he hugged me, his first hug in years, and he said, "I'll miss you. I talk more to you than to anyone else."

I had my last conversation with my father the day before he died. He called to see if l had passed my comprehensive exams in psychology. I told him yes and he was pleased. Then I begged off—people were coming to dinner and I needed to fix a salad. He said, "I'm proud of you." The next day he had a stroke and went into a coma. I was with him in the ICU when the machines bleeped to a stop.

My father would have given his life to save mine. He was embarrassingly proud of my accomplishments and naively certain that I would succeed. But he had a double standard about sex and rigid views about women. In short, we had a typical complicated father-daughter relationship, albeit probably closer than most such relationships in the 1950s because both of us were big talkers.

All fathers are products of their times. The rules for fathers have changed a great deal since the 1950s, when to be a good father, a man stayed sober, earned a living, remained faithful to his wife, and didn't beat the kids. Men weren't expected to hug their daughters, tell them they loved them, or talk to them about personal matters. In 1994, fathers were expected to do all the things they did in the 1950s, plus be emotionally involved. Many fathers didn't learn how to do this from their own fathers. Because they missed any training, they felt lost.

Most fathers also received a big dose of misogyny training as boys, and nowhere did this hurt them more than in parenting their daughters. They were in the awkward position of loving a gender that they have been taught to devalue.

Historically, mothers have been seen as having great power to do harm with their mistakes. Fathers have been viewed as having positive power by simply paying attention to their daughters. When daughters were strong, credit was often given to fathers. But in my experience, strong daughters often come from families with strong mothers.

While most girls in the 1990s were connected to their mothers by close, if often conflicting ties, with fathers they had varied relationships. Some girls barely spoke to their fathers, while others had warm relationships and shared common interests. One client said, "I hardly know my dad exists. We have nothing in common." Another said, "My favorite thing about Dad is that he plays duets with me every night after dinner. We both love the violin and have had this time together since I was three years old."

Fathers also have great power to do harm. If they act as socializing agents for the culture, they can crush their daughters' spirits. Rigid fathers limit their daughters' dreams and destroy their self-confidence. Sexist jokes, misogynistic cracks, and negative attitudes about assertive women hurt girls. Sexist fathers teach their daughters that their value lies in pleasing men. In their own relations with women they model a power differential between the sexes.

Some fathers, in their eagerness to have their daughters accepted by the culture, encourage their daughters to be attractive or lose weight. They produce daughters who believe their only value is their physical attractiveness to men. These fathers undervalue intelligence in women and teach their daughters to undervalue it too.

On the other hand, feminist fathers can be tremendously helpful in teaching their daughters healthy rebellion. They can encourage daughters to protect themselves and even to fight back. They can teach daughters skills, such as how to change tires, throw a baseball, or build a patio. They can help them understand the male point of view and the forces that act on men in this culture. The best fathers confront their own lookism and sexism. Fathers can model good male-female relationships and respect for women in a wide variety of roles. Fathers can fight narrow definitions of their daughters' worth and support their wholeness. They can teach their daughters that it's okay to be smart, bold, and independent.

In the 1970s, I did research on father-daughter relationships. I interviewed high-school girls, one-fourth of whose fathers had died, one-fourth of whose parents were divorced, and one-half of whose parents were together. I was interested in how daughters' relationships to fathers affected their self-esteem, sense of well-being, and reactions to males.

I quickly found that the physical presence of the father had little to do with the quality of the relationship. Some girls whose fathers lived in the home rarely spoke to them, while other girls who never saw their fathers were sustained by memories of warmth and acceptance. Emotional availability, not physical presence, was the critical variable. I noted three kinds of relationships: supportive, distant, and abusive.

Supportive fathers had daughters with high self-esteem and a sense of well-being. These girls were more apt to like men, to feel confident in relationships with the opposite sex, and to predict their own future happiness. They described fathers as fun, deeply involved, and companionable.

However, the majority of fathers fell in the distant relationship category. They may have wanted relationships, but they didn't have the skills. Girls with distant fathers said they liked the income their fathers brought home, but they appreciated little else. Besides being the breadwinner, often the father had only one other role: rule enforcer. Distant fathers were generally perceived as more rigid than mothers, less understanding, and less willing to listen. As one girl put it, "If Dad moved out, we'd be poorer, but there'd be more peace around here." These distant fathers were often well-meaning but inept. They worked long hours and had less time and energy for the hard work of connecting with adolescents. Distant fathers didn't know how to stay emotionally involved with their complicated teenage daughters. They hadn't learned to maneuver the intricacies of relationships with empathy, flexibility, patience, and negotiation. They had counted on their wives to do this for them.

Some distant fathers had more than a skill or time deficit. Because of their socialization to the male role, they did not value the qualities necessary to stay in close long-term relationships. They labeled nurturing and empathizing as wimpy behavior and related to their daughters in cold, mechanical ways.

The third category was the emotionally, physically, or sexually abusive father. These were the fathers who called their daughters names, who ridiculed and shamed them for mistakes, and who physically hurt or molested their daughters.

Katie's father was a supportive father. However, because of his illness, Katie had taken too much responsibility for him. Holly's father lacked the skills necessary to help his daughter. Dale was well-meaning but distant. Klara's father also fell into the distant category. He was a rigidly sex-typed father who imposed his definitions of femaleness on his daughter. These fathers all played important roles in the lives of their daughters, for good or ill.

KATIE (17) AND PETE

Pete was a single parent whose wife had died in a car accident when Katie was three. An invalid, homebound with muscular dystrophy, Pete managed to support himself and Katie as a copy editor for the local paper.

When Katie was in high school, he insisted she come to therapy. He was concerned that she was letting her love for him keep her from living her own life. Katie came in under duress, claiming that she could share all her thoughts and feelings with Pete.

Katie was so loving and insightful that she seemed too good to be true. Unlike most teenagers, she had a sense that her work was important to others. She took care of Pete, worked at a nearby drugstore, and studied. Time after time she managed to make good decisions about a life filled with problems.

I asked about her relationship to Pete. "He's always trusted me," she said. "When I have a problem, he insists I figure it out for myself. He says that I'll make the right decision. We can talk about everything: sex, boys, drugs, menstruation, you name it. He's the best listener in the world."

When I asked her if she missed having a mother, she paused and looked out the window. She said, "I don't remember my mother. Of course, I wish she were with us, but I have a better father than anyone I know."

When I asked about Pete's health, her tone changed. Her face darkened and she said softly, "He's getting worse and I hate to leave him for long. I'm worried about his future."

While she detailed his health problems and his poor prognosis, her voice was clear and firm but filled with pain. She had thought a great deal about what she wanted to give to Pete, but less about what she needed to keep for herself. I respected her devotion to her father and I wanted to be careful and not fix what wasn't broken, but on the other hand Katie needed to think more about her own life. Pete was right: she needed more friends and more fun.

When I shared my thoughts with her, Katie said, "Dad is so great that I don't miss friends. I know that sounds weird, but I like my life just like it is."

I wanted to meet this great dad, so I drove to their small suburban home one Saturday afternoon. Pete lay on a daybed covered with quilts and three Siamese cats, his telephone and typewriter within arm's reach. He was thin and frail with a big smile and an outgoing manner.

Pete and Katie joked about my black coat being attacked by white cat hairs. We talked about the ice storm that had frozen our city over the weekend and Katie's skills as a cook. No one seemed eager to broach the topic of Pete's health.

I complimented Pete on the wonderful job he had done raising Katie. He laughed. "She raised me. She's tons more mature than I am."

I agreed that Katie was mature, but I noted that she needed more of a social life. I suspected that some of her reluctance to engage with peers came from worry about her father, but some probably stemmed from ordinary teenage social anxiety.

"Usually I respect Katie's judgment, but she needs to look at herself in this area," Pete agreed. "She's more comfortable with me than she is with kids her age. She hates to fail and she knows she can succeed with me."

I offered to be Katie's "social-life consultant," and she agreed to come in for a while. I could tell she was humoring us.

I changed the subject. "How will things go when Katie graduates from high school?"

Pete and Katie exchanged looks and Pete laughed. "We have a big difference of opinion there. We have my wife's insurance money. Katie can go to school anywhere she wants. She can get into Harvard or Yale, her grades are first-rate."

"I want to go to college here," Katie interrupted.

Pete continued, "Katie has things all planned out. She wants to live at home and care for her sick old pa. I won't let her do that."

"You've never told me what to do and you can't start now," Katie said.

We all laughed.

But then Katie's eyes filled with tears and she said, "You are all the family I've got and I won't leave you. I couldn't enjoy being anywhere else. I'm not staying to take care of you. I'm staying because I want to."

Pete shook his head no.

"I'll live in the dorms if I can come home every day for a visit," she said.

"What do you think I'll be doing?" Pete joked. "Snorting coke, losing my money in poker games?"

Katie stood up for her position. "I think you'll be doing what you do now and you need my help to do it. You can hire someone for some things, like shopping and cleaning, but I'm going to visit daily and that's that."

"You've raised a stubborn daughter," I said. "I suggest you accept Katie's offer. It's not unhealthy or wrong for families to stick together."

"I don't have any choice," Pete said. "I don't think Katie will start taking orders now."

Katie wouldn't take orders, but I sensed that she was healthy enough to respond to conversation and encouragement. I knew that at some level she was aware that she was hiding from peers. On the other hand,

I admired this family's closeness and didn't want to pathologize a healthy relationship and a strong girl. "There are many ways to compromise. We can talk about this when she comes to my office."

"I think Katie will do what she wants." He smiled at her. "She's my cross to bear."

HOLLY (14) AND DALE

I met Holly at the hospital after she attempted suicide. Alone in a white room, she was dressed in the regulation hospital gown, but with her hair properly spiked and a *Rolling Stone* magazine by her side. When I introduced myself, she was polite but distant. I asked her about the suicide attempt. Holly stared out the window at the harsh November day and said, "My life is over." The rest of our time she answered questions in noncommittal monosyllables.

Holly's dad, Dale, came into her room and filled me in on their lives. Holly's mother had fallen in love with a neighbor and slipped away one day while Holly was at kindergarten and Dale was at work at the Goodyear plant. They never saw her again. Dale was devastated by the abandonment and the responsibilities of single parenting.

After his wife left, Dale's days were all the same. He came home, fixed dinner, did the dishes, and parked himself in his recliner in front of the television. Many nights he fell asleep before the ten o'clock news. He rarely made it to Holly's school programs and had no outside interests of his own. Once a coworker tried to set him up for a date, but Dale refused. He wasn't taking that kind of chance again.

Dale had arranged for Holly's physical care and supervision, but he had neither the energy nor the understanding to deliver much emotional support and companionship. He knew almost nothing about her thoughts and feelings. Clearly, he cared about his daughter, but he had no ideas about how to express his caring in helpful ways. He and Holly had talked so rarely that now that Holly was in a crisis, they had no foundation for working things through.

I suggested to them a combination of family therapy and time alone with Holly. They looked at each other and simultaneously nodded slowly.

In my first session with her, I was struck by her self-sufficiency. After her mother left, Holly had quickly learned to care for herself. She kept her bedroom neat and washed and ironed her own clothes. She was only vaguely aware that other girls had more friends and activities and parents who took them on outings. She never studied, but her grades were satisfactory.

In elementary school, she watched television with Dale, but by junior high she dropped TV in favor of music. Holly became obsessed with the music of Prince. She papered her walls with his posters and record covers. She joined his fan club, and once a week she wrote long letters to her idol. She played his music until she had all the lyrics memorized, and because Prince wore purple, Holly dressed exclusively in purple. Because Prince mentioned in an interview that he liked red hair, Holly dyed her hair red.

Dale hardly noticed this until the school counselor called to say that students were teasing Holly about her purple clothes and outrageous hair. She also was worried that Holly had few friends and she encouraged Dale to sign Holly up for a club, sports, or drama classes.

Dale asked Holly if she would join a club and she said no. He offered to pay for her lessons in whatever she wanted and she declined. Dale bought her new brightly colored T-shirts and Holly put them in a drawer unopened. Dale sensed Holly's problem might be related to her home life, but he was unsure what else to do. He gave up and returned to his television.

Then Holly met Lyle, a skinny ninth grader who had a studded black leather jacket and a tattoo that read "Live fast, die young." Like Holly, Lyle had chosen music as his way of dealing with his aloneness. He listened to music virtually every waking minute that he was not in class. He was in trouble at school for blasting music during lunch break. They met in the back row of English class. Holly noticed that Lyle had slipped a Sony Walkman into the school and shyly asked him if he liked Prince. Lyle, unlike most of the boys, didn't think that Holly's teased hair and purple outfits were a liability. He told her that yes, he liked Prince. He asked Holly to come to his house after school and listen to music.

By the weekend they were going steady. Holly transferred much of the devotion she'd lavished on Prince to Lyle. She called him first thing in the morning to wake him and met him at the corner south of school for a cigarette. She wrote notes to him during classes, ate lunch with him in the school cafeteria, and then, after school, went to his house. In the evenings she spent hours on the phone to Lyle.

Dale was relieved that Holly had a friend. He told me, "Lyle is a strange agent, but he is a good person." Dale sensed that so much closeness so fast might not be healthy, but he was unsure what to do about it. He brought up sex to Holly and she angrily told him that she could handle it. He doubted that but was uncertain what to say or do next.

For three months Holly lived for Lyle. Then Lyle broke off the relationship abruptly. He told Holly that he wasn't ready for a serious relationship and wanted more time to practice his guitar and hang out with musicians. Lyle's mother called Dale to warn him about the effect this news would have on Holly. She said that while they liked Holly, she and her husband felt that things were moving way too fast and that Lyle needed to slow down. After all, these were ninth graders. They had spoken with Lyle about their concerns and he agreed to cool it. Before she hung up, she told Dale that Holly and Lyle had been sexually active.

Dale was stunned by the news. He suggested a pregnancy test but

Holly refused. In fact, she refused to discuss Lyle with him at all. When he came home at night, she fled to her room and slammed the door. For a few days Holly cried nonstop, refusing to eat or go to school. Her eyes were red and her face puffy from grief. She called Lyle daily but the talks didn't go well. Her pleading made him even more determined to break up. Then one day Holly swallowed all the pills in the house.

Fortunately, Dale came home at lunch to check on Holly. He found her asleep in a pool of vomit and called 911. That is when I entered their lives.

Slowly I began to build a relationship with Holly. Once a week she showed up in a different purple outfit and we talked about Prince. I encouraged her to bring a tape and we listened together. To test me, she played "sexy" Prince songs. Afterward I commented on whatever I could praise.

"I like the line about staying until the morning light."

She shrugged and said, "That's his old stuff. Listen to this."

After listening to the song, I asked, "What does this song mean to you?"

Holly said, "It's two against the world. Undying love."

"Undying love is such a beautiful idea. We all want that with our families and friends," I responded.

"Are you bringing up my mother?" she asked angrily.

Holly often answered my questions by quoting Prince's songs. I listened and pulled themes from the lyrics for further consideration. I waited for Holly to use her own words. Finally, I suggested that she write a Prince-style song about her feelings.

The next week Holly handed me a song. It was Prince-like with themes of loneliness and abandonment. She grinned when I praised it. After that, Holly and I communicated mostly via her songs. She brought a fresh one each week: a song about her mother's leaving, another about her anger over the divorce, a song wondering where her mother was and why she didn't call, and a song about how cruel kids could be. I listened, discussed the writing, asked what meaning the songs had in her life.

Otherwise, I gently encouraged her to make a friend. Because of her mother's abandonment and because of teasing by girls, Holly didn't trust females. She shook her head no to my suggestions about talking to girls. I suggested music lessons and maybe joining a band.

After many months I felt we had a strong enough relationship that I could bring up sex. I suggested a doctor's appointment for an examination. I told her basic facts about sexuality that, as I put it, "all girls wonder about and are afraid to ask."

We talked about how vulnerable she'd been to the first person who said "I love you." Lyle was a decent guy, lonely and naive like Holly, but the next person might be different. I pointed out that *I love you* are the first words that psychopaths say to girls.

Holly was vulnerable to a common adolescent girl's mistake— using her sexuality to get love. She needed affection, not sex, and most of all she needed affection from her father. We discussed how she and her father were strangers to each other, and I invited Dale in for a visit. That first joint session he was even more awkward than Holly. He sat stiffly with his arms folded across his chest and said "yes, ma'am" to my questions.

"We don't talk," Holly said accusingly.

"Your mother was better at that," Dale said. "I never had much experience talking to kids."

I asked if they wanted to be closer. Holly twirled her hair around her little finger and nodded shyly. Dale choked up but finally said, "That's all I want. What else am I alive for?"

I recommended that they go slowly. Neither had much experience communicating and both could easily be overwhelmed by failure. I said, "Perhaps you could cook a meal together or drive around and look at Christmas lights."

When I suggested they attend a holiday concert, both looked alarmed. I backed down and suggested they talk ten minutes each evening about how their day had gone.

The next session they reported that the talks were difficult at first but easier with practice. Dale asked about Holly's school. She told him about lunchtime in the loud cafeteria. Holly asked what her dad did at work, and after all these years he explained it to her.

In therapy we gingerly approached their long-buried feelings about Holly's mother leaving. Dale said, "I tried to put it behind me. I couldn't change it, so what was the point crying about it?"

"I was afraid to bring it up because Dad always looked so sad," Holly said. "After the first month, I didn't mention Mom anymore. For a long time, I cried myself to sleep."

I asked both Holly and Dale to write letters in which they expressed their true feelings about their absent family member leaving. These letters were not for sending (indeed, we didn't even know where to send them) but for Holly and Dale's reworking of the painful events.

The next week Holly and Dale read their letters aloud. At first Dale's letter was formal and emotionally constricted, but later more passionate. Years of pent-up anger came tumbling out, and after the anger, sadness, and after the sadness, bad feelings about himself. He was a failure as a husband, he wasn't able to communicate clearly or to show affection. He blamed himself for his wife's leaving.

Holly listened closely to her dad's letter and handed him Kleenex. She patted his arm and said, "It wasn't your fault, it was mine."

She read her letter, which, like Dale's, began in a formal, polite way and built up steam over time. Her first and strongest emotion was loss—her mother had chosen to leave and never see her again. She suspected that something must be wrong with her, some secret flaw she couldn't identify. She had grieved since it happened, unsure how to express or even acknowledge such painful feelings.

Ever since her mother left, she hated to be touched or praised by women. If a teacher patted her, she cringed. Instead of moving toward women for support, she tried to toughen herself so she wouldn't need it. She didn't like to visit girls at their homes. She got too jealous watching them with their mothers.

She blamed herself for her mother's abandonment. She was "a mouthy little kid." After her mother left, Holly stopped being mouthy, she almost stopped talking. She no longer trusted that words could help her.

Since her mother's abandonment Lyle was the first person she let in emotionally. He gave her hope that she was lovable. He listened to her, held her, and told her she was beautiful. When he left, the pain was horrible. It reminded her of her mother's leaving and convinced her that she was unworthy of the love of another human being.

At the end of that session, both Holly and Dale were crying. I realized that Holly and Dale desperately needed each other. Neither of them felt lovable, and the only person who was close enough to change that basic feeling about themselves was the other. In what I hoped would be a self-fulfilling prophecy, I said, "You two can teach each other how to show love."

That's what we worked on. Dale had been distant because of his own unprocessed pain and because of a lack of relationship skills. Indeed, this same lack of skills had probably cost him his marriage. Holly had been distant because she was abandoned. Her dad made it easy to stay distant. Prince was the perfect love object since he was a thousand miles away and totally inaccessible. She could love him without taking any risks.

Gradually Holly and Dale formed a caring relationship. They

talked more about personal topics. For example, Holly asked about Dale's friends at work and he said he avoided them. He told her they read *Playboy* and talked about women in a way that made him uncomfortable. Holly told him about the way boys teased her at school and about her discomfort when boys touched her in the halls. That led them into a philosophical discussion of the relations between the sexes. They both had things to learn and teach.

Dale became a more involved parent. He limited himself to an hour of television a night and spent the rest of his time talking to Holly or looking at her homework. He asked to see Holly's school papers and wanted reports on her day. Most teenagers would fight involvement at this late stage, but Holly was so lonely that she welcomed his attention. He wasn't a harsh critic and she learned to trust her dad with her failures as well as her successes. He turned out to be always on her side, supportive of whatever she did.

They went to a Kiss concert at the city auditorium. Holly shared her songs with Dale and he offered to pay for guitar lessons. Her mother had a good voice and he hoped Holly had inherited that from her. Holly set her songs to music and began sharing them with a local band called Power Peach.

When we interviewed girls for this update, one of our happy surprises was how close most of them were to their fathers. In the 1960s, the main role for fathers had been breadwinner. Mothers had been in charge of the children, and fathers, while loving, were often more distant figures. By the 1990s, both parents were often working and dads were stepping up their engagement with children. By today, dads are even more engaged. Family structures are more democratic. In general, women have permission to be assertive and men have more permission to be vulnerable.

Most fathers today want their daughters to be strong and bold. They are likely to value feminism rather than fear it. They model with their wives the respect they want their daughters to receive. Many coach their daughters in sports or share mutual passions for music, art, or backpacking, and they have great power to foster their daughters' confidence and authenticity.

We know, of course, that there will always distant and even abusive fathers, but almost all the girls we interviewed reported loving relationships with their dads. In fact, except for physically absent dads, none of our focus group girls reported distant relationships. The most-repeated descriptor of fathers was "funny."

Jordan said she and her dad run two miles every morning. Kendyl said she and her dad were puzzle fanatics and competed to see who could solve Sudoku puzzles faster.

"I love my dad. He works at home, so we're together a lot," said Marta. "My mom has a busy job and travels for work most weeks. I'm closer to him."

Olivia said sadly, "My dad has cancer and he's really stressed out. That makes him grumpy. He's too tired to do much with me, but I'm trying to be there for him."

"My dad is a great cook," said Aspen. "He'll see something on the internet and he and I will cook it together. Last night we made an Indian meal with pakoras, curry, and naan."

Especially in this era of #MeToo, fathers want to help their daughters become strong, confident women. In the best cases, we're seeing a new kind of father, one who is actively countering sexism. For example, Maddie's dad told me, "I used to comment on women's appearance, but now that Maddie is a teenager, I never do that. I don't want to objectify women."

"I try to treat my wife the way I want my daughters to be treated," my neighbor Grant said. "I make a point to ask about their social lives. I am teaching them how to stand up for themselves."

ANIKA (17)

Anika is the oldest of three children who lives with her parents in a small town in Iowa. Her dad is the guidance counselor at her high school. Her mother teaches middle school in the same town. I interviewed Anika in Omaha at a trendy coffee shop. She was eager to talk about her dad and started with her earliest memories of her relationship with him. She tossed her long dark hair off her face and said, "When I was little, I adored my dad. I thought he was perfect. He sang and read to me for hours at a time. He wrestled with my brother and me and made us laugh. He was so kind. I couldn't wait for him to come home from work."

Anika's eyes twinkled as she laughed aloud at a memory. "When I was young, I wanted to marry my dad and I asked him once if he would marry me if Mommy died."

I asked if she had experienced enough time with her dad and she nodded readily.

"He's always included us in everything he did. If he was building a dog kennel or planting trees, we helped him. He taught us to cook and take well-composed photos. Since I was three years old Dad has always spent Saturday afternoons with me. We'd do whatever I wanted. We'd go on adventures together. We'd sing and dance and go out for ice cream. On rainy days, he'd read aloud to me all afternoon. If the story was a sad one, I'd want us to act it out. That way I could cry and deal with my emotions. We acted out Charlotte's death scene in *Charlotte's Web* about three hundred times.

"Since I started high school, I am usually too busy to spend Saturday afternoons with my dad, which makes him feel sad. Now and then we'll squeeze in some time together. We'll go to the library and check out books, then go read at a coffeehouse. It's like being alone, together.

"As a girl I thought he was perfect, but now I see him as a whole person. He makes mistakes. He can be impatient. In fact, a lot of my flaws are his flaws." Anika made a rueful face and we both laughed. She continued. "But he apologizes if he makes a mistake. He is not perfect, but he is close. Still, it was hard to let go of my illusion."

I asked what their issues are now. Anika said, "My dad is a really emotionally open guy and he wants me to tell him everything. I don't have his personality. I am more like my mom *and* I am a teenager. I don't want my dad to know all about my life."

She paused and sighed. "Sometimes I push back when he grills me for information about my day. That hurts his feelings. He takes it personally and it isn't personal. I want my own life.

"He can bug me sometimes, but in some ways I love him more as I know him as a real person. Still, it was hard to let go of my belief that he was perfect."

"He sounds like an amazing man," I noted. "Does he have bad days or bad moods?"

"He has a difficult job," Anika acknowledged. "He deals with children who have been abused or sexually assaulted. He sees the kids who have behavior problems or are suicidal, but he leaves all that when he walks in our front door. He comes in with a smile on his face. Pretty soon he is cooking us dinner and cracking jokes. More than anything, he is intentional about his time. He's made a commitment to give his family his attention. I respect how passionate he is about life. He is always looking for beauty. He taught me to do that, too."

"What else have you learned from your father?" I asked.

"I see how hard he struggles to be honest and kind. He treats my mom really well and he has taught us kids how to be in a healthy relationship. I have high standards for any boy I date."

Anika tossed her cup into the recycling bin and pumped her fist when it hit its mark.

"I still want to marry someone like my dad."

As I drove home, I thought about the lovely relationship Anika had with her father. I noted that her issues with her father centered around individuation. He had been close and connected to her and now, when she wanted more space, he felt sad and hurt. Today, engaged fathers like Anika's are experiencing feelings that are old hat to mothers. Anika and her peers are ready to grow into their own lives and their fathers are thinking, *Wait. Stay with me a little longer.*

LUNA (19) AND STEVEN

"Ten years ago, I was hired by a national environmental organization to be their point person on environmental advocacy issues in Nebraska," explained Steven, a laid-back fortysomething with a goatee and shiny black reading glasses. "Luna was in middle school at the time. When I'd pick her up from school, Luna always had her earbuds in. Nevertheless, I'd tell her about my work and how I'd been hired to fight this oil pipeline, and why it posed a threat to our state. I felt like I was talking to myself. But eventually one earbud popped out, then another one, and then Luna turned to me and said, 'Dad, you have to stop them!'"

Luna laughed and squeezed her dad's knee. We were seated in armchairs around a fireplace at an Indian restaurant and lounge, chatting over chai and vegan samosas.

"I remember that day," Luna said. "In middle school I didn't want to pay attention to anything my dad said. I was listening to Lady Gaga on my iPod, but then my dad said some things that piqued my interest and, more importantly, pissed me off. That's what got me interested."

"Before we jump into your activism, can we back up a bit? What was your relationship like when Luna was a little girl?" I asked Steven.

"I thought she was a cool human being," Steven said. "From birth, she's been interesting, fun, funny, and smart. I loved going to the park with her, loved being silly with her and hearing what she thought of the world. I wasn't much of a disciplinarian; I just wanted to convey to her, 'I'm on your side.'"

"My parents split up when I was pretty young. I didn't have time to experience them as a mom and dad together," Luna explained. "I love my mom, but she was much more of a parent, whereas dad wasn't strict. The rules he set were important, but I always felt I could be honest with him about . . . well, anything. I'm really glad I had the father I did. He let me figure out who I was."

"It was always important to me to show up," Steven added, propping his hiking-booted feet on a sari-print ottoman. "We've had some great adventures together."

"We started getting really close as we became involved in activism," Luna added. She propped her feet next to her father's; she was wearing glittery purple Converse high-tops. "It was like having a partner in crime. Whenever we darted off someplace, it was just the two of us, and whatever we did, Dad was always there encouraging me."

"How did the two of you transform into the powerhouse father-daughter activism team I keep seeing in the newspaper?" I asked.

"The more my dad told me about what was going on in our state, the more I felt compelled to get involved," said Luna. "I especially felt that as a teenager, I needed to be a voice for the youth of our state because we're going to have to deal with any environmental fallout from the pipeline for the rest of our lives. So we started going to protests. Then I testified before the state legislature when I was in ninth grade."

"Before that, you went with me to DC," Steven reminded her. "I told my supervisor I wanted my daughter to come with me to meetings at the State Department, Environmental Protection Agency, and congressional offices. I figured she'd just listen and observe, but I still thought it would be a valuable experience for her. Instead, whenever we walked into meetings, Luna identified herself as an activist representing the youth of Nebraska. She held her own with the rest of our delegations, and she could get away with asking tough questions because she was this charming teenager. That was the beginning."

Over the next few years, Luna became a fixture at environmental rallies and legislative hearings. She testified several times before the state legislature, always making the connection between environmental peril and the future of the state's young people.

"The first time I testified, I was fourteen and terrified," Luna admitted. " But afterward, I felt breathless with joy, because I had a voice and I had used it. That same year, we went to DC for a rally. We made a human chain, three people thick, around the White House. It was incredible to be surrounded by sixteen thousand people who cared about the same things I did."

"I remember when we came to Lincoln for one of the early legislative hearings, I told Luna she could just come and watch," Steven added. "I made it clear that she didn't need to participate. Instead, she sat down and wrote her incredibly powerful testimony in less than an hour."

"How has this changed you?" I asked Luna. "All of this has unfolded in the midst of your adolescence. How did your peers react to your activism? "

"My high-school teachers were supportive and my administrators always went out of their way to ask me about how my trips and events went," Luna said. "My friends knew what was happening—like, they thought it was cool when I did a TEDx talk and went to the PowerShift conference—but it's high school. Everyone is preoccupied with their own lives."

"How is your relationship with your dad unique?" I asked.

"Whenever I bring up my dad, my friends always say, 'He's the sweetest. I love your dad,'" Luna said proudly. "Some of my friends have had horrible experiences. Maybe they're terrified of coming out to their parents so they live secret lives. Or their parents just don't give a shit about the things that matter most to them. I have friends whose parents have told them, 'Poetry is a waste of your time.' That guts me. Poetry has done so much for my confidence and mental health. To not believe that your parent is going to be respectful of who you are . . . I just can't imagine that. Having a supportive dad has made all the difference for me."

"How would you describe adolescent girls today?" I asked.

"Girls my age are eager to identify as feminists," Luna replied. "They'll go to protests and hold up signs. Activism now is personal.

"I've gotta be honest, after watching Hillary Clinton—who spent her entire life doing everything right, checking every educational and professional box—lose the election, I felt like, 'What is the point of getting involved in politics and public service when someone like Trump can come in and win anyway?'" Luna shook her head in dismay.

"I think old fogeys like me can learn a lot from Luna and her friends. I'd like to see more intergenerational conversations," Steven said. "For example, some of the bands I really like are musicians in their twenties. A lot of my peers would never consider the importance of contemporary music. We need to get people talking to each other rather than categorizing each other."

Luna nodded in agreement.

"Most of all, we have to remember to take care of ourselves and each other. Activism gets tiring. Especially when you're young and you want so many changes; the most important thing is to take care of yourself and your friends. Oppression really weighs on you, and there is no power in the movement if you're all sick and depressed. Just take a minute and listen to Beyoncé when you're really sad."

These new, positive relationships that girls have with both their fathers and mothers allow the generations to enjoy each other's company and work together toward common goals. In spite of the time all members of the family spend online, when parents and children talk to each other, they enjoy it.

In our interviews and focus groups, we were repeatedly impressed by how respectful girls were of their parents today. They possessed a real understanding of how hard their parents were working to give them safe homes and experience-filled lives. They admired their parents' work ethics and skills. Many said that their parents were their best friends. This may be the best news we can share about the changes in our culture since 1994. We hope these attitudes of respect and love lead into decades-long relationships that remain relatively friction free.

EIGHT

Divorce

Julia (14)

Jean, an animated woman dressed in a business suit, reported that her daughter had been arrested for being a minor in possession of alcohol. Julia, dressed in pink stretch pants, an oversized sweater, and shark earrings, groaned and folded her arms across her chest.

"I had one beer."

I listened as Jean explained their complicated family. Julia's parents had divorced two years ago after her father became involved with a younger woman. He had since married the younger woman and moved to a nearby town. They had a baby girl born three months ago. Since the birth of his new daughter, Julia's father hadn't seen Julia. He called a couple of times, but he was busy with the new baby and his new wife. Jean hadn't even told him about Julia's arrest.

Jean worked at an accounting firm and they'd scraped by on her earnings. Jean, Julia, and Reynold, Julia's ten-year-old brother, had moved to a smaller house in a less expensive part of town. The children had to change schools and Julia had been cut off from her closest friends.

A year ago in Parents Without Partners, Jean had met Al, a father of three boys and owner of a small printing company. Right away she had liked his kindness and sense of humor. He liked her efficiency and common sense. For several months they met on Saturday nights for dinner and a movie. They combined their children for some family picnics and miniature golf outings. Three months ago they were married.

Jean, Julia, and Reynold had moved again, into Al's home with his sons. This fall Julia attended her third junior high in two years. Jean said, "Reynold hasn't had much trouble. He's got brothers now and he's a jock who found friends right away on the softball team. But the divorce hit at a bad time for Julia. She was just beginning seventh grade. At her first new school she was shy and didn't make friends. At her next school she made friends with the kids who were smoking and drinking. I'm sure her arrest is connected to all the changes."

I thought to myself that most teenagers, like plants, don't do well with moves.

Julia curled her feet under her and nestled into the couch. "I know Mom and Dad weren't getting along, but I was fine. I haven't been happy since the divorce."

She looked at her mother. "Al's not a bad guy—he's good to Mom— but I hate his sons. They're spoiled rotten. I have to pick up after them and do their dishes. Al lets them get away with murder. They're jerks."

"It's true that Julia does more than her share. Al's boys never have had chores. Al's a softy," Jean said.

"Most stepfamilies need some counseling, especially if there are teenagers," I said. "Making a new family is so difficult that everyone needs a consultant."

Julia said, "For a long time I wished my parents would get back together. Now I just wish that Reynold and I could live alone with Mom. I don't like all the noise and mess at Al's."

Jean touched her daughter's arm. "You're not home very much."

"I try not to be," Julia said.

"Last week Julia was busted at a party," Jean said. "Afterward, one of the mothers suggested we get together and make rules. We all work so no one is home after school to supervise."

Julia interrupted, "Mrs. Snyder's a creep. Don't you dare get involved in that. Everyone drinks. You don't know anything about it."

"Kids are different now," Jean said with a sigh. "I had a roller-skating party for Julia's eighth-grade birthday and it was an eye-opener. The kids talked filth. The rink had security people to check for drugs. Believe me, skating rinks were different when I was a kid."

"Of course things are different," Julia responded. "Why do you treat me like they aren't? You have the same stupid rules for me that your mother had for you. Don't you understand that I can't live by those rules and have any friends?"

Jean looked at me. "I just want her to be safe."

Clearly Julia had too much to handle—her parents' divorce, the loss of her father, the new living situation and school, and a new stepfather and stepbrothers. Plus, she had all the issues that hit girls with puberty. Like many adolescent girls whose parents divorce, she turned to friends. She found a crowd who kept her away from home and gave her a sense of belonging. She used alcohol to forget.

Julia needed a place to talk about all her losses. She needed to reconnect with her father. I suspected that she needed some guidance about sexuality, a drug and alcohol evaluation, and maybe a support group for teen users. If she could sort through the pain, she wouldn't need to medicate it away.

I recommended family therapy. The rules regarding housework should be fair. Al's boys could use more discipline. Jean agreed to discuss this with Al.

I asked Julia if she would like to come in alone. Julia uncurled her legs and looked hard at me. "Yes, as long as you don't lecture me."

I promised I wouldn't.

My own thinking about divorce changed during the years I was a therapist. In the late 1970s, I believed that children were better off with happy single parents rather than unhappily married parents. Divorce seemed a better option than struggling with a bad marriage. By the 1990s, I was more aware of the effects of divorce on children. In some families, children didn't notice their parents were unhappy, but divorces shattered them, at least for a while. As one girl said when I asked her how she felt seeing her father one weekend a month, "I try not to think of it; it hurts too much. I try not to feel anything."

Of course, some marriages are unworkable. Sometimes, especially if there is abuse or addiction involved, the best way out of an impossible situation is the door. Adults have rights, and sometimes they must take care of themselves, even when it hurts their children. Living in homes with unhappy parents who have stayed together for the sake of the children is by no means ideal for anyone. But divorce often doesn't make parents happier. Certainly, it overwhelms mothers and fathers, and it cuts many parents off from relationships with their children.

Many times, marriages don't work because people lack relationship skills. Partners need lessons in negotiating, communicating, expressing affection, and doing their share. With these lessons, many marriages can be saved. And if these lessons aren't learned in the first marriage, they will have to be learned later or the next marriage will be doomed as well.

In the 1990s, most adults experienced at least one divorce, and many children lived with one parent. Divorces almost always make families poorer. Often families must move and teenagers find themselves in new schools surrounded by strangers. They have left their longtime friends, who could have helped them through this. Often they worry about money for clothes, cars, and college.

Divorce is particularly tough for adolescents. Partly that's because of their developmental level and partly it's because teenagers require so much energy from parents. Teenagers need parents who will talk to them, supervise them, help them stay organized, and support them when they are down. Divorcing parents often just don't have that kind of energy. Adolescents feel an enormous sense of loss—of their parents, their families, and their childhoods. And, unlike younger children, when they express their pain, they are likely to do it in dangerous ways.

Adolescents' immature thinking makes it difficult for them to process the divorce. They tend to see things in black-and-white terms and have trouble putting events into perspective. They are absolute in their judgments and expect perfection in parents. They are likely to be self-conscious about their parents' failures and critical of their every move. They have the expectation that parents will keep them safe and happy and are shocked by the broken covenant. Adolescents can be unforgiving.

Just at a time when feeling different means feeling wrong, divorce makes teenagers feel different. If a parent wearing the wrong kind of shoes can humiliate a teenager, a parent who is divorcing causes utter shame. Teenagers are so egocentric that they think everyone knows about the divorce in all its details. They are ashamed of their families, which they see as uniquely dysfunctional.

Adolescence is a time when children are expected to move away from their parents but check back frequently for their support and guidance. When the parents disconnect, the children have no base to move away from or return to. With divorce, adolescents feel abandoned, and they are outraged at that abandonment. They are angry at both parents for letting them down. Often they feel that their parents broke the rules and so now they can too. They no longer give their parents moral authority. Instead they say, "How dare you tell me what to do when you've screwed up so badly."

Until late adolescence, children don't think of their parents as people with needs separate from their own. Rather, they are seen as providers of care. Most teens aren't able to empathize with their parents and prefer their parents to be married even if they are unhappy. They find it frightening that parents can break their bonds to each other. If parent-parent bonds can be broken, so can parent-child bonds.

Often there's bitterness between the parents that makes it difficult for them to discipline their teenagers. Teens can and do manipulate divided parents. They pit them against each other or live with the one who has the fewest rules and the least supervision. Teenagers are not always good judges of what they need and often choose to live with the parent who promises to buy them the new stereo or take them on vacation. The parent who insists on schoolwork and chores is often the parent they avoid.

Legal actions, particularly custody battles, tear adolescents apart. Often they end up blaming both parents for the anguish they experience and so they have no one left to trust. They discount adults and rely only on peers for comfort and companionship.

Divorce is particularly difficult for teenage girls, who are already stressed by cultural forces. Girls deal with this situation in various ways. Some get depressed and hurt themselves, either with suicide attempts or more slowly with alcohol and drugs. Some withdraw and sink deep within themselves to nurse their wounds. Many react by rebelling. And miraculously, others cope well.

TARYN (14)

Lois called for an emergency appointment after her daughter shoved her. That afternoon in my office she spoke softly, glancing nervously at her daughter with every sentence. Her daughter, Taryn, dark-haired and muscular, was much more outspoken. She interrupted, contradicted, and insulted her mother at every juncture. Taryn was good at blaming, and Lois was good at accepting blame. Watching the two of them interact, I could see how conflicts might escalate into violence.

Until two years ago, when her parents divorced, Taryn had led the life of a pampered only child. Her father was a banker and her mother was an audiologist. They lived in a small community a hundred miles from our city, where Taryn was the biggest duck in the puddle. Her father's grandparents had been the founders of the town. Everyone knew and respected her family.

Then Lois went to a convention in Los Angeles, and when she came home she asked for a divorce. She had had an affair at the convention, but that wasn't really the issue. The affair made her realize that the marriage wasn't working, that the relationship with her husband was strained beyond fixing. She announced that she wanted to move to a city where she could build a life of her own.

I looked at this small, shy woman and was amazed at her boldness. "I know the affair was wrong. I've apologized to Randy and to Taryn, but the divorce was right for me," Lois said. "I have never been happier than this last year."

Taryn groaned. "Yeah, but what about me and Dad? You ruined our lives."

Lois spread her palms upward in a hopeless gesture and looked beseechingly at me. I could tell that she wanted to defend herself but felt too guilty. I asked Taryn to tell me what happened after the divorce.

"At first, I stayed with Dad, but that didn't work out. He spent all his time at the bank and the country club."

She glared at Lois, who continued the story. "Taryn wasn't getting much supervision. Her grades dropped and she skipped school. Randy couldn't control her. He had always left the discipline to me. Finally, he gave up and sent her here."

Lois looked at her daughter. "After the separation, I tried to stay close, but she was too angry. When Randy brought Taryn down, I was eager to reunite with her but also afraid. I had my own life for the first time, a good job and friends. I didn't want everything screwed up by Taryn's anger."

"Nobody wants me." Taryn tossed her black hair. "I'm pissed. I miss our big house. Now we're in a cramped apartment. I miss my boyfriend. I hate Mom's friends and the kids at school. This whole thing is an enormous fucking drag."

Lois said, "It's hard for her. She knew everyone in town and was involved with everything—music, sports, and the church. A city is a big adjustment. I thought we could work things out, but recently Taryn has been hitting me." She showed me a bruise on her left arm. "I don't know how to handle this."

Taryn scowled. "I didn't hit you, I pushed you. You always overreact."

We spent the rest of that first hour working out a contract about hitting. It was agreed that if Taryn hurt her mother again, she would be grounded for a week. Lois left feeling relieved, while Taryn left angry that I had been influenced by her mother.

The next week I saw Taryn alone. Like many teenagers, she was much more pleasant when her mother wasn't around. She said that she hadn't hurt her mom since we talked and then quickly changed the subject to the divorce. She had hated living with her dad, who was depressed and self-absorbed. She had hated eating frozen pizzas and doing the laundry herself.

She had missed her mother who was a good homemaker. Even though Lois had worked, she always had time for Taryn. She helped her with homework, sewed school costumes, decorated for holidays, and fixed gourmet meals. She arranged parties that everyone in town loved. In short, Lois had catered to Taryn and her father.

Taryn said, "After Mom left, there were nights when I sat alone in our big old house, looked at pictures of Dad, Mom, and me. I cursed Mom for being selfish and breaking up our family."

As we talked, things seemed a little less simple, even to Taryn. Her father was financially successful but hard to live with. He had expected Lois to take care of the house and of Taryn. He drank after work and some days he came home boisterous, other days sullen. He directed most of his anger at Lois, who wasn't good at standing up for herself. Watching her mother, Taryn decided that she would never take anyone's bad treatment. Still she was angry when her mother made the same decision.

Taryn said, "One reason I'm mad at her now is that she was such a great mom when I was little."

"What happened after your mother announced she wanted out?"

"Dad and I worked on her," Taryn said. "Dad told everyone about her affair. Both sides of the family pressured her. She practically had a nervous breakdown."

I tried to smile. "Your mom sounds like she can be as stubborn as you."

We discussed Taryn's current social life. She had been popular in her hometown, but here she was a loner, going from a school of 225 students to one of 3,000. Even if she wanted to make friends, it would have been tough. But she hadn't wanted to. Taryn had missed her boyfriend, who had been her main confidant. He wrote her letters for a while, but by now he had another steady girlfriend.

Taryn had all the ordinary vulnerabilities of early adolescents, plus the pain of losing her family. Her trust level was zero, and she was too angry and discouraged to make friends. I was amazed she talked to me, and when she left, I congratulated her on her willingness to trust a new adult.

Our next session began with Taryn describing a blowup with Lois. She shouted when she told me about her mother's refusal to buy her a television for her room.

"She says she can't afford it, but I know she could borrow the fucking money."

I asked her if she had any other feelings besides anger about the incident.

"I'm embarrassed. I know it's wrong to call her a bitch. She is a bitch, but I shouldn't call her that." She said, "I want to kill her I get so mad."

We talked about anger control. I recommended she punch a pillow the next time she felt angry. I also suggested that she jog until she had "outrun" her anger. It's hard to be angry when physically exhausted. I encouraged her to write. "Write everything you can think of. Get those feelings out of your chest and onto a piece of paper. Then you can throw the paper away."

Taryn brought me her writing. At first it was pure rage—her mother was the source of all pain in her life and virtually all evil in the universe. But gradually as she wrote the anger softened. She began to write about the issues that the divorce raised for her—the loss of her life as she knew it, missing her boyfriend, her fear of a new school, and the lack of trust that relationships could work.

I was pleased when the writing became more Taryn-focused. She had been so obsessed with her mother that she hadn't cared for herself. Too much anger, like too much compliance, stops growth. It's impossible for blamers to take responsibility for their lives and get on with it. After several months, Taryn acknowledged that she had expected her mother to live solely for her, but now she could see that this wasn't realistic. It set both of them up to fail in certain ways. It kept Lois from having a life and Taryn from learning she could make herself happy. Taryn still had angry times, but her temper tantrums were over. Between arguments, Lois and Taryn had some fun together.

As Taryn's anger waned, she had more energy for her own life. She mourned her past, but then she set some goals for her future. She improved her abysmal grades. She exercised and even considered going out for track. She fought back her fears and talked to kids in her classes.

AMY (12)

Joan brought Amy in for counseling because she and Chuck were divorcing. The previous year Amy had been lively, lighthearted, and fun-loving. When I met her a year later, she was quiet, withdrawn, and serious.

Joan was an articulate schoolteacher who was venomous on the subject of her husband, Chuck. He was evil incarnate, the Adolf Hitler of husbands and without a good motive to his credit. She poured out her anger while Amy shrank deeper into my couch. Amy looked like she was vanishing as her mother talked; her serious little face grew smaller, her body more childlike.

Joan explained how she and Chuck had tried counseling, but that Chuck, even though he was a therapist himself, wouldn't cooperate. She had done her best, but he sabotaged her efforts to save the family.

And now that she had filed, he was doing everything he could to destroy her life and turn Amy against her.

Joan listed her concerns about Amy. She had lost five pounds since May. She wasn't communicating and was avoiding friends and activities. Joan finished by saying, "I think she's depressed by her dad's behavior."

I asked for examples of Chuck's behavior. "Do you have all day?" Joan asked. "We're fighting for custody and he keeps pressuring and bribing Amy to choose him. He puts me down constantly and he sets me up to be angry. Last week he called to change visitation three times. He disappoints Amy by not coming when he says he will."

"He comes when he says," Amy protested.

Joan continued as if she hadn't heard. "We have psychologists evaluating Amy for the custody decision, but I wanted someone to help her with the stress of the divorce."

With some reservations, I asked to talk to Amy alone. In the last few months she'd talked to attorneys, judges, and psychologists and her trust for adults was at an all-time low. From her point of view, I was just one more adult who was supposed to be helping but wasn't.

I asked how her summer was going and she answered so softly I had to ask her to repeat herself. She said, "It's rained a lot and I haven't been able to swim as much as I like to."

She was giving careful answers to me and probably to everyone else as well. She'd learned that what she didn't say didn't get her in trouble. I talked to her about divorce, how it stresses out kids and makes them feel alone and weird. I said that I'd seen lots of kids who were sad and mad about their parents' divorce. I told her some stories about other teens who had worked through their parents' divorces and moved on. Amy relaxed as I talked and asked me questions about those kids. But when I asked about her, she resumed her frozen face.

I said, "Most kids hate to choose which parent to live with."

"Both of them want me and I hate to hurt their feelings." Amy shook her head miserably. "Besides, some days I hate Dad and some days I hate Mom. Some days I hate them both."

I asked about living arrangements. "Mom and I still live at home for now. Dad has an apartment in the town where he works. I don't know anyone there and I can't stand his place. Mom says that she'll have to move, though, especially if Dad gets me."

She sat up straight and said, "I don't want to live with either of them right now. They're both screwed up. I want to run away from home." We talked about running away—its dangers and appeals. Amy, like most twelve-year-olds, wanted to run to family. Older kids often want to go to the coast or to move in with friends. Amy dreamed of going to her grandmother's house in Minnesota. She asked for her parents' permission, but neither had agreed to that.

Once she opened up to me, Amy loved to talk. She told me about starting her period at her dad's house. She had supplies at her mother's, but nothing at her dad's, and she had to ask him to go buy her pads. Later her mom got in a fight with him because he hadn't brought her home. She'd wanted to share Amy's first period. As Amy said, "She thought it should be a mother-daughter thing."

She told me that both parents tried to buy her love with presents. "If I wanted to, I could ask for a racing bike or television right now." Worst of all was how her parents talked about each other. "They both pretend they don't rag on each other, but they drop hints all the time that the other one is the craziest, meanest person they know."

Her biggest worry was starting junior high the next year. If she lived with Dad, it would be a new school where she had no friends. If she lived with Mom, all the kids would know her parents got divorced. She said, "I don't know how I'll get my homework done. Mom helps me with math and Dad knows French."

She told me how ashamed she was of the divorce. She had tried unsuccessfully to keep it secret and had been embarrassed when kindly adults offered her sympathy. She avoided her friends because they might bring it up. She was sure she had the strangest parents in America.

"They have lots of competition for strange, believe me," I said.

She smiled for the first time that day, and I caught a glimmer of what the predivorce Amy must have been like.

I ended the session by calling Joan in and suggesting that Amy go spend a few weeks with her grandmother while the adults worked things out. After she returned, we'd talk again and maybe Amy could be in a divorce group for young teens.

Joan said, "Chuck will never agree with this." I offered to call him. Chuck was immediately angry when he heard I'd seen Amy. I talked to him about releases, consent to treatment, and confidentiality. Then, after he calmed down, I asked him how Amy was doing. He said, "Since the separation, she's a different kid." Of course, he had his own theory about Amy.

"Just between you and me," he said, "Joan is the biggest bitch on the planet."

I listened patiently while he bad-mouthed Joan. As he talked, I thought how miserable these two people had made each other and how right it was that they divorce. But unfortunately, because they had Amy, they couldn't really separate. In fact, in some ways they would need to negotiate and coordinate efforts even more now that they lived in separate households. And the same things that destroyed the marriage could keep them from adequately parenting Amy over the next few years.

I reminded myself that underneath the parents' anger was pain. No doubt they both needed guidance sorting through this failed marriage. But my job was to help Amy. I feared that unless these parents settled down, Amy was at high risk for depression and, perhaps later, delinquency. I wasn't sure these parents were capable of putting Amy's needs first and working as a team, but I had nothing to lose in trying to help them do this. I suggested Chuck and Joan come in for some divorce counseling.

I told Chuck that it's better to talk about Amy in therapy than in an attorney's office. It's cheaper and nonadversarial. Perhaps because he himself was a psychologist, he had to agree. Chuck said he was willing, but he doubted Joan would do it. Maybe by the time Amy came home from her grandmother's and started junior high, her parents would be doing what mature adults do in this situation, which is putting aside their own emotions and needs to care for the children.

JASMINE (12)

Long before I met Jasmine I'd seen her parents in marital therapy. Joe and Georgeanne were decent, likable people but their marriage wasn't working. They had married right out of high school because Georgeanne was pregnant. Joe was an extrovert and an excitement seeker, while Georgeanne was quiet and liked routines. She seemed always to be in the shadows when Joe was around. On the other hand, Joe spent many nights at home when he would have preferred a social outing. They had compromised for years; probably they'd compromised too often and too much.

They did all the things couples do to save their marriages. They tried communication exercises, read self-help books, and went on dates and a second honeymoon. But the spark was gone. Without ever really arguing, they were ready to call it quits.

Now they wanted help divorcing. Both of them loved Jasmine and wanted to keep the divorce from damaging her. They weren't sure what to tell her about the divorce or how to handle living arrangements and money. I suggested that together they give Jasmine a brief but honest account of why they were divorcing. I encouraged them to make it clear that they both loved her and would keep on caring for her. Also, I recommended that they keep Jasmine's life as routine as possible. Then I asked to see Jasmine.

Jasmine was small and blond like her mother, talkative like her father. When I first met her, she'd known about the divorce for three days. She had been stunned by their announcement. I asked how she felt when her parents told her the news. Jasmine said, "At first I thought it was a joke. Then when I caught on they were serious, I wouldn't even listen to them. I put my hands over my ears and ran out of the room."

She looked out my window. "I still think they'll get back together. This is just a phase they are going through—what do you call it? Middle-age crisis. But in the meantime, they shouldn't do this. They don't even fight. We have fun together."

I asked her if she'd told her friends yet. She nodded her head and said, "I told my best friend. She's trying to understand, but she can't. I got mad at her yesterday because I was jealous. She has a family and I don't. I haven't told any other kids, but word gets around quick. Dad moved out yesterday and there was a U-Haul truck parked in our driveway."

Jasmine had all the usual worries: Where would she live? Would she see both her parents? Would there be enough money? Would she be forced to choose?

"I thought divorce was what happened to other families—you know, families where the dad drank or beat the kids," Jasmine said, holding her palms up in front of her. "I can't believe my parents would do it."

I recommended she attend a divorce group for teenagers and she agreed. We talked about what else she could do to deal with her feelings. Jasmine said, "The main thing that helps is my cat. I lie on my bed with Orange and listen to music. I tell her everything."

After the initial visit, I alternated sessions between Jasmine and her parents. I talked to Joe and Georgeanne about living arrangements and joint custody. They were both struggling with their own issues but remained committed to helping Jasmine through it all. Joe found an apartment in the neighborhood so that Jasmine could walk between homes and so that her friends and school were handy.

For more fractious couples, joint custody doesn't often work. All the issues that sabotaged a marriage also sabotage joint custody. But Joe and Georgeanne were low-key and rational and they could agree on basic issues. They could communicate about Jasmine without fighting. They did have some differences about rules and expectations, but that was to be expected. Jasmine could learn to behave differently in different houses. What was important was that the parents not criticize or second-guess each other.

Both felt okay about their time with Jasmine. They tried to make it as ordinary as possible. Jasmine had chores, schoolwork, orthodontist's appointments, and outings with both parents. Money was tight, but money had never been a big deal to this family. They all knew how to have fun without spending a lot. Joe and Jasmine hiked and played sand volleyball. Georgeanne took Jasmine to art galleries and museums.

Both, Joe and Georgeanne were needy after the divorce. Georgeanne spent six months on antidepressants. Joe got so lonely in his apartment that he thought he'd go crazy. But somehow they managed to keep their own pain from interfering too much with their parenting. Both of them were grown-ups in the truest sense of the word.

I saw Jasmine once a month for the first year. In addition, she attended a support group. The kids helped one another talk about feelings and cheered one another on through the tough times. She also had her best friend and her beloved Orange.

At our last session we talked about the year. Jasmine looked relaxed and vibrant as she talked, very different from the shaken and shocked girl of a year ago. I admired the way Joe and Georgeanne had stayed emotionally committed to Jasmine.

Jasmine liked her living arrangements. At her mom's, her bedroom was old-fashioned and filled with mementos from the past. Her bedroom at her dad's was art deco with built-in bookcases. She had a carrying case for Orange and took her to both homes.

Still she nurtured a small hope that her parents would get back together. She was sad about the divorce, but no longer mad.

"They tried to make it work and they couldn't," she acknowledged. "I know my parents are just people and make mistakes like everyone else."

She admitted that both her parents seemed happier. "Mom's more outgoing now that Dad's not around. She's stronger than I thought she was."

Jasmine wrinkled up her face. "Dad's dating someone. I'm not ready for that, and I try to avoid her."

She was pleased that her parents got along fine. They both attended her events. Jasmine put it this way: "They like to get together and brag about me. They love me and that gives them a bond."

One of the things that helps saplings survive a hurricane is their root system. With divorce, the root system splits apart. Girls are often unsupported, at least temporarily. They face the strong winds without the support of a home base, and they are at risk of blowing over.

Still, divorce is not always avoidable and it's not always a mistake.

Parents and girls have some control over the effects of divorce. Girls are likely to do well if they come from families in which the parents have a working relationship, in which the girl feels loved by both parents, and in which the family is not economically depressed. Girls do better if they are neither manipulated nor allowed to manipulate, if they have adequate supervision and a safe environment.

Jasmine's parents handled the breakup of her family in a resilient manner. Julia had a tougher time because of all the stepfamily issues and the emotional loss of her father. Amy, whose parents were bitterly feuding, had the hardest time. Taryn learned that her mother was a person with a life independent of Taryn's. In the years following the divorce, she became responsible for herself. Divorce, like all experiences that are properly handled, can be an opportunity for growth.

The National Center for Health Statistics shows that divorce rates were almost twice as high in the 1990s as they are today. In 1994, American culture was chaotic and permissive. People of all ages were restless and the economy was strong enough to allow divorce financially. Most important, people could divorce without great loss of social status.

Currently divorce rates are at their lowest point in forty years. The 2015 rate was eighteen divorces per one thousand married women. People stay together for emotional stability and for economic necessity (housing costs, health insurance, and childcare expenses). Also, as institutions fail us, what we have left is relationships. Often, adults who have difficult relationships choose to stay together and learn to get along.

The biggest exception to the above generalization is that online relationships and pornography precipitate more marital crises and divorces than they did in 1994. Most adults were not online in 1994, and online pornography was not widely available. By now, many men are addicted to pornography, and adults of both genders sometimes have "secret correspondences" with other adults. Marriages crumble because of these new digital behaviors.

Girls' reactions to divorce haven't changed much over the years. Divorces almost always cause daughters pain. Often, girls feel angry at their parents and are likely to act out in self-destructive ways. Girls today still struggle with the challenges of parents who move away. They feel abandoned and vulnerable just when they most need the support of family to cope with the new world of adolescence.

It's impossible to evaluate the effects of most divorces at the time of the event. None of us knows what another person's marriage is really like. It's hard to predict how children will feel about the divorce over time. Sometimes these disruptions work out for the best. Sometimes, over the course of a few years, the kids are doing well and the adults are happier. On the other hand, if over time people are not happier, it's easy to wonder if the divorce was a mistake. And this outcome assessment is often complicated by the fact that one parent may be happier, while the other remains mired in grief or anger.

In general, children benefit from falling divorce rates. However, when divorce is necessary, single parents, like all parents, do best when they are embedded in a supportive community. Desi's parents divorced, at least in part, because her father reconnected online with an old girlfriend. While that's a very modern cause of divorce, even after the bitterest of separations, families move on. Desi is proof that teenagers eventually adjust to their new normal, heal, and find happiness again.

DESI (18)

"Until I was a freshman, our family was pretty stable. I got along with both of my siblings. Or you know, as well as siblings get along." Desi shrugged and her glossy brown ponytail swung from side to side.

"When my parents split, things got harder. Going back and forth between our house and my dad's apartment was depressing, and spending time with my siblings was hard because we weren't always in the same place at the same time."

"Were your parents conscientious about supporting you during their divorce?" I asked.

"At first I felt like I had to choose a side. When my parents separated, everything was so intense. My dad had an affair with an old girlfriend he found on Facebook, and my mom was furious with him. We all were. Now they're better about not talking badly about each other, but for a while all I heard was, 'She did this' or 'He did that.' I was stuck in the middle."

Desi and I met at a divey coffeehouse after school; she had squeezed our conversation in between spring musical rehearsal—she was tap dance captain for a revival of *Mary Poppins*—and a Young Life [a Christian youth group] meeting.

"By now, I have a good relationship with my mom. When I was a younger teenager, it felt like she was against everything I believed or wanted to do. And then during the divorce, there was a time when I wasn't close to either of my parents. I just hid in my bedroom."

Desi paused to check an incoming text, fired off a quick reply, and smiled apologetically.

"When they first separated, I was so upset and always had an attitude with my mom. We argued all the time because both of us wanted to be right and wanted to have the last word." She laughed. "We are *so* similar.

"As I've gotten older, I've seen that she has my best interests at heart. As I've grown up, I am more honest with her about things going on in my life. That has made our relationship stronger."

"What about your dad?" I asked.

"Our relationship was better when I was younger. We'd play tennis and wrestle and watch the US Open together. Now that I'm closer with my mom, it's hard for me to connect with my dad. I feel like I have to prioritize one or the other since the divorce, and I'm still mad about his affair. I can't believe he cheated on my mom and on Facebook of all things!"

"Have there been periods in your adolescence that were especially difficult?"

"Middle school was the toughest time for me. Seventh grade was the worst."

Desi shivered, as if she was mentally transporting herself back in time.

"Everyone was figuring out who they were, there was lots of drama between girls and friend groups.

"During that time, my parents started to argue more. If my mom and dad yelled at each other in the morning, my entire day was ruined before I even left the house. My best friend's parents were going through a divorce and I wondered if that would happen to my family. On top of that, I was obsessed with how I looked. I was a hot mess."

"Did that change when you headed to high school?" I asked.

"My best friend went to a different school, which was devastating. Freshman year, a lot of my new friends got into drugs, and I didn't want any part of that, so I removed myself from their lives. My older brother had used drugs and it was a nightmare for our family. He ended up going into rehab."

"How are you different from the girl you were three years ago?" I asked.

"It's not an exaggeration to say that Young Life changed everything for me. I went to Young Life camp the summer after my sophomore year, and after that I started to take on leadership roles. I met my best friend, Elsie, at camp. Our group would get together and talk about the Bible and about how our lives were going. Actually, it was mostly just talking about our highs and our lows, not about the Bible. We just knew that we could say whatever we wanted and it would stay there. Everyone was trustworthy."

"Finding a safe community must have felt reassuring in the midst of the chaos of high school," I offered.

"Totally. I mean, it's high school. There were cliques within the group and gossip even within Young Life. But it was mostly a safe, positive place.

"Senior year, I started working with the middle-school Young Life chapter, Wyld Life. Elsie and I lead the group at my old school. I love collaborating with her; we know each other's strengths and weaknesses and support each other in becoming leaders. All the younger girls look up to us. Those girls' biggest challenges are social status, popularity, and their relationships with their parents. We've been there. We give them perspective.

"I want to model praying and talking to Jesus," Desi continued. "I want to show them it's okay to communicate and be open about anything, because it helps when other people know your true feelings."

"How is your brother doing? Was his time in rehab helpful?"

"Oh my goodness, you'll never believe it," Desi began, enthusiastically tapping her fingers on the tabletop. "He's been clean for two years, and he came out of the closet six months ago! He has a boyfriend named Parker and they're adorable together." She grabbed her phone to show me photos of the two men.

I couldn't mask my surprise. "I would have assumed that, as a Christian, you might not be so enthusiastic about having a gay brother," I said.

Desi shook her head emphatically. "Everyone should get to decide who they love and what they believe. Loving my brother doesn't conflict with my faith."

"I'm impressed with how well you know yourself," I said. "I'm glad you're serving as a mentor for younger girls."

"My faith definitely helped me get to this place. I still pray and ask God to guide my life, and to help me know how to take care of my parents, but also take care of myself. I journal a lot. Writing is how I process my feelings. And, I read the Bible every day and I know he's always listening.

"When my parents told me they were splitting up, I didn't know how I'd live through that. I was devastated. Over time, I've realized that the more I talked to God, the better I felt. He knew I could overcome this; he knew I'm strong enough."

Divorce remains one of the most traumatic life events a child can experience. Postdivorce life is not easy at first and, sometimes, it never feels easy again. However, recent research shows that most families recover from divorce and that, after five years, many family members are as happy or happier than before the divorce. Positive outcomes depend on honesty, trust, good communication, and fairness, all things that are hard to negotiate in any system.

It is heartening to observe the trend toward lower divorce rates. At the very least, this means that children's lives are less disrupted. It also may mean that families are actually happier, with parents who love each other and know how to handle conflict, negotiate differences, and express affection.

NINE

Depression and Self-Harm

MONICA (15)

Monica was brought to my office by her kindhearted and slightly out-of-touch parents. Born when her mother was approaching menopause, Monica was an only child. Her parents were concerned about her lack of friends and her depression. Her father thought Monica had no friends because, with her IQ of 165, she was too smart for other kids. Mom thought it was because their family was different. The parents were both professors, bookworms, and political radicals. Monica hadn't been exposed to many common childhood experiences, such as television, Disneyland, camping, or sports.

Her mother laughed. "We're an odd family. We talk about philosophy and science at dinner. We know more about chaos theory than we do about movie stars."

Monica said flatly, "It's my looks. I'm a pimply whale."

Monica's parents were eager to turn her over to someone younger and more knowledgeable about teens. I agreed to meet with Monica and discuss "peer relations." Monica wasn't optimistic, but she was desperate.

Under her drab, tentlike clothes and depressed demeanor, Monica had real personality. She delivered insightful comments about her situation with a wry twist. She had the social scene down. She said, "All five hundred boys want to go out with the same ten anorexic girls." She added, "I'm a good musician, but not many guys are looking for a girl that plays great Bach preludes.

"Boys get teased if they even talk to me," she moaned. Most boys treated her as if she were covered with invisible ink. A few actually harassed her. One boy called her the Killer Whale and pretended he was afraid she'd smash up against him. Her Spanish lab partner couldn't look at her without smirking.

Monica had given up on girls, too. She told of sitting with all these "tiny girls who were on diets and complaining how fat they were. If they think they're fat, they must view me as an elephant." Some girls giggled about her and teased her. Most just chose prettier friends. No one was all that eager to be seen with her on Saturday nights.

Monica had more perspective on her problems than most girls her age, but unfortunately insight does not take away pain. She told me ruefully that she hated her fat body and, hence, herself. She showed me her poems, which were full of despair about her large, unloved body.

She said, "Let's face it, the world isn't exactly waiting for girls like me."

She'd resisted the culture's definitions of what was valuable in girls, but she was tired. She said, "When I walk down the halls, I feel like a hideous monster. I understand my parents' point that looks aren't that important in adulthood, but I'm not an adult."

I encouraged Monica to fight her depression by exercising regularly.

Monica said that she came from "a long line of slugs." She agreed to break tradition and walk and bike. She chose these activities because she could do them alone and without wearing a swimsuit.

At first she had trouble. She told me, "I hate to sweat. Ten minutes out and I'm red in the face and sweating like a marathon runner." Once, when red-faced and panting, she biked by a tennis court and some guys pointed at her and laughed. She thought of a million excuses not to exercise, but she managed to make her goal of biking or walking three times a week.

She also decided to fix herself up and bought some "semipunk" clothes. She had her hair cut by someone who knew what she was doing and she started wearing a little makeup.

She respected the fact that her parents were not big consumers of mass culture. She said, "In some ways it's been good. I wasn't exposed to all these messages that women were sex objects and that bodies were what mattered. But I wasn't prepared for real life."

When I asked her to elaborate, she explained, "I guess I thought we'd all sit around and discuss books we'd read. I was shocked by how superficial everyone was."

We talked about what kinds of relationships Monica wanted. She wanted to be appreciated for her wit and her musical gifts. She wanted to be seen as a person, not a dress size, and she wanted friends who cared more about her ideas than her weight.

I suggested we start slowly. Rather than worrying about popularity, we focused on making a few new friends. Monica liked the idea but was hesitant about the actions required to carry it out. She'd been rejected so often that she was reluctant to take more risks.

Because she was a Suzuki viola student, I used the Suzuki method as a metaphor for how we would work. Dr. Suzuki believed that any student could learn to play the most difficult classical works. All that was necessary was that the steps be small and the practice regular. Thus, a small child practices holding the bow, touching the bow to the strings, curving her fingers correctly, and playing a note beautifully.

Eventually this child will play a Vivaldi concerto. We could have the same success with social experience. Eventually small steps would lead her to a fuller and richer social life.

Monica pushed herself to speak in class and to smile in the halls. It was scary because sometimes she was rewarded, other times scorned. I encouraged her to focus on her successes instead of her failures and to view her occasional rejections as stones in the path to a healthy social life. She learned to walk around them.

Monica joined writing and political clubs at her school. One day she announced to me that she was "tearing up the Young Democrats with her political satire." Another day she reported she'd been elected secretary of the Writers' Club. "It's a job reserved for terminal geeks," she said proudly.

I encouraged her to think of boys not as dates, but as friends. Monica selected a sensitive poet from her writing club. She shyly tried a joke on him and he laughed. He began joking with her. After a few weeks, he offered to let her see his poetry.

At the same time that she made some friends, she remained aware that there were many students who would never give her a chance. She said, "I can see people size me up as unattractive and look away. I am not a person to them."

Monica came in for therapy most of her sophomore year. Gradually she began to enjoy exercise in spite of all her predictions to the contrary.

She, like most adolescent girls who do not fit our cultural definitions of beautiful, needed a lot of support to make it through this time. Her self-esteem crumbled as she experienced taunts and rejections. Still, Monica built some friendships that held. She spent time with her poet friend and a few others. She could actually go out on Saturday nights, an experience that helped her depression enormously.

Monica had found a niche in an alien environment. She was happier, but still aware of how tough life was going to be for her. She knew that she would never be a pretty package and that many guys were intimidated by her smarts. She knew that some people were so put off by her plain appearance that they never gave her personality a chance.

She made a good adjustment to a rough situation. She didn't deny her brightness or musical talents so that she could fit in, but she developed some skills for diffusing the tension her gifts created. She used humor to redirect some of her pain about being chubby.

Monica was lucky in that even though the culture of the 1990s was hostile to her development, she had many resources of her own. Her life had exposed her to ideas not explored by popular culture—she had some perspective on her experience. Her parents were feminists who decried the narrowness of women's roles and their lack of public power. They did all they could to help her through adolescence—music lessons, a bicycle, new clothes, and therapy. They encouraged Monica to be true to herself and resist the message that she got from peers. They knew she was wonderful.

Monica had a mild case of depression, which makes some young women sluggish and apathetic, others angry and hate-filled. Some girls manifest their depression by starving themselves or carving on their bodies. Some withdraw and go deep within themselves, and some swallow pills. Others drink heavily or use sex as a sedative. Still others refuse to go to school, a common problem in the 1990s. Whatever the outward form of the depression, the inward form is the grieving for the lost self, the authentic girl who has disappeared with adolescence. There's been a death in the family.

This death occurs in numerous ways. Some adolescent girls may destroy their true selves in an effort to be socially acceptable. Others strive to be fully feminine and fail. They aren't pretty enough or popular enough in just the right ways at the right times. Others make the sacrifices necessary to be fully feminine, even as they are aware of the damage they are inflicting upon themselves. They know they have sold out and blame themselves for their decision. They have chosen a safer path, but it's a path with no real glory. When they lose their subjective fix on the universe, they are adrift and helpless, their self-esteem hostage to the whims of others.

Some girls are depressed because they have lost their warm, open relationship with their parents. They have loved and been loved by people whom they now must betray to fit into peer culture. Furthermore, they are discouraged by peers from expressing sadness at the loss of family relationships—even to say they are sad is to admit weakness and dependency.

All girls experience pain at this point in their development. If that pain is blamed on themselves, on their own failures, it manifests itself as depression. If that pain is blamed on others—on parents, peers, or the culture—it shows up as anger. This anger is often mislabeled rebellion or even delinquency. In fact, anger often masks a severe rejection of the self and an enormous sense of loss.

Adolescence is a time when development and culture put enormous stress on girls. So many things are happening at once that it's hard to label and sort experiences into neat little boxes. And there are many casualties. For example, a girl who is suffering from a mild case of adolescent misery may try to kill herself, not because her life as a totality is so painful, but because she is impulsive, reactive, and unable to put small setbacks in perspective. Some girls are suicidal because of trauma and others because of the confusion and difficulty of the times. Girls who threaten suicide need different kinds of attention, but all are potentially dangerous to themselves and their threats must be taken seriously.

In my first ten years as a therapist, I had never seen a client who cut or burned herself. By the 1990s, it was an infrequent, but not surprising, initial complaint of teenage girls. Girls dealt with their internal pain by picking at their skin, burning themselves, or cutting themselves with razors or knives. As more young women came to my office with this problem, I asked myself, why was this happening now? What cultural changes had fostered the development of this emerging problem?

Just as depression can be described as anguish turned inward, self-harm can be described as psychic pain turned inward in the most physical way. There were some possible explanations: girls were under more stress in the 1990s, they had less varied and effective coping strategies to deal with that stress, and they had fewer internal and external resources on which to rely.

In my experience, behaviors that arose independently and spontaneously in large numbers of people often suggested enormous cultural processes at work. Self-harm may well have been a reaction to the stresses of the 1990s. Its emergence as a problem was connected to our girl-poisoning culture. Self-harm could be seen as a concrete interpretation of our culture's injunction to young women to carve themselves into culturally acceptable pieces. As a metaphorical statement, self-harm could be interpreted as an act of submission: "I will do what the culture tells me to do"; an act of protest: "I will go to even greater extremes than the culture asks me to"; a cry for help: "Stop me from hurting myself in the ways that the culture encourages"; or an effort to regain control: "I will hurt myself more than the culture can hurt me."

Once girls begin to cut and burn themselves, they are likely to continue. Inflicting harm on the body becomes cathartic. Physical pain is easier to bear than emotional pain. In the absence of better coping strategies, self-harm becomes a way to calm down. With time, this habit becomes more ingrained, so the sooner young women seek help, the better.

What is the treatment? Ideally, we will change our culture so that young girls have less external stress to contend with in their lives. But for now, young women must learn better coping strategies and develop more internal and external resources to cope with stress.

Therapy can teach girls to identify early that they are in pain. They need to label their internal state as painful and then think about how to proceed. They must learn new ways to deal with intense misery and also new ways to process pain.

Fortunately, this tendency to inflict harm on the body when in psychic pain is quite curable. Young women can be taught to process pain by thinking and talking instead of punishing themselves. Most young women respond quickly to guidance about how to stop this behavior and develop more adaptive ones, as these examples from my 1990s therapy sessions show.

TAMMY (17)

Tammy came in after her mother discovered her cutting her breasts. Alice had awakened around three a.m. and noticed a light on in Tammy's bedroom. She went in to check on her and found her sitting on the bed surrounded by bloody newspapers, a razor in her hand. Alice woke Brian and they drove Tammy to the hospital. The doctor stitched up the deeper cuts and made an appointment for the family with me.

Alice and Brian were pale with fear and anxiety. Brian could narrate the events of the night. Alice couldn't stop crying. Tammy's face was red and puffy from tears, but she wouldn't look at me or speak above a whisper.

In spite of the current crisis, the family seemed to be a rather typical, traditional one. Brian was the minister of a small church and played saxophone in a jazz band on weekends. Alice taught piano lessons from home. Tammy was the third of four children. The older two were in college and the youngest, a ten-year-old boy, was doing fine. There was a history of depression on Alice's side of the family, but otherwise this family was unique for its lack of previous problems.

The family took long summer vacations every year. Often on Sunday nights they played music and sang together. Alice had served as a PTO president and a Girl Scout leader. Brian was a slightly absent-minded man who shut his eyes during the violent scenes in movies and fainted at his prewedding blood test.

Even with her puffy face, Tammy was a pretty girl with long blond hair and alabaster skin. She was dressed in a leather jacket, designer blue jeans, and stylish knee-high boots. Brian reported that she was a good student and an easygoing daughter. She made the honor roll every semester and was a twirler in the high-school band. Like her parents, she loved music, sang in the church and school choirs, and played flute with her school orchestra. Brian said, "She's the best musician of all the kids."

Alice added, "We're in shock about this."

I spoke to Tammy alone.

"Do you know why you did this?" I asked gently.

Eyes averted, she said, "After a fight with my boyfriend."

We talked about Martin, whom she had met her sophomore year at all-state music camp. Martin played bass for the biggest school in the state. He was everything a high-school girl could desire: good-looking, athletic, and popular.

Tammy said, "All the girls were after him. I was shocked that he picked me."

"What's the relationship been like?"

Tammy sighed. "We fight a lot. Martin is jealous."

"What else?"

"He does things my parents wouldn't like. He smokes pot and drinks." She paused and looked at me suspiciously.

"Are you sexually involved with him?"

She nodded miserably.

"How do you feel about that?"

"I don't know. I'm afraid of getting pregnant."

She spoke softly but rapidly. "Martin's really into sex. This New Year's Eve, he had a party and rented porn videos for all the couples to watch. The guys liked it, but we girls were really embarrassed."

"When did you have the fight that led to cutting yourself for the first time?"

Tammy brushed her hair off her face. "It was the weekend after New Year's Day. We went to a party and I had a wine cooler. Martin was mad because I talked to a friend of his. He took me home early and pushed me out of the car. I fell down on our driveway and he just drove off. That's the night I was so mad I didn't know what to do."

"Try to remember exactly how you felt."

Tammy said, "I slipped into my room so Mom and Dad wouldn't see me. I thought I was going crazy. There were scissors on my dresser and the idea of cutting myself came to me. I don't even know how I did it. But later I had cuts on my arms and I felt better. I could go to sleep."

She looked at me. "Do you think I'm crazy?"

I said, "I think you are scared."

Tammy said, "After that first time, it happened again. Whenever Martin and I fought, I felt this need to cut myself. I couldn't relax until I'd done it."

"Has Martin ever hit you?"

Tammy nodded. "Don't tell my parents. He doesn't mean to, but he's hot-tempered. Afterward, he's really sorry."

I said, "I must tell them enough to keep you safe."

I called Alice and Brian in and said that I'd like to work alone with Tammy for a while. I explained that she'd developed the habit of hurting herself physically when she was in emotional pain. Fortunately, her self-harm was a new habit and therefore easier to change. I limit Tammy's time with asked them to Martin to visits to their home. Tammy looked down at her hands.

Alice said, "Martin seems like a great guy."

"Parents don't always know what's going on. We want to keep Tammy safe, emotionally and physically," I said. Tammy looked at me gratefully.

I thought to myself, *This minister and his wife have no idea how complicated the world has become for their lovely flute-playing daughter.* I was careful not to betray Tammy's confidence, but I said, "Tammy has some decisions to make."

DANIELLA (15)

Daniella was very different from Tammy. She was younger and, to quote her, "trapped in the halls of a junior high." She was dressed in a way that signaled "I am different" with her head half shaved and half green. She had a nose ring, eight earrings—mostly of skulls and snakes—a tattoo of a dragon on her left arm and tiny tattoos on every finger. She wore a stained T-shirt with a FREE TIBET logo, black jeans torn at the knees, and heavy boots.

She was the oldest daughter in a family of artists. Her mother was a dancer and her father a sculptor. Daniella's family was financially poor but culturally enriched. They couldn't afford trips, new cars, or nice clothes for their daughters, but they could afford cheap tickets to the symphony, used books, and therapy.

Daniella's parents, Stephen and Shelly, were warmhearted, quirky people who seemed baffled at being in a therapist's office. Shelly's first comment was to compliment my overflowing bookcase. She said, "I see you like Jung. So do I."

I asked why the family was in my office. Daniella looked out the window. Shelly and Stephen looked at each other. Stephen said, "We hate to tell on Daniella. We made her come today."

Shelly said, "We've been worried since she began junior high, but last Saturday night we discovered that she was burning herself with cigarettes. We decided we had to do something."

"Before junior high, Daniella was the star of the family," Shelly continued. "She was such a joy. The school classified her as highly gifted, so she qualified for special tutors and programs at the university. Her artwork made it to the state fair."

"She had everything going for her," her father added. "She had friends and was the comedian of the school. She stayed up all night reading and then went to school the next day and did fine."

Shelly said, "She was so competent and independent. We weren't prepared for her to have trouble. We didn't see it coming."

I turned to Daniella, who was perusing my bookshelf with interest, and asked, "What happened with junior high?"

Daniella spoke slowly and with great precision. "I hated being warehoused and sent from room to room at the sound of a bell. I felt like a cow in a feedlot. I got teased when I took gifted classes and bored in the regular classes. I liked art class, but I'd just get into a zone and the bell would ring."

"How about the other kids?" I asked.

"Do you know the slogan 'Sex, drugs, and rock and roll' from the sixties?" I nodded and she continued. "Now that's 'Masturbation, booze, and Madonna.' I don't fit into that scene."

"Daniella changed from outgoing to introverted," Stephen said. "She didn't like anyone. The phone stopped ringing for her."

"Junior high wasn't the worst thing in my life," Daniella said. "I was sad about the environment. I couldn't sleep at night because I was worried about oil spills and the rain forests. I couldn't forget about Somalia, either, or Bosnia. It just seemed like the world was falling apart."

As a therapist in the '90s, I often saw these problems in bright, sensitive girls. Adults expected them to be mature emotionally, but they reacted to their own pain and to global tragedies with the emotional intensity of adolescents. Though bright girls I worked with were perceptive enough to see through the empty values and shallow behavior of their peers, they had the social needs of adolescents. They felt utterly alone in their suffering. They had the intellectual abilities of adults in some areas and could understand world problems, and yet they had the emotional abilities and political power of teenagers.

Daniella avoided mainstream kids and gradually found a few of her own kind. She discovered the smoke-filled back room of the local coffeehouse where the alternative crowd gathered to talk. She made friends with gays and lesbians, with runaways, school dropouts, and unhappy intellectuals like herself. She pierced her ears and then her nose. Unfortunately, this crowd had its share of problems. Many were into drugs both as painkillers and experience producers. Soon Daniella was smoking pot and dropping acid.

School, meanwhile, grew even more difficult. Daniella was the only girl in her class with a nose ring and tattoos. Kids giggled and pointed at her when she walked past. By the time she was in ninth grade, she'd read more on the environment than her science teachers. The easy classes made her cynical about education. Her grades dropped. She skipped school and went to the park to smoke pot.

Stephen and Shelly knew that Daniella's life wasn't going well at that point and had encouraged her to try therapy. She refused. Then her best friend moved to California and Daniella became a loner again. The week before I met her, they'd found her with the cigarette burns.

The next week I met with Daniella alone. She wore the same boots and jeans with a T-shirt that said LIFE SUCKS AND THEN YOU DIE. I thought of the Allen Ginsberg line about "the drunken taxicabs of Absolute Reality." They had crashed into Daniella in early adolescence.

I told her about reading *The Diary of Anne Frank* in my small town thirty years earlier. I said, "When I discovered the evil that people do to each other I wanted to die. I didn't really want to be part of a species that produced the Nazis."

Daniella agreed with me and said she'd felt that way when she heard the public radio reports about women being raped in Bosnia. She felt that way when she read that Stalin killed even more people than Hitler, that the Khmer Rouge killed six million Cambodians, and that the Serbs practiced ethnic cleansing.

"The Holocaust wasn't an isolated event, you know," she told me. "It happens all over."

I replied, "What saved me was reading Willa Cather, Jane Austen, and Harper Lee. Shortly after I read about Anne Frank, I discovered them. It was summer and I would take my book and go to the woods. I would read and watch the wind in the trees. I sat on my back porch at sunset and read. These women were such good antidotes to superficial people and shallow ideas."

Daniella said, "Going to the park with my friend helped me, but now he's gone."

"Tell me about burning yourself."

"That happened automatically, "Daniella said. "I was smoking in my room and I felt helpless and angry. The next thing I knew I was burning my arm and it felt good. It felt clean. I was careful to burn only my upper arm, so I could hide the marks. Afterward I felt calmer."

"You were turning all your rage at the world against yourself," I said. "You need a better way to express rage and to fight back."

We talked about protest marches, recycling, boycotts. All those suggestions seemed too abstract. Daniella's despair could be assuaged only by direct action. Even though she was young, I encouraged her to work at the local soup kitchen for the homeless. She needed to make the world better for real people. Daniella agreed to look into that.

Daniella came in for many months. Mostly I encouraged her to talk and write about her pain. As we became acquainted, she talked more about her current life. One of her gay friends was HIV-positive. A girlfriend of hers had overdosed and almost died.

She developed an emergency plan for those times when she was tempted to burn herself. She would pull out a notebook and write every painful, angry emotion she was feeling. She needed to get those emotions out of her body and onto a piece of paper.

She later shared some of this writing with me. She wrote about the snobby girls at her school who teased the poor students. She wrote about the backstabbing and pettiness, the scramble for the right clothes and the right friends. She wrote about the poverty her hardworking parents had faced their entire lives. She wrote about children in Somalia, old people freezing in the Bosnian winter, and homeless people.

She wrote until the craving to burn herself passed. Sometimes it didn't and she asked one of her parents to hold her and comfort her until she could sleep. Sometimes she called me and I talked her down. And, of course, sometimes the craving was too strong and she gave in and hurt herself. But this happened less and less as she learned to talk and write about her problems.

It helped that Daniella was enjoying her life. She liked the other volunteers and many of the clients at the soup kitchen. When she saw homeless people on the streets, she often knew their names and stopped to chat. She knew she would be fixing them soup later. Even though her contributions were small, they took the edge off her despair.

By now Daniella's appearance had changed slightly. Her hair was returning and shone a lovely auburn color. The last session we invited her parents to join us.

Shelly said that Daniella was laughing again and playing with her younger sisters. The phone was ringing and she had the most interesting friends. Stephen said that he was pleased that Daniella was again working on her art. The tone of her work seemed slightly more optimistic. She had rejoined the land of the living. Daniella gave some credit for her changes to therapy, which she compared to spring-cleaning. "You get the dust off everything and sort through stuff. You get to throw a lot of junk away."

In the 1990s, many girls were the victims of sexual trauma. They were rebellious, risk-taking, and out in the world getting into all kinds of trouble. Most adults didn't understand what their lives were like. But, after the chaotic and difficult 1980s and early 1990s, girls began to make steady progress. On every measure of mental and social health, adolescent girls showed real improvement.

However, today depression rates for girls are skyrocketing and, by age seventeen, 36 percent of girls have been or are depressed. Additionally, according to the 2014 National Survey of Drug Use and Health, many girls report being depressed by age twelve. These results are puzzling in light of what we know about girls feeling happier with their families.

Why are depression rates so high today? Most research can't help us with causality. It shows us what goes together with what, but not why.

However, just as eating disorders increased with advertising and mass media featuring extremely thin women, we can be reasonably certain that changes in our culture are causing this widespread epidemic of depression and anxiety. Terrorism, pornography, school shootings, the decline of faith in institutions, overt racism, global climate change, political polarization, and other cultural factors all play a role. Also, girls ache with the loneliness that comes from life lived online.

In his book *Lost Connections*, Johann Hari suggests that we think of depression as disconnection. In 2019, we are disconnected from our histories, our future, our bodies, our institutions, and one another. He posits that we humans exist because we lived in tribes and took care of one another. Adults worked together and children played together. People sat around fires at night and told stories. This tribal way of living lasted well into the last century in many places. Communities were vibrant connected places. Today we are almost universally disconnected from our tribes or communities.

Additionally, many families are facing severe economic problems. They may not have access to health care or affordable housing. Many teens participate in free-food programs or live in temporary housing or homeless shelters. Others have incarcerated or drug-addicted parents and live in foster care or with extended family.

Twelve-year-old Avery's mom is addicted to drugs and her dad is in prison. She lives with her widowed grandmother. The house is run down and her grandmother doesn't have the money or energy to fix it. She has diabetes and high blood pressure, and Avery is afraid that her grandmother might die soon. If that happens, she'll have no place to go. Avery told us, "I'm afraid my dad will die in prison. My mom might die too. My life feels like an egg that could crack at any moment."

When Skylar's mother lost her job at a convenience store, she moved her family into a homeless shelter. Skylar and her mother sleep in the women's dormitory, isolated from her brothers, who must sleep with the other boys and men. She takes a city bus to school and stays at school until the last child leaves the after-care program. She has a hard time studying at the crowded raucous shelter. Skylar is a responsible girl who would like to be a marine biologist, but right now, she has a hard time just keeping herself in clean clothes and shoes.

"I feel like stability is a word that applies to other people but not me," she told us. "I hate the shelter, the dependency, and the poverty. I feel ashamed even though I haven't done anything wrong. I feel angry at girls who are lucky enough to live in houses and buy new clothes. Sometimes, I feel like giving up."

The most useful research on girls and depression correlates depression with technology and social media use. Between 1994 and 2007, happiness scores for girls were on the rise. Then, scores decreased rapidly with the advent of social media and smartphones. For example, Vanderbilt University reported that teen visits to emergency rooms with suicidal thoughts and behaviors doubled between 2008 and 2015. In 2016, three times as many twelve- to fourteen-year-old girls killed themselves as did in 2007.

If we consider some of teenage depression as grieving for the lost self, it follows that social media causes depression by isolating girls from their true selves and even substituting a virtual self for a real identity. When this happens, girls feel insecure, confused, and lost. Depression and suicide rates reflect girls' deep sorrow about their disconnect from their authentic selves.

With social media, girls are now vulnerable to peer pressure and other influences every hour of the day. Online bullying, fear of missing out, exposure to pornography, and sexual harassment all contribute to girls' rising depression and anxiety rates. As one girl in our focus groups said, "Instagram makes my day a 'most likes' contest."

In addition to pressure to look sexy and thin, selfies and videos show others having a wonderful time on a beach, in a park, or at a café with friends. Girls can easily feel that everyone's life looks perfect but theirs.

"I see all these pictures online of perfect faces and bodies. My friends text me that they are with other friends or on a cool vacation. I feel like such a loser," Aspen lamented. "I have constant opportunities to feel inadequate."

Girls often construct a false self on social media. They post pictures and videos that show them in beautiful places looking their best and happiest. Often the discrepancy between what they post and how they feel is enormous. The online self is practically perfect and highly desirable. The off-line self may barely leave her bedroom. This marketing of self is a pernicious kind of fake news that hurts all girls.

Most girls today start using smartphones in sixth or seventh grade, the time when puberty and middle school begin. During this time, meanness is at its peak and most adolescents experience their greatest struggles. They are innocent, eager to be liked, and uncertain about boundaries. They face sharp learning curves in many different areas at once, and they live in a time when a rumor or a comment can ruin their reputations.

Adolescent girls simply don't have the skills and the emotional and cognitive maturity to cope well with the intensity and pain they face. They try to sedate themselves with social media or other addictions, but that medicine tends to inflict more pain. At some point, girls need to know that pain is their friend. It's a signal to them that something needs to change. If they can listen to their pain and learn from it, they can find ways to feel better. That's a lot to ask of a thirteen-year-old. By eighteen, many girls possess that skill, but the journey is arduous.

"Most of my friends have diagnosed themselves with anxiety or depression," said Marta. "Schools don't teach us what we need to learn—how to get along with others, find a job, use a bank—stuff we need for basic survival. They don't educate us on emotional health."

"When one boy in our class killed himself, we all just gathered at his locker and cried," said Izzie.

"I have friends with debilitating problems like cutting and OCD," said Jordan. "They are kind, sweet people who try to act like nothing is wrong. It's frustrating because I can't help them. I mean, I'm only fourteen myself."

"When my friends are depressed, I'm the person they call," Olivia told us. "It's terrifying. I've put suicide prevention apps on so many people's phones."

In our focus groups, we talked with the girls about how to help their friends. We acknowledged that no one solution fits all girls, and we tried to allow the girls themselves to suggest possibilities. One was simply to ask troubled friends about suicide and, if it is an emergency, to call a suicide prevention hotline or accompany the friend to a parent or counselor.

"When my friends have mental health problems, I offer support and ask how to be helpful," said Aspen. "I encourage them to talk to an adult they trust."

"I invite them to participate with me in an activity, like running or choir," said Olivia.

Jada nodded in agreement. "The most important thing is let your friend know that you care," she added. "Girls really need to hear that." She took Aspen's hand and added, "But, please, don't carry the burden of saving a friend alone. Share your concerns with people you trust."

An occasional companion of depression, self-harm refers to girls cutting, burning, or injuring themselves in other ways as a way to deal with various kinds of despair. In 1990, 3 percent of girls harmed themselves to relieve emotional pain. By 2008, rates were much higher. A Centers for Disease Control study published by the American Medical Association reported that in 2016, girls between ten and fourteen made three times more emergency room visits than they had in 2009. Most of these visits were because of self-harm or suicide attempts.

Girl today are hurting themselves in response to cyberbullying and loneliness, but they also learn how to adopt these behaviors on social media. Their friends who cut themselves reveal their scars on Snapchat or in texts. As Jada explained it, "It's almost like they are in contest to see who has the most cuts or the deepest scars."

CHRISTINA (15)

Christina attends the arts and humanities high school in our city. She spends her free time working with watercolors, oil paints, and charcoal. Her favorite bands are Imagine Dragons and 21 Pilots. She has a teal stripe in her short bob and loves reading dystopian fiction.

On paper, Christina appears well-adjusted and lucky. Her grades are consistently high and she has won prizes for her paintings. She lives in a stable family with a mom who is a potter and a dad who is a graphic designer. She has an orange cat named Chunky.

But Christina doesn't feel lucky. She's not in the popular crowd and has been bullied at school and online. Even though she is empirically attractive, she thinks she is the ugliest girl in school. Because of Facebook and Instagram, she knows exactly who is hanging out with whom and when she is being left out.

She can barely drag herself out of bed and she has trouble being polite to her family at breakfast. When we spoke to her, she felt as if she were a shell of her former self. She couldn't say why she felt so blue. She knew she was stressed about being bullied and about academic pressures. Soon she would need to take the ACT and apply for college. She couldn't even decide what to eat for lunch or what shirt to wear. Deciding about life after high school was unimaginable.

Recently Christina became a "cutter." She started harming herself because she felt numb all the time and feeling physical pain made her feel alive. She told us that she felt "clean" when she cut herself, as if all the negative energy was flowing out of her. She also said that many girls she knew cut themselves as a way to deal with stress and depression. It didn't seem weird or horrific to her. She said that at her school a handful of girls wore bandages on their wrists and arms as if to prove, "I am sadder than you."

She believed some girls just cut themselves to get attention, but most were like her, and just wanted to feel better. "Most parents don't even know this is going on," she added.

Christina was lucky. A teacher noticed her scars and alerted a counselor, who in turn called a meeting with Christina and her parents. She started therapy after only a few experiences of self-harm and hopefully she will have a relatively easy experience of breaking this self-destructive habit and learning new ways to deal with her pain.

Ariel's cutting habit was more entrenched. Even with the help of a therapist, it took time and a great deal of emotional fortitude for her to heal.

ARIEL (14)

"When I was in sixth and seventh grades, I'd have flashes of really dark thoughts. I'd be in our car, hoping another car would hit us. Or if there was a severe weather warning, I'd hope a tornado would flatten our house and kill me."

"My mom had already put me in therapy, just to help me deal with middle-school stuff. My therapist, Tanya, asked me about my day-to-day thoughts, and I told her about my fantasies of death. I truly thought they were normal."

"How did Tanya respond?" I asked.

Ariel laughed. "She told me I was dealing with depression. I was actually surprised, isn't that nuts? I thought it was normal to imagine dying all the time."

In addition to depression, Ariel began experiencing anxiety attacks in middle school, brought on by academic pressure and complicated relationships with her peers.

"Last year around this time—that was seventh grade—was the peak of my depression and anxiety. I was surrounded by mean people. Even if they weren't mean *to me*, their attitudes were terrible and they were cruel to some of the other girls in our class. To tune them out, I started smoking pot and drinking. It's the only way I could be around them."

"Did you ever think about ending those friendships?" I asked.

"It's not that easy," Ariel replied. "Your friends can be the worst people, but they're still your friends and they have your back. I didn't want to be all alone."

"Did you talk to your mom about what you were dealing with?"

"I didn't tell her about anything," she admitted. "I didn't know how to describe my feelings. It's not as if one big thing was causing my anxiety. Some girl would be mean to me in first period, and then I'd fall down in the hallway and get embarrassed, and then right before the end of the school day, I'd get a science test back with a bad grade. It was everything adding up, and I just didn't know how to stop it."

She continued, "Around this time last year, I began having breakouts of hives. I went to a dermatologist who thought stress was the cause. Every few days I'd get these itchy red patches on my chest, stomach, and arms. At some point—and I know this was irrational—I decided that the next time the hives appeared, I was going to cut myself."

Ariel took a few deep breaths before continuing. "I did that for months. I'd get stressed or sad, then I'd cut myself. It made me feel better."

"Once you progressed to cutting yourself, did your parents find out?" I asked.

"From their conversations with Tanya, my parents knew I was dealing with anxiety and depression. But they didn't figure out I was self-harming until last year, when it was peaking. I was in a secret Facebook group with other girls who were cutters. We'd write how it cleared us out and took away our sadness. Once, when I forgot to close out the browser, my mom saw that page. She doubled my sessions with Tanya and hid all the knives in our house."

"I know you're no longer cutting yourself. What helped you stop?" I asked.

"Change happened in stages," Ariel replied. "Even with my parents and Tanya supporting me, I was aware that this was something I had to figure out for myself. No one but me could change my behavior. It sounds silly, but I started covering my eyes with a cold washcloth when my skin was blotchy. I wouldn't let myself look at it, and then if I couldn't see it, I couldn't decide to cut myself."

"That sounds simple and smart," I told her.

"Once I decided I didn't want to harm myself, it wasn't hard to stop," Ariel explained. "It's a mental thing. I know I'm luckier than some girls, but I was able to work through it on my own."

"What are your new ways to deal with depression?" I asked.

Ariel's expression lit up. "I swim!" she said, beaming. "It takes my brain somewhere else. When you're swimming laps, you can process everything, plus it calms me down. Underwater, nothing feels impossible.

"My friend group has changed, too. Now I hang out with the swim team kids. I'm not around pot or booze as much as I was in middle school."

"Do you have friends who've struggled with depression? Girls you can share experiences and support with?" I asked.

"Um, all of them." Ariel laughed sadly. "Depression is the biggest thing going on with my friends. Just last night I was talking with my friend Neveen and she said, 'I feel so connected to the world around me, that when someone gets hurt, I feel hurt, and when there's stuff going on around the world, it physically hurts me.'"

Ariel wiped tears from her cheeks with the back of her hand. "I feel exactly the same. I see news of children being bombed in Syria, or school shootings all over the US, and sometimes it's more than I can handle," she said. "But I'm determined to manage my depression in healthy ways from now on, even if it's hard. I believe I can do it. Even after everything that's happened to me, I believe in myself."

Ariel's experiences may be unique in their severity, but her tumultuous emotions, peer struggles, and depression are typical for our era. Therapy helped Ariel, as did exercise and her own resilient nature.

We talked to all the girls in our focus groups about ways to combat despair and stress. The girls themselves came up with many coping tools: limiting time online, hanging out with friends, getting out of the house, spending time with animals, playing or listening to music, meditating, exercising, taking on volunteer work, and reading. Jada recommended that when girls feel depressed, they find someone to help. She said that doing a good deed made her feel better. Just talking about skillful coping seemed to help girls feel more confident that they had some tools in their emotional arsenals.

For our part, we encouraged therapy, support groups, and confiding in parents and school counselors. We urged participants to turn off their phones and go outside, read a book, sing, listen to music, or talk face-to-face with friends. We emphasized that the girls already possessed many of the skills of happiness—gratitude, friendship, empathy, and kindness.

TEN

Anxiety

THE AMERICAN COLLEGE Health Association reported that in 2016 anxiety had overtaken depression as the most common problem of freshmen in college. Indeed, 62 percent of young women reported experiencing "overwhelming anxiety," with panic attacks their most common complaint.

At first glance it's difficult to parse this rise in anxiety. Family life has stabilized and girls' own lives are less chaotic. Yet our culture has become isolating, polarizing, and fear-producing. Girls fear failure, ostracism, bullying, and ridicule on social media. They fear school shootings. No place feels truly safe. Many suffer from sleep problems, social anxiety, and obsessive-compulsive behaviors.

Students report being too busy and overscheduled. They are slogging through homework until late at night and waking early for school or sports practice. Good grades are important to most girls and they feel pressure to achieve the grades and test scores they need to attend certain colleges or to secure scholarships. Sometimes the pressure comes from parents, but often girls are more stressed about their grades than are their parents.

In our focus group, Maddie mentioned that she was frustrated by precalculus. She wanted an A but didn't think that was possible; the class was simply too hard for her. She told us that she cried from stress during her final exam. Fortunately, her kind teacher patted her arm and said, "School is just school." That teacher helped her put things in perspective. Still, Maddie wants straight As in all her advanced placement classes. She hopes to be accepted to a prestigious college. She told us, "School forces me to think about my intellectual inadequacies."

"I'm convinced I should only take weighted classes, but that means I can't take interesting electives like pottery or psychology," Aspen told us. "At my school, if you aren't in AP classes, you aren't worth talking to."

"In my first semester of high school, I was so anxious about school work that I couldn't sleep," said Jordan. "My hair started falling out in the shower."

"I feel a lot of academic pressure," agreed Amalia. "I work at a clothing store on weekends. I'm on student council and in marching band. I never have time to sleep. Oh, and my parents want me to be a doctor." She threw up her hands in mock frustration and the other girls laughed.

"I haven't had one night off since school started. Usually I study about four hours every night," said Olivia. "People judge us if we don't have high expectations."

Girls are also fearful of school shootings and terrorists. Most schools now practice lockdown drills and employ secure entrance monitors, but threats of violence and chronic reports of shootings in the national news keep girls on edge.

Olivia told our focus group about a boy at her high school who was popular and seemed "totally normal." Last fall, he wrote a suicide note and brought a gun loaded with one bullet to school. He planned to kill himself during an all-school assembly. Another student saw the gun and reported it, and school officials were able to intervene.

Izzie shrugged and saide, "School shootings are so common, why couldn't one happen at my school?"

Kendyl, a freshman in college, still lives at home. She confessed that she's afraid of her intro-level survey courses with hundreds of students. She told us that the university has almost no security regulations and students could easily conceal weapons in their backpacks.

"I sit in class and wonder, 'Which students might have weapons? How would I get out of here?'" she admitted.

All the girls in our focus groups became animated on the topic of school shootings. Their levels of fear surprised us. We didn't expect them to know exact details about security procedures and district safety policies. The students could spell out the gaps in their schools' security down to the last unlocked door, and every girl believed that her school's security was inadequate.

"Last year, the school had two locker raids and found BB guns in lockers," said Amalia. "The police discovered a switchblade hidden in mulch outside the school. A person could just walk into my school and shoot people."

"My school is close to downtown and in a sketchy neighborhood," said Jada. "It's pretty secure inside, but not outside on the steps. Monitors check backpacks before school, but who knows what kids have in the backpacks after they go to lunch."

Putting aside the issue of school shootings, there are a litany of other anxiety-producing topics on adolescent girls' minds. African Americans, immigrants, and people of color fear slurs or racial violence. Asylum seekers and undocumented immigrant youth fear sheriffs, police, and ICE agents. Students who fall into any minority categories are harassed. Muslims and Jews are fearful of hate groups.

Unquestionably, in recent years our streets have become meaner and racism more prevalent.

JAMILA (17)

Jamila lives on the north side of Omaha, Nebraska, in a neighborhood known for its high crime rate, as well as for ongoing tension between police and residents. When she was nine years old, she watched police line up her older brother and his friends, strip-search them, and threaten them, even though the adolescent boys had done nothing wrong; they had merely congregated at a playground after dinner to enjoy the cool evening breeze, since none of them lived in air-conditioned apartments.

That experience forever changed Jamila's perception of law enforcement. She no longer views police officers as allies whose job it is to "serve and protect." She avoids police at all costs and notes bitterly that since receiving her driver's license six months ago, she has been pulled over four times for "driving while black," once for failing to signal when changing lanes, and another time for slowly proceeding through a four-way stop. In two of those instances, she was forced to exit her car and submit to a pat-down at busy intersections.

"You can't tell me a white girl in the suburbs would be treated this way," she noted.

Jamila's oldest brother, Anton, is serving seven years at the state penitentiary for possession of a recreational amount of marijuana. He was arrested and prosecuted as an adult near the end of his senior year of high school. In his letters and phone calls from prison, he talks about feeling like a slave, herded from one spot to another, living without any humanity or freedom.

Before his arrest, Anton was a popular, fun-loving basketball player, destined for a junior college scholarship. Now, he's chronically depressed and has lost all sense of future orientation. Jamila and her mother hope that, when he's released just after his twenty-fifth birthday, they will be able to convince him to reconsider college or trade school. For now, Jamila prays nightly that he'll remain safe in prison, protected from gang activity and abuse by guards.

"A lot of the girls I've interviewed point to academic stress as their biggest source of anxiety," I told Jamila, "followed by fear of school shootings or worries about the future of our country or planet."

Jamila laughed ruefully. "I mean, I get it," she said. "I worry about my grades, too. I know college is my best chance for a good job. But I'm far more stressed about police brutality and the endless racism that surrounds us. Every time I walk to the corner for a soda, I'm afraid something bad might happen. I worry my little sister will be shot or assaulted by cops or called the N-word when she's riding the bus or playing at the park. That's the stuff that keeps me awake at night."

Jamila grapples with all the issues other girls her age face, plus the added burden of living in a country with deeply embedded racism. Her anxiety, first and foremost, is tied to her family's survival. While her fears differ from those of many girls we interviewed, Jamila's story is far from atypical in America today.

Many students today traumatize one another with constant news flashes about their emotional distress. Gracie worried about her depressed friends and felt responsible for them. She said, "A friend of mine just got out of the hospital after a serious suicide attempt. I don't know whether I should talk with her about what happened or just move on as if nothing is wrong."

She told us that sometimes when her friends say they are suicidal, other kids tell them to just do it and get it over with. One boy even dares people to kill themselves. Gracie said that some days she is afraid to go to school. She just can't face the meanness and she worries that another friend will tell her that she's on drugs or cutting herself.

Finally, the digital world generates anxiety. Psychologist Sharon Begley reported that almost half of all teens use their phones before they get out of bed in the morning. Some psychologists believe that smartphone use is more like an obsession than an addiction. Begley found that social media both increases and decreases anxiety. In the short term, using social media calms students down, but over time, it makes them more anxious.

When students are deprived of smartphones, they show physiological signs of stress such as an elevated heart rate. In a 2010 study, two hundred students surrendered their phones and all social media for twenty-four hours. Afterward, they described themselves as "miserable, antsy, jittery, crazy, and anxious."

The best strategy for controlling social media is to start with strict limits and then hold to them. However, this is easy to say and hard to do. Once hooked, it's difficult for girls to cut back. Cutting back isn't just a matter of willpower; girls are dealing with a highly addictive compulsive behavior.

High-school girls who balance technology most effectively spend about an hour a day on social media, much less than most of their peers. Girls become stronger and more resilient if they spend time talking to adults, enjoying in-person meetups with their friends, reading, and relaxing outdoors. They also benefit from self-calming practices such as mindfulness, yoga, or prayer.

Megan and Anne-Marie experience almost all the common kinds of anxiety teens face. Fortunately, they support each other and practice yoga for stress management. Anne-Marie also draws deeply on her faith in God.

MEGAN (15) AND ANNE-MARIE (16)

Megan and Anne-Marie are cousins who live two blocks apart and attend the same Catholic high school. When I interviewed them, Megan was dressed in a dark tunic and plaid tights. She had arranged her long hair into a tight braid and wore no makeup. Anne-Marie had curly black hair and hazel eyes and sported a miniskirt and tank top.

Both girls love to sing and play piano. Anne-Marie is a strong Catholic, but Megan does not believe in church and isn't sure about God. Her parents insist that she attend weekly Mass with the family, but when she moves out after graduation, Megan plans to take a break.

Both girls take medicine for anxiety, and Megan struggles with stress eating. Both cousins have been hurt by bullying at school and on social media. As Megan said, "It's easy to get pushed around if you're not popular."

Anne-Marie told of a girl at her school who had been beaten up by bullies who had been harassing her online.

"No matter what messages they're sending to parents, schools don't know how to handle bullies," she said.

"Who are these bullies?" I asked. "Is it individuals or one specific group of kids?"

"They are the ones in sports or who have rich parents, great clothes, swimming pools, and all the video-game consoles," Anne-Marie replied, jokingly feigning a yawn.

Both cousins felt ambivalent about social media, which they believed contributed to cruel behavior among their peers. But, like many girls we interviewed, they weren't willing to part with their devices and online accounts.

"We see way too many six-pack abs and everyone seems more

successful and happy than us," Anne-Marie said, "but we like to stay in touch with our friends."

"I've seen a lot of creepy things online," Megan added. "This one guy with a foot fetish keeps asking me for pictures. But generally, I can ignore that stuff. What hurts the most is mean chatter and judgmental comments from people we know."

Megan told me that some of her friends had unexpectedly dropped her. They announced on social media, "We don't like Megan anymore. Sorry, not sorry."

Megan never understood why. Though this happened two years ago, she still feels faint when she sees them.

Anne-Marie chimed in about another challenge she had faced. In sixth grade, while watching *Glee*, she realized she was a lesbian. Her church teaches that homosexuality is a sin and she felt condemned by God. She suffered constant panic attacks that made it hard to breathe. She was terrified and afraid to turn to her parents for help. Megan encouraged her to tell her parents and sat beside her when she did. At first, they were upset, but they calmed down after a few weeks and promised Anne-Marie that they would never withdraw their love or support. They weren't going to condemn their kind, loving daughter.

As she told me about coming out, Anne-Marie began shaking, but she acknowledged that life was better now. She sees a supportive therapist who has taught her deep breathing practices to calm herself during panic attacks. She and Megan are regulars at Lotus House of Yoga and have made a pact not to look at social media on Sundays.

"We're stressed out most of the time, but we're learning new ways to calm down," Anne-Marie said. "At least we have each other."

More girls are depressed and anxious today than at any other time in modern history. We see this in rising suicide rates and a documented upswing in emergency room visits. Self-harm is increasingly common. In fact, there are videos online that show girls how to hurt themselves. Our focus groups report that in some social groups, girls compete to show off the most dramatic scars from self-harm. This devastating and destructive behavior is spreading via social contagion. Parents, school officials, and medical professionals need to be more aware of this phenomenon and take action as soon as they see evidence of it.

Many girls see therapists and report that it is helpful. High schools often have girls' support or empowerment groups. In general, parents are eager to assist their daughters. We can all work to give girls encouragement, love, and protection from their online behaviors. Since LGBTQ teens are at higher risk for suicide, they especially need our attention and understanding. But all adolescents benefit from connecting with one another, their communities, extended families, and the real world.

ELEVEN

Worshipping Thinness

HEIDI (16)

Heidi arrived in my office after gymnastics practice. Blond and pretty, she was dressed in a shiny red-and-white tracksuit. We talked about gymnastics, which Heidi had been involved in since she was six. When we met in the 1990s, she had just been selected to train with coaches at our local university. She trained four hours a day, six days a week. She didn't expect to make an Olympic team, but she anticipated a scholarship to a Big 10 school.

Heidi glowed when she talked about gymnastics, but I noticed her eyes were red and she had a small scar on the index finger of her right hand. (When a hand is repeatedly stuck down the throat, it can be scarred by the acids in the mouth.) I wasn't surprised when she said she was coming in for help with bulimia.

Heidi said, "I've had this problem for two years, but lately it's affecting my gymnastics. I am too weak, particularly on the vault, which requires strength. It's hard to concentrate.

"I blame my training for my eating disorder," Heidi continued.

"Our coach has weekly weigh-ins where we count each other's ribs. If they are hard to count, we're in trouble."

I grimaced in disapproval. Heidi explained that since puberty she had had trouble keeping her weight down. After meals, she was nervous that she'd eaten too much. She counted calories; she was hungry but afraid to eat. In class, she pinched the fat on her side and freaked out.

The first time she vomited was after a gymnastics meet. Coach took her and the other gymnasts to a steakhouse. Heidi ordered a double cheeseburger and onion rings. After she ate, she obsessed about the weigh-in the next day, so she decided, just this once, to get rid of her meal. She slipped into the restaurant bathroom and threw up.

She blushed. "It was harder than you would think. My body resisted, but I was able to do it. It was so gross that I thought, 'I'll never do that again,' but a week later I did. At first it was weekly, then twice a week. Now it's almost every day. My dentist said that acid is eating away the enamel of my teeth."

Heidi began to cry. "I feel like such a hypocrite. People look at me and see a small, healthy person. I see a person who gorges on food and is totally out of control. You wouldn't believe how much I eat. I shove food into my mouth so fast that I choke. Afterward, my stomach feels like it will burst."

I explained that bulimia is an addiction that's hard to break. It requires enormous willpower to fight the urge to binge and purge. And unlike people with other addictions such as alcohol or cocaine, bulimic women can't avoid their drug of choice. Heidi would need to learn controlled eating. Fighting the urge to binge is just one part of the treatment. She also needed new ways to deal with her own psychic pain. Bulimia, like all addictions, is a way to run from pain. Heidi needed to learn to face her feelings. I suggested she record how she felt at the time of binges. Later we would examine her writing.

Heidi's father was a pediatrician and her mother a homemaker and a member of the Junior League. The oldest of three children, Heidi said that she had experienced a wonderful childhood. Her family had taken trips every summer—one year to the coast of Maine, another to Sanibel Island in Florida, and another to Alaska.

She loved elementary school. She'd been busy with her family, church, and gymnastics. She was the kind of girl other kids like—easygoing and energetic. Heidi paused. "I had the perfect life—great parents, good friends, and my own bedroom with a canopy bed and a balcony. I had walls full of ribbons and trophies."

"When did it stop being perfect?" I asked.

"After my thirteenth birthday things got tough. I graduated from my neighborhood school and moved into a consolidated school. School was harder; gymnastics was harder. I gained weight when I started my periods. Coach put me on a diet."

Heidi sighed. "Social life got harder. The girls were competitive. I hated the gossiping. With boys, everything got sexual. I was friends with some of the guys in the neighborhood, but we stopped hanging out together. We didn't know how to handle our friendships anymore."

I asked how Heidi felt about her appearance and wasn't surprised to hear that she had felt ugly in junior high. "Appearance was all we talked about. I tried not to get caught up in it, but I couldn't help it. I wanted to be pretty like everyone else."

As is often the case, Heidi's bulimia began with anxiety about weight gain. She was in a high-risk category—women who make a living or have an identity based on being thin. This category includes gymnasts, dancers, actresses, and models. Many acquire eating disorders as an occupational hazard. However, once bulimia is entrenched, it functions—like alcohol or other chemicals—as a stress reducer.

We ended our first session with a talk about expectations. Heidi said she felt pressure to be attractive, athletic, and popular. She was amazingly successful at meeting these expectations, but she was paying a big price. Her perfectionism was taking its toll on her physical and emotional health. She needed to cut herself some slack. Eventually, unless she conquered bulimia, she wouldn't be athletic, attractive, or popular.

Next session Heidi came with careful notes on her bulimia. She had binged at home late at night after all her work was done. Usually she went to bed and tried to sleep, but almost always she was too anxious to settle down until she had binged and purged. Then she slept, only to wake the next morning hungover and ashamed.

Heidi wrote that before bingeing she felt tired, she worried about her tests, or she was upset about practice or her boyfriend. We discussed ways she could deal with those feelings besides bingeing: she could talk to someone, write in a journal, listen to music, or learn relaxation techniques. Heidi agreed to write in her journal before she binged. She didn't think it would stop her, but it might slow her down and maybe she would learn something about herself.

We talked about how bulimia had changed her life. She no longer enjoyed family dinners or social occasions where food was served. It made her nervous to be around normal eaters. She could either pick at her food or binge, but she'd lost the ability to have an ordinary meal. She was afraid that Sunday dinners with her grandparents would cause her to lose control, so she avoided them. She missed her grandparents and she knew they missed her.

Heidi was exhausted from the time and planning that bingeing required. Sometimes she stayed up past midnight to have the kitchen to herself. Sometimes she missed outings because she knew the house would be empty and she could binge in private. She said, "My parents don't try to stop me, but I hate to do it when they are around. I don't want my little brothers to find out."

"My boyfriend knows and is really supportive, but it hurts our relationship," she said. "I won't eat out with him. Sometimes I want him to take me home so I can binge. I'll make up an excuse to end our date." She looked at me. "I hate to say this, but I'd rather binge than make out.

"I get really moody if anything interferes with my bingeing," she continued. "I'm irritable before and depressed afterward. It seems like I'm never happy."

I congratulated Heidi for being in therapy. "You have the discipline and capacity for hard work that will be required to fight this," I told her. "You'll make it back, I can tell."

THE FOOD ADDICTION

In the 1990s, bulimia was the most common eating disorder in young women. It started as a strategy to control weight, but soon it developed a life of its own. Life for bulimic young women became a relentless preoccupation with eating, purging, and weight. Pleasure was replaced by despair, frenzy, and guilt.

Over time young women with bulimia are at risk for serious health problems: often they have dental, esophageal, or gastrointestinal problems, and dangerous electrolytic imbalances that can trigger heart attacks.

They experience personality changes as they grow to love bingeing more than anything else. They become obsessed and secretive, driven for another binge and guilty about their habit. They experience a loss of control that leads to depression. Often, they are irritable and withdrawn, especially with family members.

While anorexia often begins in junior high, bulimia tends to develop in later adolescence. It's called the college girl's disease because so many young women develop it in sororities and dormitories. While anorexic girls are perfectionist and controlled, bulimic young women are impulsive and they experience themselves as chronically out of control. They are more vulnerable to alcoholism than their anorexic peers. Unlike girls with anorexia, young women with bulimia come in all shapes and sizes.

Bulimic young women, like their anorexic sisters, are oversocialized to the feminine role. They are the ultimate people pleasers. Most are attractive, with good social skills. Often, they are the cheerleaders and homecoming queens, the straight-A students and pride of their families.

Young women with bulimia have lost their true selves. In their eagerness to please, they have developed an addiction that destroys their central core. They have sold their souls in an attempt to have the perfect body. They have a long road back.

PRUDENCE (16)

Prudence and her mother came to my office one sunny winter afternoon. Marvelene was a plump, middle-aged woman dressed in a stylish red wool suit with a faux fur collar. Prudence, also plump, wore blue jeans, a faded sweatshirt, and Birkenstocks.

Prudence told me that she started bingeing three years ago and now binged twice a day, sometimes three times. She described her binge episodes as a kind of craziness when she fell into a trance and inhaled whatever was around.

"We tried locking up the food," Marvelene said, "but Prudence bashed open the pantry with a hammer. When she wants to binge, there is no stopping her."

Marvelene said that Prudence never ate normally. If she wasn't bingeing, she was starving herself.

"She's always on a diet. She won't eat anything except when she binges."

"I want to lose weight, but I can't," Prudence told me. "I weigh more now than ever."

"This is all my fault." Marvelene sighed. "I'm always on diets."

I asked about the family. Marvelene worked at the telephone company, as did her husband. In fact, they met there eighteen years ago. Marvelene said, "I'm definitely not one of those modern women who stands up for herself. I have a hard time saying what's on my mind."

"She's the family servant," Prudence said. "She lets Dad push her around and apologizes for any mistake she makes. She needs to get a life."

I was struck, as I often am, by how closely daughters observe their mothers and by how strongly they feel about their mothers' behavior. Prudence described her father as a good provider, but quiet. Marvelene put it this way: "Prudence means the world to him, but he doesn't have much to say to her. He's not the type to show his feelings."

"Are there other children in the family?"

Suddenly the tone of the interview changed. Marvelene sighed and Prudence bit her lip. Marvelene said, "Prudence's older brother was killed three years ago in a car accident."

"I don't want to talk about Greg," Prudence said.

I looked at the two frozen-faced women. I suspected that the family had hardly discussed Greg's death and that most of their grieving was still ahead of them. I knew this work needed to be done, but not in this first session.

Instead we talked about Prudence's school, which was in the wealthiest part of town. The population was suburban and homogenous. Most of the girls had designer clothes, straight white teeth, and beautiful hair. Hardly any girls were even chubby. It was a perfect breeding ground for eating disorders.

Prudence laughed. "When I first went there, all the girls looked alike to me. It took a while to learn to tell them apart."

She gestured toward her somewhat unconventional outfit and said, "I refuse to play the designer-clothes game. I'm not a Barbie doll. I'm embarrassed to have bulimia. It's such a preppy disease."

The next time I saw Prudence I asked to see a picture of Greg. She pulled out her purse and showed me his senior-class picture. "Greg wasn't like most brothers. He was my best friend. He didn't mind having me around, even when his buddies were over. He gave me advice and protected me. The worst thing Greg could say was that he was disappointed in me. That would shape me up fast. He got on my case if I made Bs. He taught me to ice-skate."

I asked, "How was he killed?"

Prudence bit her bottom lip. "He was out with friends after the state basketball tournament. I knew he would be drinking but I wasn't worried because his group had a designated driver. That night their designated driver was drunk and hit a bridge outside of town. He wasn't hurt, but Greg died instantly."

She told me about the memorial service at the high school. More than one thousand people came. The high-school choir sang, and the captain of Greg's basketball team gave the eulogy. She told me of the church service. "Everyone in the family put something in the casket for him to take along. Mom and Dad put in his fishing pole, basketball, and his yearbooks. I put in my teddy bear, Misha."

Prudence cried as she told me about their last serious talk. Greg had warned her about junior high and all the temptations she would face. He'd advised her to avoid sex and alcohol at least until high school.

"I've followed his advice about sex," she said. "I really don't want to get involved anyway."

She continued, "After he died, we stopped talking about him. Mom shut his bedroom door, and we acted like he was away at camp or sleeping in late. I felt our family would fall apart if I brought it up.

"The only person who could have helped us through this was Greg," she said. "He knew the right things to say."

I handed Prudence a Kleenex, and five minutes later she continued. "I was mad at God. Why couldn't he have taken an old person who wanted to die or a child murderer on death row? Why did he have to take the best person in the world?"

She cried more, but afterward she said, "It feels good to talk about it."

"You have lots of catching up to do," I said.

I felt hopeful after that session. Prudence, like many bulimic young women, had learned to deal with feelings by bingeing and purging. It seemed likely that as she faced her biggest pain, she'd be able to face others and talk rather than binge when she was upset.

Over the next few months we talked frequently about Greg. Prudence brought in other pictures of him and letters he had written her from basketball camps. She told me stories about their adventures together. She talked about Greg with her mother and Greg's old girlfriend. She even tried to talk to her dad, but he said firmly, "Pru, I can't do it."

One day I suggested she find something in the natural world that reminded her of her brother, something that could help her feel connected to him whenever she saw it. The next session Prudence told me that her brother reminded her of cattails because he was tall, thin, brown-haired, and loved the water. When she missed him, she walked to a nearby creek with cattails and thought of him.

Prudence found that she actually binged less on the days she talked about her brother. She learned to deal with other pain by facing it as well—by writing in her journal or talking to someone she trusted.

I encouraged her to take better care of herself. I told her the

Overeaters Anonymous slogan: HALT—Don't get too hungry, angry, lonely, or tired. She learned to identify her feelings and not to label everything as hunger. She learned to rest when she was tired, tell people when she was angry, or find something to do when she was bored.

Prudence liked the OA group. It was a relief to hear others talk so honestly about their eating disorders. She was heartened that some of the women were in recovery and doing well. She liked the support and conversations about feelings. She had a consciousness-raising notebook in which she kept track of lookist, sexist remarks. She brought in ads featuring thin women. She hated how women were portrayed as vacant-eyed sexual objects with no personality. Prudence prided herself on her independence, and she grew even more outspoken in her resistance to being "bimbo-ized."

Then she decided to fight the incredible cravings to binge. This is a necessary and critical step in recovery, but it's terribly difficult. From my clinical experience, I've learned that fighting the urge to binge is at least as hard as fighting the urge for drugs. It requires incredible self-discipline and emotional pain tolerance. Prudence learned to call on her brother for help. She formed a picture of his face in her mind and talked to him, asking him for the strength to fight binges. When she succeeded, she thanked him.

Of course, Prudence wasn't always successful. But gradually she was able to reduce her binges to once a day. After four months in therapy, she had a binge-free day. Some of her energy was returning and her skin and hair looked healthier. She reported that there were days she didn't even think about weight.

Prudence was a good talker, more sensitive to her own and others' feelings than the average teenager. Slowly she defeated her addiction. She made a commitment to live an examined life. After months in therapy, she said to me, "Greg would like who I am now."

STARVATION IN THE LAND OF PLENTY

Anorexia is a problem of the prosperous nations. It is, to quote Peter Rowen, a question of "being thirsty in the rain." Anorexia is both the result of and a protest against the cultural rule that young women must be beautiful. In the beginning, a young woman strives to be thin and beautiful, but after a time, anorexia takes on a life of its own. By her behavior an anorexic girl tells the world, "Look, see how thin I am, even thinner than you wanted me to be. You can't make me eat more. I am in control of my fate, even if my fate is starving."

It is the good girls—the dutiful daughters and high achievers— who are at the greatest risk for anorexia. Anorexia often begins in early adolescence with ordinary teenage dieting. But instead of stopping the diet, perfectionist young women continue. They become progressively obsessed with weight and increasingly rigid in their thinking about food. They see themselves in a competition to be the thinnest girl around, the fairest of the fair.

The word *anorexia* implies an absence of hunger, but in fact anorexic girls are constantly hungry. They are as obsessed with food as any starving people. They have many of the physical symptoms of starvation—their bellies are distended, their hair is dull and brittle, their periods stop, and they are weak and vulnerable to infections. They also have the psychological characteristics of the starving. They are depressed, irritable, pessimistic, and apathetic, and they dream of feasts.

Family members try everything to make their daughters eat— pleading, threatening, reasoning, and tricking. But they fail because the one thing in life that anorexic girls can control is their eating. No one can make them gain weight. Their thinness has become a source of pride, a badge of honor.

Anorexic young women tend to be popular with the opposite sex. They epitomize our cultural definitions of feminine: thin, passive, weak, and eager to please. Often these young women report that they are complimented on their appearance right up until they are admitted to hospitals for emergency feeding.

Anorexia is a metaphor. It is a young woman's statement that she will become what the culture asks of its women, which is that they be thin and nonthreatening. Anorexia signifies that a young woman is so delicate that, like the women of Chinese history with their tiny bound feet, she needs a man to shelter and protect her from a world she cannot handle. Anorexic women signal with their bodies, *I will take up only a small amount of space. I won't get in the way.* They signal, *I won't be intimidating or threatening.* (Who is afraid of a seventy-pound adult?)

SAMANTHA (16)

Against her will, Samantha was brought to my office by her German-Lutheran mother. Wilma kept her coat on and her arms folded across her ample chest as she explained that her husband wanted to come but was in the fields. The corn needed to be brought in before the predicted snow fell that weekend. Wilma reported that the family doctor had diagnosed Samantha with anorexia. She hadn't had a period in several months and her cholesterol level was so low it could trigger a heart attack.

Wilma said that Samantha used to be a cheerful and peppy girl. By the time she came into therapy, she rarely smiled, and she was irritable and lethargic. Once she'd been a strong worker on the farm; now she could do only the lightest of chores. When she was home, she hardly spoke to the family and spent all her time exercising or studying in her room. Samantha was a straight-A student, a cheerleader, and she was popular with her classmates, but, Wilma said, "She doesn't enjoy those things like she used to."

As her mother talked about her health problems and behavior changes, Samantha listened without emotion. She was five feet six inches tall and weighed ninety-nine pounds. Her head clearly showed the outline of her skull, and her eyes were watery and sunken. Her light brown hair, though attractively arranged, was dull and brittle. She dressed in a blouse and heavy sweater to disguise her thinness. She had the furry arms that often come with anorexia. This is called lanugo and is the soft, woolly body hair that grows to compensate for the loss of fat cells.

I asked Samantha what she thought of her mother's description of her. She said, "She's exaggerating. I eat plenty. Just last night I had pizza and ice cream."

Wilma looked doubtful and said, "Only a spoonful of ice cream and less than one piece of pizza. You took off all the cheese first."

"I don't like cheese," Samantha said. "You know that."

Wilma said, "She plays tricks on us with food. She pretends to eat but really just rearranges things on her plate. She says she ate at school, but we'll find out from her friends that she didn't."

"Has your personality changed in the last year?" I asked.

"I am different now, I admit it. I don't have as much fun, and I get stressed out. I have trouble sleeping."

"When did you begin to lose weight?"

Samantha said, "I went on a diet." She pointed at her mom. "You encouraged me."

Wilma shook her head sorrowfully. "Yes, and I tried to lose weight with her. Only I stopped after a week of misery and Samantha never stopped."

I suggested Samantha keep track of her eating and exercising so that we could talk about patterns. I stressed that Samantha couldn't get well unless she decided that anorexia was her enemy and made a conscious decision to fight back. Otherwise, she'd perceive me and her family as her enemies, trying to make her do something she didn't want to do. She'd fight us and she could win.

"It is painful to watch Samantha eat a dinner of lettuce and a few grapes when I know she's starving," Wilma said. "But we've learned that we can't make her eat. We tried and Samantha lost weight even quicker."

I gave her my book on eating disorders and scheduled an appointment with Samantha for noon the next day. I wanted to see Samantha alone with a sack lunch.

Samantha arrived wearing a blue sweatshirt with white kittens on the front and blue jeans that looked ironed. I pulled out my cheese sandwich and apple and suggested we eat as we talked. Samantha showed me her lunch—two crackers, celery and carrot sticks, and a small bunch of grapes. She explained that she had had a big breakfast and wasn't hungry.

I asked what triggered her anorexia. "I broke up with Brad," Samantha said. "We dated all through junior high. I thought I could trust him and that we'd be together forever."

I put down my sandwich. "Why do you think he dated someone else?"

"He teased me about my thunder thighs. He wanted someone thinner."

Samantha nibbled on a carrot stick. "I was much better at dieting than my mother or my friends. I lost five pounds the first week and then three the second. Twice I fainted at school."

She smiled in memory of the time. "I got lots of compliments. My friends were jealous, and guys who wouldn't have considered me before asked me out."

Samantha's most important event was her weigh-in time, first thing in the morning. If she lost weight, she felt great, but if she gained, she was distraught. Nothing else, not grades or social success, had much effect on her well-being.

She learned to love the "high" she experienced from fasting. She began running three miles a day, then five and then eight. Even though this running exhausted her and depleted her limited energy reserves, she wouldn't cut back. She devised tests for herself to prove her control over food. For example, she invited her friends over for a party and, weak with hunger, watched as they devoured lasagna and ice cream sundaes. She baked brownies for her family and would not even sample the ones fresh from the oven. She watched other people scarf down food with their animal appetites and felt superior. Samantha had done what many girls with anorexia do: she had reduced her complicated life to one simple issue—weight.

Samantha had her own rigid ways of thinking about herself and was impervious to the influence of others. She had brainwashed herself into thinking that anorexia was her friend. She was in my office because her parents and doctors wanted her to fight. We were her enemy, not the anorexia. She lied, distorted, and hid her eating to protect herself from those who wanted to help her.

Therapy must be a kind of reverse brainwashing. I attacked the anorexia, but not Samantha. As she finished her meager lunch, I asked her questions that I learned to ask from psychologist David Epston. "If anorexia is your friend, why is he making you so tired and weak? Why is he encouraging you to do something that has made your periods stop and your hair fall out?"

"I don't know what you mean," she responded.

At the end of that hour, I said, "We will continue to explore the lies that anorexia has told you, the lies that are costing you your life." I also told her I would work with her only if she agreed to stop her long-distance runs for now. I explained that these runs might trigger a heart attack. She resented my limits, but agreed.

Work with Samantha proceeded laboriously. I assigned her consciousness-raising work. She was to look at models and movie stars and ask, "Who picked this thin, passive type as our standard of beauty?" I asked her to think about women she really respected. Were they weight and appearance conscious?

With Samantha, as with most anorexic women, the biggest step was her realizing that anorexia was not her friend but her enemy and even her potential executioner. One day Samantha realized at last that anorexia had lied to her. She said, "He promised I would be happy when I was thin, and I'm miserable. He promised I would accomplish great things and I'm too tired to even do what I used to do. He promised me friends, and everyone is mad at me. Anorexia has stolen all the fun out of my life."

That was the day I felt Samantha would recover.

COMPULSIVE EATERS

In this culture we are all socialized to love food. Rich, sweet foods are connected to love, nurturance, and warmth. We associate grandmothers and parties with cookies and cakes, not carrot sticks. Emotional nourishment is linked with physical nourishment. Many of our words for those we love are food words, such as sweetie, sugar, and honey. In addition to the emotional power of food, it has a chemical power that's addictive as well. We all have experienced that sedating effect after Thanksgiving dinner.

Young women who eat compulsively have learned to use food as a drug that medicates away their emotional pain. This is harmful because they do not learn to deal with emotional pain and because they become obese, which sets them up for much more pain and rejection. In America, it's virtually impossible to be heavy and feel good about oneself. A vicious cycle has begun.

Compulsive overeaters are often young women with a history of dieting. They diet and feel miserable, then they eat and feel better, but meanwhile their dieting makes their metabolism grow more and more sluggish. Over time weight loss becomes associated with control, and weight gain with out-of-control behavior. Soon it's not just their eating but their lives that are out of control.

Writer Susie Orbach distinguished between "stomach hungry," which is genuine physical hunger, and "mouth hungry," which is a hunger for something other than food—for attention, rest, stimulation, comfort, or love. Compulsive eaters are mouth-hungry eaters. All feelings are labeled as hunger. Compulsive eaters eat when they are tired, anxious, angry, lonely, bored, hurt, or confused.

Treatment for compulsive eating is similar to the treatment for bulimia. Young women need to identify their real needs and not label all need as hunger. If they are restless, they need stimulation; if they are tired, they need rest; if they are angry, they need to change or escape the situation that angers them. Of course, compulsive eaters need to learn controlled eating. Often, they can benefit from a support group such as Overeaters Anonymous.

Violet was living on the streets when we first met, but soon after she moved into a shelter for homeless young women. She had a more difficult life than many compulsive eaters, but she shared essentially the same issues. Violet associated food with love and nurturance. Like many compulsive eaters, she was a good-natured, hardworking people pleaser. Violet was good at caring for others, but when she needed care, no one was around. Food was her pain medicine.

Violet (18)

I met Violet in the 1990s when I worked at our local homeless center. During the day, homeless people and transients came there to shower, use the phones, pick up mail, escape the weather, and play cards. As a volunteer, my job was to make coffee and put out trays of donuts and rolls. I was to enforce the rules—no swearing, no alcohol, no obscenities, and no weapons. Most of our customers were men, but increasingly during the time I worked there women and families had come to the center. Cigarette smoke filled the room with a blue haze by midmorning. I was struck by how many of the homeless were hooked on caffeine, sugar, cigarettes, and alcohol.

I noticed Violet right away because she was an unusual age for a shelter visitor. She looked about eighteen, maybe even younger. She was chubby and dressed in jeans, a T-shirt, and plastic flip-flops. Like most of the people at the center, she had bad teeth. When I first saw her, she was playing cards at a table of regulars. They joked with her and offered her smokes and advice on survival.

Later, when the men hit the streets, I visited with Violet. She had just run from what she said would be her last foster-care placement. She'd had six and that was plenty. She'd also lived on the reservation with her mother, who was sick and alcoholic, and she'd lived in an institution for difficult kids with no place else to go. She was ready to be on her own and said, "I'd rather live on the streets than have anyone tell me what to do."

I worried aloud that she might get raped being on her own, and she looked at me strangely and asked, "Do you think that hasn't already happened?"

Violet came to the shelter for several months. Like many of the local homeless, she sold her blood and "volunteered" for drug studies at a pharmaceutical company. She wove leather armbands that she sold on the streets. Violet made enough money to buy herself and her friends food. She bought presents for children whenever they turned up at the shelter.

One morning she showed me all the scars on her arms and leg—from a knife fight with her mother's ex-boyfriend and from a foster father who believed in physical discipline. Another day she said, "You're a shrink. I wonder what I should do about this tendency I have to eat everything that isn't nailed down." She told me how she always associated food with comfort. Her fondest memories were of her childhood visits to her grandmother's. There she'd had a calm, clean place to play and rest. She said her grandmother was a good cook and always had oatmeal cookies and angel food cake for her to enjoy. "Mom never had food around, only booze. Grandma's place had good food."

She lit a cigarette. "I had lots of bad homes. Food was the one thing I could count on. No matter how wrecked I was, eating helped me feel better. But there was never enough food. That's what worries me now. I eat until my stomach hurts, and then I'll keep on eating."

I said, "It sounds like you've got things pretty well figured out."

She smiled. "I know what's wrong, but how do I fix it?"

Eating filled a deep need that Violet didn't know how to fill in other ways. I knew she could learn healthy ways to take care of herself. Because she was such a good worker, I was sure she could work her way into a decent job and a more stable life. I started to tell her this, but Violet waved her hands. "Whoa. Don't get too deep on me."

I apologized. "We shrinks have a tendency to do that." Then a man at the shelter asked me to make some more coffee.

A few weeks later, Violet told me that she thought her eating was related to her fears about sex. "I figure that if I'm fat enough, maybe guys will leave me alone." She laughed. "It's a kind of armor, soft armor, but it works pretty well."

Another day I said, "Everyone counts on you to cheer them up." She was pleased by my observation. I continued, "I wouldn't want you to change, except maybe to follow some of that sensible advice that you give other people."

She looked at me. "Like what?"

I answered, "Like getting off the street. I'll help you when you're ready."

I wish I could say that Violet's story had a happy ending, but after a few months she left for California to pick fruit with a man she met at the center. She sent me a postcard from the Central Valley. It said: "I miss my shrink. I'll be back. Don't worry."

I never saw her again.

Violet came from an extreme situation, but in terms of dynamics, she was similar to most compulsive eaters. She learned to associate love with food and to use food to comfort and nurture herself. Her sexual fears were quite typical of compulsive eaters. Many date the start of their compulsive eating to an incident involving sexual abuse. Others are fearful of men or their own sexual appetites and see their weight as a form of protection.

If I could have seen Violet in therapy, I would have encouraged her to examine her feelings carefully at the times when she felt tempted to gorge. No doubt she had pain from her accumulated life experiences. She had abandonment issues and physical and sexual abuse issues to deal with. She had learned that while people let her down, food was an ever-faithful friend.

I would have taught her to respect rather than run from her feelings. I would have encouraged exercise as a way to fight depression, manage stress, and feel better about her body. I would have taught her to set limits with others and even to ask for help. We could have found money for her to go back to school or get some technical training so that she'd be employable. I would have found her a good dentist.

Beauty is the defining characteristic for American women. It's the necessary and often sufficient condition for social success. It is important for women of all ages, but the pressure to be beautiful is most intense in early adolescence. Girls worry about their clothes, makeup, skin, and hair. But most of all they worry about their weight. Peers place an enormous value on thinness.

This emphasis on appearance was present when I was a girl. But girls experienced increased pressure to be thin by the 1990s. We had moved from communities of primary relationships in which people know each other to cities full of secondary relationships. In a community, appearance is only one of many dimensions that define people. Everyone knows everyone else in different ways over time. In a city of strangers, appearance is the only dimension available for the rapid assessment of others. Thus, it becomes incredibly important in defining value.

In the 1990s, the omnipresent media consistently portrayed desirable women as thin. Girls compared their own bodies to our cultural ideals and found them wanting. Dieting and dissatisfaction with bodies had become normal reactions to puberty. When unnatural thinness became attractive, girls did unnatural things to be thin.

Unfortunately, girls were not irrational to worry about their bodies. Social desirability research in psychology during that time documented our prejudices against the obese, who researchers found were the social lepers of our culture. One study found that 11 percent of Americans would abort a fetus if they were told it had a tendency to obesity. By age five, children selected pictures of thin people when asked to identify good-looking others. Elementary-school children had more negative attitudes toward the obese than toward bullies. Teachers underestimated the intelligence of the obese and overestimated the intelligence of the slender. Obese students were less likely to be granted scholarships.

Girls were terrified of being fat. Girls heard the remarks made about heavy girls in the halls of their schools. Fat meant being left out, scorned, and vilified. No one felt thin enough. Because of guilt and shame about their bodies, young women were constantly on the defensive. In the 1980s and 1990s, rates of eating disorders exploded upward. When I spoke at high schools, girls surrounded me with confessions about their eating disorders. At colleges, when I asked if any of the students had friends with eating disorders, everyone's hands went up. Studies reported that, on any given day in America, half of all teenage girls were dieting and that one in five young women had an eating disorder.

Today, girls still live in a lookist culture that values thin women. Bulimia is still the most common eating disorder, although the incidence rates of all eating disorders have dropped slightly. Since the 1990s therapists and medical professionals have become much more sophisticated about treatment. We have many excellent treatment programs such as the Renfrow Center. The public is much more aware of the dangers of eating disorders.

In recent years we've seen a spike in the percentage of young women who are obese. Diabetes rates for teens are soaring. The American diet is sugar and fat-filled, and many teens exercise less as they spend more time indoors and on devices. Once obese, girls have a difficult time losing weight. Heavy girls are still ostracized, but we have a heartening new concept in our culture—body positivity. A number of confident, interesting women are writing, blogging, and YouTube-ing about their experiences of being fat in our current culture, yet thriving and achieving new levels of self-acceptance and professional success.

The internet heightens adolescents' pressure to be beautiful. Via social media, girls constantly see ads for body products and diets and they cannot escape images of girls with flawless skin and coltish legs. Girls today are more likely to have cosmetic surgeries and exercise compulsively to achieve more sculpted bodies. The American Society for Plastic Surgeons reported a 98 percent increase in procedures between 2000 and 2012. As Marta told us in one of our focus groups, "There are lots of fake boobs and butts out there."

Maddie described the world of high-school girls this way: "The comparison game is huge. I size up every girl I meet within five seconds and decide if she is prettier than me. All girls do this. It's exhausting.

"I try to remind myself that every girl, including me, is created in the image of God," she continued. "But it's hard. At football games, maybe half the boys watch the cheerleaders, but I guarantee you that all the girls do, just to see how they compare."

"Most girls I know are skinnier than me," Maddie added with a sigh. "I see body shaming of those who don't conform to the ideal. Most girls look down on girls who are heavier than them."

She added, "Right now, the big deal is a thigh gap. If you've got the ideal body shape, there is space between your thighs when you are standing."

"For my friends," Izzie said, "it's waist trainers. I just bought one of those. Words cannot describe how uncomfortable it feels. I can't breathe, but dammit I'm gonna be hot!"

YouTube stars are becoming as influential as movie stars. Many are beauty gurus who talk about fitness and makeup. They encourage Herculean efforts on appearance. Some offer tutorials on editing images for maximum sex appeal.

In 2019, girls watch makeup tutorials by Pixiwoo, Michelle Phan, and Luxy Hair and spend their discretionary money on cosmetics. Most believe that being beautiful is a responsibility. "Makeup is a huge factor in girls' lives," said Aspen. "Almost all girls wear at least foundation and mascara, because they think they look naked without it."

In our focus groups, we discussed the never-ending pressure to be beautiful. Olivia said that even though she didn't want to wear makeup, her friends pushed her to do it. Her best friend told her that she looked like an egg without it. She worried that her peers thought she was ugly. Eventually, she straightened her hair and wore mascara. Clearly, she told us, "makeup isn't optional."

Izzie announced that when she posts a photo on Instagram, she watches to make sure she gets at least ten likes in fifteen minutes. If she doesn't, she takes the photo down. The other girls chimed in that they did the same thing.

"Thinspiration is in fashion now," said Kendyl. "All of us try to look sexy and thin in our photos."

"I've had a crappy body image since sixth grade," said Jada. "I hate to see pictures of myself and I'm terrified to be seen in swimsuit. A girl in P.E. suggested I go on a diet. I cried and cried. I've been in sports for years and I know that if I could be skinny, I would be. I desperately want to be thin, but I don't have the power to decide what my body looks like."

"A few weeks ago, a girl told me I'm so skinny that it's disgusting," said Aspen. "There is such a narrow range for ideal."

All our focus group participants had at least one friend with an eating disorder. Amalia's locker mate ate only carrots. Amalia told the group, "She was diagnosed with anorexia and hospitalized. She almost died."

Addie told of coming back to school three months after her jaw surgery. "Everyone thought I looked great because I'd lost twenty pounds. I'd been almost starving. Part of me thought the praise was sickening, but another part of me liked being noticed. I didn't want to gain the weight back."

"My mom has dieted her whole life," said Kendyl. "She wants me to diet with her. She made our family retake our Christmas picture to make sure everyone looked their thinnest."

We all laughed at the weirdness of that. Jordan said wryly, "Misery loves company."

Public education and eating disorder treatment protocols have changed for the better since 1994. We possess a great deal more knowledge about eating disorders than we did two decades ago. Therapists have access to more effective treatment methods, and experts have established excellent treatment centers. Young women are speaking out against the pressure to be thin. Girls' empowerment movements are coalescing around these issues.

Many girls are more interested in fitness than they were in 1994. Participating in sports, jogging, swimming, or any kind of physical activity such as rock climbing or biking can be an antidote to worries about a beautiful, thin body.

Sara and I thought about this as we watched Kate's winter basketball tournament. She was the first female athlete in our family. Sports weren't available in the 1960s and Sara, who famously achieved her high-school P.E. credit with an independent study walking class, didn't participate in them in the 1990s. In contrast, Kate was a gifted athlete on her school's varsity team.

We sat in the bleachers and watched her team, the Eagles, battle it out for a spot in the quarterfinals. The girls, sporting blue-and-white uniforms, wore their long hair in braids or swinging ponytails. They ran up and down the court with confidence and focus. We were struck by how muscular, competitive, and aggressive they were, yet they constantly cheered and comforted one another. The Eagles high-fived with every score and jumped into the air with glee when a play went well.

We felt proud of and amazed by these strong, bold girls. We wondered if we would be more comfortable with competition and aggression if we had played sports. At that game, we both hit on the same conclusion, that athletics could be a route toward body positivity and empowerment for adolescent girls.

The tragedy of eating disorders will change only when our culture changes. When young women are valued for their characters, personalities, creativity, intelligence, and efforts, we will see girls' attitudes toward their bodies change. Individual girls are sometimes strong enough to resist the pressure to be thin and adults can help. Every one of us can help by valuing girls—*and all people*—for their intelligence, character, compassion, and resilience.

TWELVE

Drugs and Alcohol

RITA (16)

Rita looked as if she'd stepped out of an MTV video. Her brown hair
was decorated with feathers and beads, and she was dressed in a skin-
tight animal print dress. But Rita's personality didn't match her flam-
boyant clothing. She was soft-spoken, almost shy, and eager to be
liked. In a tentative way, she told me that she had just been arrested for
drunken driving. This embarrassed and scared her. Her dad was an
alcoholic and the last thing she wanted was to follow in his footsteps.

"I'm here because I want to get fixed while I'm young," Rita said. "I
don't want to live a screwed-up life like my parents."

Rita was the oldest of three children. Her dad was a salesman at a
discount furniture store, and her mother was a homemaker. Things had
been bad for as long as Rita could remember. Her mother had arthritis
and couldn't work. Her dad was a womanizer and a compulsive gambler who worked long hours, then hit the bars or keno parlors. He
wasn't around home often, but when he was, it was chaos and misery.

"I was hit a lot myself," she said calmly. She showed me a scar above
her left eye where she'd been hit by a beer bottle. "But that wasn't the

worst of it. Dad said horrible things when he was drunk, like 'You'll never get a man, you're too ugly,' or 'Too big of a bitch,' or 'Too much of a slut.'" She shuddered. "I stayed out of Dad's way. I lay awake and listened to him yell at Mom. Sometimes he hit her, too."

She pushed her long hair back from her face. "When I was fourteen, I told my dad that if he ever touched Mom again, I would kill him. He knew I meant it too. He hasn't hit her since then."

As we talked, it quickly became clear to me that Rita carried way too much responsibility for a sixteen-year-old. Like many parental children, she took better care of others than she did of herself. She worked too many hours at the country radio station. She comforted her mother, and on the days her father couldn't make it out of bed, Rita called his boss with an excuse. She helped her brothers with their homework while ignoring her own.

Rita had a boyfriend, Terry, who at nineteen was already a heavy drinker and a gambler. He worked part-time at a keno parlor. He had met Rita at a street dance and been immediately attracted to her. That night he danced with her and invited her to a barbecue at his place on Sunday. Rita brought a cake and did all the cooking.

"He's nicer than Dad." She shrugged. "I know he's got problems, but he never gets mad at me."

She paused, embarrassed. "I know dating Terry is dumb, so don't feel like you have to point that out."

I decided to save the topic for another day. Like many daughters of alcoholics, Rita was choosing men like her father. Love was connected to anger, violence, unpredictability, and shame. She dated Terry in the hope that this time the story might have a happy ending. She dated him because the familiar was comfortable, even if it was the familiar chaos of a relationship with an alcoholic.

Even though Rita considered herself an adult, she really wasn't. She hadn't developed any identity except that of helper. She hadn't thought through issues like her own sexuality or career plans. She had no personal goals or sense of direction. She had bad judgment about relationships, and she was uneasy socially and failing in school.

Like most girls who have been emotionally or physically abused by their fathers, Rita had internalized many of the messages that he sent. She didn't think that a decent guy would like her or that she was worthy of a loving relationship. She saw her value to men in primarily sexual terms. As is true of many women with abusive fathers, Rita was patient, tolerant, and good-hearted, all qualities that helped her survive in the home of an alcoholic. She was competent and responsible, but under the surface Rita believed her value was in serving others.

I wanted to help her develop a sense of herself independent of this family. She needed guidance in even imagining good relationships. She was unsure what a healthy man would be like. Men were like boys to her; they needed patience, care, and humoring. Women were either like her mother—weak and ineffectual—or like herself, required to take on the weight of the world and handle it without complaint.

Rita had a genetic tendency toward alcohol abuse, she had observed the misuse of alcohol, and she was under a great deal of stress and unsure of herself. Alcohol was her way to deal with pain. I recommended she find a support group.

Rita was ready for change. She had a difficult background to overcome and limited support. She was young and overburdened, but she had energy, honesty, and openness. I was hopeful that Rita would avoid a "screwed-up life like my parents." At the end of our session I asked Rita when she would like to come back. She tossed her lovely hair and said, "Tomorrow."

In the 1990s, many more adolescents were using alcohol and drugs. Teenagers did this for a variety of reasons: psychological problems, social pressure, and familial factors. Some of the reasons had to do with complicated psychological processes, and other reasons were as simple as availability. Usually peers determined what intoxicant was most likely to be used.

Alcohol was the drug of choice of most teens. It was cheap, powerful, and sold everywhere. But drugs were much more available than most parents suspected. Most of my clients had been offered drugs by the time they were in seventh grade. By eighth grade, they knew students who regularly used drugs.

My own rural state had problems. The interstate that dissected Nebraska was a national conduit for drugs, and the small communities along I-80 had drug problems. Teenagers from towns like Alvo (population 144) and Aurora (population 3,717) came to my office with drug habits that once could be found only in cities. As one of these girls put it, "The drug business at my school is major."

I want to emphasize that not all drug and alcohol use is pathological. Healthy, reasonably well-adjusted teenagers use drugs and alcohol. Some experimentation is normal. Drinking at parties is widespread and not necessarily a sign of anything except a desire to fit in and do what others do. It's important not to label all drug and alcohol use in teenagers as addiction. The labeling process can do harm. Rather, kids and adults need guidelines for what is normal experimentation and what is self-destructive use.

Drug and alcohol use are appealing to teenage girls, who are often confused, depressed, and anxious. Alcohol and marijuana are popular because they offer teenage girls a quick, foolproof way to feel good. Amphetamines help girls avoid hunger and eat less. Plus, imbibing often enhances status with friends.

How do we identify girls who are at risk for addictions? Thirty percent of the children of alcoholic parents become alcoholic. But I don't want to overstate this. Teenage girls from other families sometimes develop serious abuse problems. Peers play a role. In general, teens whose friends are heavy users are more likely to use. Certain patterns, such as drinking to escape reality or drinking to get wasted, are more dangerous than others. Drinking alone or being secretive about drugs and alcohol are destructive habits. But each girl must be evaluated separately. Often drug and alcohol use are symptoms of other problems.

Particularly with teenage girls, it's important to try to understand the context in which use occurs. Often, heavy use is a red flag that points to other issues, such as despair, social anxiety, problems with friends or family, pressure to achieve, or negative sexual experiences. Girls use alcohol or drugs for different reasons, and responses must be tailored to each unique situation.

KELLI (15)

Dressed in green polyester pants and a yellow golf shirt, Kevin looked provincial in spite of his international work as an agronomist. Roberta, a public health nurse, was sweet-faced and matronly. "We found pot in Kelli's bedroom," Roberta said.

"We have known Kelli was on something for months now," Kevin said. "She and her boyfriend, Brendan, act too goofy sometimes."

I asked about alcohol, and Roberta said, "Kelli wouldn't touch the stuff. She's a vegetarian and hates alcohol and tobacco. She's attracted to the drugs of the sixties. She's a hippie at heart."

Kelli was the youngest of three daughters. Her older sisters were smart, successful, and attractive. Carolyn had been a straight-A student and a Miss Nebraska finalist who married an attorney and was pregnant with her first child. Christina was in her senior year at Grinnell College, where she'd been a student leader. Soon she'd be on her way to medical school.

Roberta said that they were an ordinary family who liked church, Big Red football, and community socials. Their first two daughters were easy to raise. "We mainly stayed out of their way. Other kids flocked around them. They never needed rules or curfews. We actually told Christina not to study so hard.

"Kelli is so different," she said. "She likes different food, movies, music, and people. She's attracted to strangeness. All the things that worked with the others seem to be wrong for her."

"The older girls were self-motivated while Kelli doesn't care about success," Kevin said. "She's hard to punish because she doesn't want money, television, or new clothes. Once we tried to ground her from her boyfriend and she threatened to kill herself."

"We're sure she's having sex," Roberta added. "Brendan and she are inseparable. He's a nice enough boy, but we know they do drugs together. Her sisters never drank or took drugs."

"It sounds like the older girls are a hard act to follow," I said. Kelli was desperately seeking her own niche, different from her sisters. Since they had the glorious and successful niches, Kelli was left with the black-sheep niche.

"One of the problems with your earlier success is that it makes it hard to do things differently. It was easy to parent Christina and Carolyn. But for Kelli, you may need a consultant."

"Kelli thinks we love her sisters more than her, but it's not true," Roberta said. "Kelli is just harder for us to understand."

The next week I met with Kelli, who was tall and thin with long brown hair. She wore an orange shirt, torn jeans, and combat boots with thick olive socks. She was polite but distant. I had the feeling she was enduring this session, so I filled some time by talking about my teen years in the '60s for a while.

Kelli said, "I wish I'd been alive back then. I have nothing in common with the kids of today."

"What do you like to do?" I asked.

"Hang out with Brendan. We feel the same way about things. He likes me just the way I am."

She looked at me suspiciously. "Did my mom tell you we were having sex?"

I nodded.

"It's no big deal," Kelli said. "We love each other and I'm on the pill."

I asked her what a "big deal" was from her point of view.

She tossed her hair and said, "My parents. They like to play bridge and do crossword puzzles. They watch educational television and listen to opera. I feel like the hospital made a mistake and sent me to the wrong home. My sisters were perfect for my parents. They are middle-class success stories. I'm not going to be."

I asked how she felt as she talked. "It hurts. They try to love me as much as my sisters, but they can't. My parents love it when we achieve—that's what makes us worth something. They don't know what to love about me."

"What do you want?" I asked.

"Enlightenment—what the Buddhists call 'nirvana.'"

"That's pretty ambitious."

"Brendan and I read about Buddhism. When we have the money, we're going to the Naropa Institute in Boulder."

We spent the rest of the session talking about Buddhism. Kelli knew a surprising amount for a fifteen-year-old. She was animated on this topic, and, at the end of our time, she seemed reluctant to go.

The next session Kelli wore those same boots, jeans, and socks, but this time with a rose-colored T-shirt. She brought me some drawings she'd made of the Buddha resting under the tree of his enlightenment. She said, "I hate alcohol and cigarettes. They destroy consciousness."

"How about other drugs?"

"We take mushrooms now and then, and acid." She paused. "Some of the best moments of my life have been on acid."

She liked the way LSD changed reality—the way music sounded different, colors were more vivid, and oranges tasted better. She had a battered old copy of Timothy Leary's *The Psychedelic Experience*. But she said, "I prefer a natural high."

We discussed other ways to alter consciousness. I told her about psychological research on "flow experiences." We talked about how meditating and also the creative process can alter consciousness. When I met again with Roberta and Kevin, I agreed with them that they would need fresh ways to approach Kelli. For example, maybe they could take her and Brendan to visit the Naropa Institute or help them enroll in a local course on Buddhism. Kelli needed to define herself in new ways, not as different from her sisters, not as a drug user, but as a sensitive and philosophical person.

When I talked to teenagers about drug and alcohol use, I tried to remember that curiosity and exploration were normal at this age. Healthy teenagers experimented, and it was not sensible to label every teenager who used chemicals as an addict. Except in extreme cases, it was better to deal with the problems that inspired abuse.

Relationships were powerful agents for change. I worked at connecting and at helping parents connect with teenage girls who were abusing drugs or alcohol. I also tried to find a substitute for the abuse such as a new habit that was more positive or a new identity that was less self-destructive. And I included friends in the process and encouraged teens to help one another.

Research showed that girls were less likely to be heavy drinkers if they were introduced to light drinking in their homes. Probably it was a good idea to offer girls a small glass of wine at special dinners or on holidays. That kept drinking from being viewed as rebellious behavior and taught a reasonable context for the use of alcohol.

Schools in the 1990s had early and fairly extensive education about alcohol and drug use and abuse. Students learned the signs of problem drinking and drug use. They were taught healthy limits. For example, the National Council on Alcoholism recommended the 1, 2, 4 rule. That was, "Don't have more than one drink an hour, two drinks a day, or four drinks a week total, and you'll be safe from developing problem drinking." Most girls were shocked when I shared that rule. They said, "Everyone I know drinks more than that."

To fundamentally change the rates of alcohol and drug use, our culture needed to change. For many adolescents in the 1990s, smoking and drinking stood for rebellion and maturity. The media contributed to this illusion, linking sophistication with self-destructive, unrestrained behavior instead of prudent, thoughtful behavior. Film and TV characters with self-control were often portrayed as boring geeks.

Corporate America encouraged girls to consume products such as sugar, alcohol, and nicotine to sedate their natural and understandable pain. As the cigarette companies discovered, adolescent girls were perfect targets for anyone peddling sophistication. In fact, adolescent girls were the only population group whose smoking increased between 1970 and 1990.

Advertising teaches that pain can be handled by buying and consuming products. There's big money to be made in creating wants and then encouraging consumers that these wants are needs, even rights. We are taught to go for it. We're encouraged that if it feels right, it is right. And we're told, "Don't worry, spend money."

The junk values of our mass culture in the 1990s socialized girls to expect happiness and regard pain as unusual. Advertising suggested that if we aren't happy, something is wrong. Pain was presented as something that can and should be avoided by consuming the right things. It was treated as an anomaly, not an intrinsic and inescapable part of being human.

America places enormous emphasis on the gratification of every need. It hasn't always been so. Earlier in the century, children were taught patience, endurance, and stoicism. Ideal children were able to forgo their own needs and pleasures for some greater good. Adults knew that the gratification of all wants was impossible and would be dangerous to individuals and society. It wasn't until the advent of Madison Avenue–style advertising that this ethic of self-sacrifice began to crumble.

As a society we have developed a feel-good mentality. We need to rethink our values and to break the link between negative feelings and chemical use. Ideally, we would offer our children new definitions of adulthood besides being old enough to consume harmful chemicals, have sex, and spend money. We would teach them new ways to relax, to enjoy life, and to cope with stress. We have a responsibility to teach our children to find pleasure in the right things. I wrote this in 1995, but it is true today.

The good news today is that girls are less likely to get into trouble from hard drugs or alcohol than they were in 1994. Rates of alcohol use among eighth graders are half what they were in 1994, and 40 percent of high-school seniors have never tried alcohol. Fewer girls smoke now than in 1994, but many girls are vaping. Drinking, smoking, and drug use are no longer markers of maturity. Instead, academic success and extracurricular involvement—not a high priority of many girls in the 1990s—are often the measure of maturity today.

As of the 2018 midterm elections, recreational marijuana is now legal in ten states and the District of Columbia. Both teens and their parents often prefer it to alcohol. Girls see it as safer and less harmful and indeed, by today, many researchers think all alcohol use is unhealthy. Girls also report that kids who smoke don't cause any trouble, whereas kids who are drinking often do. Every girl in our focus groups thought marijuana should be legal.

Vaping is the new smoking, with roughly two million teens currently vaping. Teens can hide vaping equipment in their clothes and even vape during classes. It's an expensive, unhealthy, and addictive habit. Most teens vape tobacco, but other drugs can also be vaped. Once teenagers realize they are hooked, they often have trouble stopping.

It is important to note that the decline in alcohol use doesn't mean that girls are not seeking sedation. Indeed, in this age of anxiety, girls are often desperately in need of quick fixes for relaxation. More girls take prescription antidepressants and antianxiety medications. They have found a new drug to stimulate dopamine release: social media.

"In eighth grade, my friend decided to take some of her dad's leftover pain pills," said Jada. "I worried about her and told my mom. I cried for an hour as she and I talked about how drugs could affect my life."

"I believe that most people who abuse drugs or alcohol have bigger problems," said Izzie. "I know a girl who hated her dad and didn't ever want to go home. She smoked a lot of pot to cope."

"Kids use drugs to be with their friends and not be left out," added Amalia. "For me, smoking a little pot helps with anxiety. The main thing I worry about with drugs is my parents finding out."

"Curiosity has gotten a lot of kids in trouble," said Jada. "Lots of kids at my school smoke weed. Some of them—mostly the black kids, which is totally unfair—have been arrested."

Aspen mentioned that some of her friends were into vaping. They do it in school hallways between classes and teachers don't notice.

Marta told us that her cousin sneaks Ativan from her mom's medicine cabinet and takes several of the pills before big exams.

Statistics tell us that, until they leave home, this generation tends to be cautious about alcohol and drugs. Sadly, when girls arrive at college, they often throw that caution to the wind and engage in binge drinking. Many college-age girls regularly drink to the point of blackouts. As Kendyl said, "You could float a battleship on what we drink at parties."

Of course, many high-school girls still use drugs and alcohol as medicine, and without external resources or family support, those habits are difficult to break. For Tiana, an unexpected pregnancy led to a new outlook on her health and lifestyle.

TIANA (17)

"My best memories are from when my mom and dad were together. Life was just better." Tiana sighed wistfully and tore a bite off her everything bagel.

"We never had to worry about what we were gonna eat for dinner or how we would make rent this month. There were never any worries when my dad was in the picture."

"When I was eight years old, my parents had the fight that broke them up. The judge said they couldn't be with each other. Once my dad left, my mom hit rock bottom. She started doing K2 and other drugs, and I became the mom of the family. My brother and sister looked up to me, and I became the one who told them what they needed to do. They were just babies when it all went down."

"Where did you go?" I asked.

"When my parents first separated, we lived in a shelter for abused women and their families. My mom worked as an orderly at the hospital from 6 a.m. to 6 p.m. We hardly ever saw her because when she was home with us, she was sleeping. She needed her rest to be good at work. It was so lonely. I was trying to care for my siblings and go to school. After I got the kids to sleep, I would watch *American Idol* and cry until I fell asleep.

"After we moved out of the shelter, it was like musical jobs for my mom. Every few months she'd start a new one, and she'd claim it would be *the* job that was going to change things for us. But we struggled all the time, and after she quit her last job we were evicted from our town house. We were homeless for eight months, just crashing with different people she knew. One lady was cooking meth in her basement."

"How did you cope with all these moves and changes?" I asked.

"I can't say I did a great job." Tiana shrugged. "During that time, I went downhill, I got ruder, and I started doing drugs and going out late at night, trying to be like the cool kids. I wasn't there for my siblings as much as I should have been.

"During middle school, my grandpa bought us a house. It was like we won the lottery. He had requirements for my mom: she had to go to work and quit using, because we had been homeless for two years before that. He didn't even make us pay rent. But when I turned fourteen, my mom lost that house. She couldn't keep up with her promises to my grandpa. When she lost our house, I moved in with my boyfriend. I lost contact with my mom because she was going down the drain. I was in eighth grade."

"Tiana, what was that like?" I asked.

"Lawrence came from a mostly stable family. His mom owned a daycare and she let me play with all the little kids. That good time lasted for five months and then I started helping Lawrence sell drugs. He was on house arrest for dealing, so I'd drive his car illegally—I was only fifteen—to make deliveries. I knew it was a terrible idea, but I wanted money for clothes and toys for my brother and sister.

"One night we got high and I didn't remember much the next day; when I bugged him about it, Lawrence admitted he had slipped some crushed Xanax into my blunt. That's the night I got pregnant.

"A few months later, I got a call from my doctor after a sports physical. At my mom's request [Tiana was by then back in touch with her mother] they had done a pregnancy test and it was positive. I was seventeen weeks pregnant.

"The doctor called and told my mom the news. She called me at school and told me to come home right away. When I got home, we talked all afternoon and all night. I was just in awe . . . I couldn't believe I was pregnant. My mom gave me three choices: abortion, adoption, or keep the baby. I told her, 'You were a teen mom. You had obstacles and I'll have obstacles too, but I want this baby.'

"Right away, I changed my lifestyle. I stopped hanging out with certain people. I got a job at Taco Bell and saved money for baby stuff. I've been there for three years; I've been employee of the month four times. I grew up and stopped worrying about myself and started worrying about what was inside me."

"What were your main emotions during your pregnancy? Were you afraid? Excited?" I asked.

"Um, all of the above." Tiana laughed. "When my mom was pregnant with me, she wrote little letters to me. So I started writing little letters to *him*. Some of them were too emotional and he won't ever see them."

Tiana cracked up remembering her turbulent pregnancy hormones. "Through it all, my true personality didn't change. I'm still outgoing, still funny, still who I was. I just adjusted my attitude and cleaned up my act."

"And Lawrence?"

"At that point I didn't want to be around drugs, so Lawrence was out of the picture. A few months before I had my baby, I started talking to his best friend, DeAndre. He became my best friend and my protector.

"During my pregnancy, me and my mom got superclose, and now she's like my best friend. I know that sounds crazy but it's true. She'd call in the mornings and make sure I was awake and heading to school. As soon as I said I was keeping the baby, she stopped bringing up any other options and said she would support me. She and DeAndre have a good relationship."

"It sounds like your pregnancy gave her something positive to focus on," I suggested.

"She's been working it out for herself," Tiana agreed. "She stopped smoking and works at my school in the cafeteria. Right now, she lives at the City Mission. Just last year, she went to rehab after smoking K2. My brother and sister went back into foster care. I visited her in rehab every week and we worked on building our relationship again."

"My head is spinning," I confessed.

"Welcome to my life," Tiana replied. "Anyway, DeAndre and I officially started dating ten days after Elijah was born. He tells him he loves him, and helps me with him, even in the middle of the night. DeAndre wants to adopt him, but in the meantime, he already *is* the father. Elijah calls him Daddy. We've talked about what it would be like if Lawrence ever gets his shit together and comes back on the scene. We've agreed we would build the relationship around Elijah and focus on what's best for him."

"Tell me all about Elijah," I invited.

"Elijah is getting to the age where he likes to talk back," Tiana said. There was pride in her voice when she spoke of her son. "He's a supersmart baby." Tiana grinned. "He knows sign language and we're teaching him both English and Spanish words. His personality is magical, but he doesn't sleep well. I'm still up with him several times every night."

"What kind of mother are you?" I asked.

"Real talk, I'm easily annoyed," Tiana admitted. "Some of those toddler behaviors make me crazy. But I told myself I'd never lay my hands on my son. Sometimes I raise my voice, but I know that if I make a habit of yelling, then as he grows older, I'll continue to do it. So I focus on using positive language. I try and praise everything he's doing and keep things loving."

"How do you balance work, motherhood, and participating in an academically challenging program? Do you ever sleep?"

"It's crazy. I work thirty hours a week or more. I try and get to homework when I can. Sometimes I turn in papers a month late. My teachers understand, for the most part, and they let me do what I need to. At the end of the day, work and my baby are my main focuses. Now and then if I have to, I'll take time off work to get caught up on school.

"I've already been accepted to the University of Nebraska, so I don't have to worry about grades and test scores like a lot of my classmates. I want to be an elementary school teacher. I don't have all As and Bs, but I'm just about getting the diploma. For me, it's not about grades, it's about showing people that I can do it."

"How are you a typical adolescent?"

"Since middle school I've drooled over guys. I still do . . . don't tell DeAndre," she joked. "I want to stay out late at night. I may not always get to, but there are nights when I do get a break. Usually we end up just driving around, hanging out with friends. Oh, and I'm moody. That's a typical teenager thing, right?"

"I'd say you have the right to be moody now and then," I said. "You're keeping a lot of plates spinning at once."

"People don't know how I do it, how I'm still up and going. I know some of my classmates see me as a role model. People want to show as much strength as I do. And I think people respect me because I don't keep secrets. People know that my mom is homeless, that I live with my boyfriend, that I had a baby.

"For me, it all comes back to Elijah. I want him to see that if you set your mind to something you can do it. I want him to know I'm never gonna let him down. If my mom hadn't quit her jobs, we wouldn't have been homeless. There were days when I went without eating so my brother and sister could eat. I'm determined—Elijah will never have to worry about those things."

Tiana's experiences played out on the extreme end of the continuum of adolescent struggles, but she managed despite great obstacles to hold on to her sense of humor and desire to create a better life for her son. As she progressed through high school, she quit running from her own vulnerabilities and faced her suffering with purpose and intentionality.

Our culture today is one that runs from pain and treats suffering—which is an inevitable part of life—as an avoidable problem. It still teaches girls the values of junk culture: shop, stay thin, and buy or consume when you feel pain.

It's heartening that girls today are less likely to use drugs and alcohol socially, but the loneliness and vulnerability they feel from living life online sets many of them up for future addictions. Adult usage rates have not diminished since the 1990s. Social media doesn't destroy one's liver or lead to hallucinations and drug overdoses, but in the long run, it may be as pernicious and toxic as any drug.

THIRTEEN

Sex and Violence

CHRISTY (14)

During my shifts at the homeless shelter in the 1990s, Christy and I talked about her life. Her mother was a state worker and her father an engineer. They were strict but loving, child-centered parents. They were also devout Catholics who taught Christy that sex was for marriage. They lived in a ritzy neighborhood and Christy was in the gifted program at school and attended summer camps for gifted kids. Because she was ahead of her classmates, she skipped third grade. But this meant that when she hit junior high she was immature socially and physically.

"I was nervous about school," Christy said. "I wanted to prove I was as cool as the other kids. I wanted a boyfriend to take me to the parties that the popular girls got invited to. I knocked myself out to get into that crowd."

I asked how she did that.

"I realized right away that being smart was trouble. I felt like I was 'severely gifted.' I got teased a lot, called a brain and a nerd. I learned to hide the books I was reading and pretend that I loved watching TV. This one guy in my math class threatened to beat me up if I kept breaking the curve, so I deliberately made Bs and Cs. My parents were mad at me, but I ignored them. I knew what I needed to do to get by."

Even though she wasn't particularly athletic, Christy joined her school's cross-country team. Some of her teammates invited her to parties. Suddenly, she had a gang of friends who were the jocks and the preps at the school. By the end of seventh grade, she even had a boyfriend.

"He was great, really sweet. We kissed and held hands but nothing else. We talked on the phone about twenty hours a week. Our parents wouldn't let us go out."

Her first boyfriend moved after the seventh grade. But soon many other boys were asking her out. She was drawn to Adam, who was older and more experienced than her first boyfriend.

"I remember this one party. We were drinking margaritas and playing this question game," Christy recalled. "Someone asked about sex. Have you ever gone all the way, or had sex in a car, or had oral sex, or sex with two people at once—stuff like that. If the answer was yes, we had to drink our margaritas. I was the only one who never took a drink and I felt so embarrassed."

Christy explained that she liked Adam and wanted to make out, maybe "go to second base," but stop before they had intercourse. She was curious about sex, but she didn't want to harm her reputation or break her parents' rules. She said that making out satisfied Adam for a while, but then they started fighting because he wanted to have sex and she didn't. Finally, she broke it off.

Several other guys asked her out right away. She accepted a few offers, but all the dates ended as wrestling matches. Some of her friends became sexually active during this time and they encouraged her to follow their example. But she said, "They want me to have sex so they won't feel guilty. I won't help them out that way.

"I wanted to date but not have sex," Christy said. "It was hard to be popular without a boyfriend, but I didn't care. I wanted to wait at least until I got my braces off. Maybe it was all that Catholic guilt."

She said, "Now mostly I go on group dates. I always make sure I pay my own way so I don't owe a guy anything. I'm careful not to get too close. I hide my looks and my intelligence. I've learned that being too smart or too pretty can get me in trouble. I want to be ordinary, to fit in."

After class at the university one day, a group of female students stood around my desk. I'd just given a lecture on sexuality in the 1990s and they had observations to share.

"Your ideas about healthy sexuality won't work in the real world," Ginger said. "No one talks about sex like you suggest. It would be too embarrassing."

Jane added, "Everyone is so mixed up that they just get drunk and do it. Then they try not to think about it the next day."

"I'm scared to go on dates," Suzanne piped up. "I'm afraid of getting raped or getting AIDS."

Marianne said, "I'm lucky that I have a steady boyfriend. We've been together since our freshman year. He's not perfect, but it's better than dating."

In unison they all said, "Anything's better than dating."

Girls faced three major sexual issues in America in the 1990s. One was the old issue of coming to terms with their own sexuality, defining a sexual self, making sexual choices, and learning to enjoy sex. Another was communicating about intimacy and embedding sexuality into relationships. The other issue concerned the dangers girls face of being sexually assaulted. By late adolescence, most girls either had been traumatized or knew girls who had been. They were fearful of males even as they were trying to develop intimate relationships with them. Of course, these two issues connected at some level and made the development of healthy female sexuality complicated.

Even today, America doesn't have clearly defined and universally accepted rules about sexuality. We live in a pluralistic culture with contradictory sexual paradigms. Girls hear diverse messages from their families, churches, schools, and the media. Every girl must integrate these messages and arrive at some value system that makes sense to her.

Paradigms collide between people. There are no clear agreements about the right ways to be sexual, so each couple must negotiate an agreement for themselves. At best, communication tends to be awkward and fragmented. At worst, no one even tries. The real crash-and-burn misunderstandings come when people with radically different ideas have sex without discussing their paradigms. For example, two people go on a date and one of them believes sex is recreation while the other believes sex is the expression of a loving relationship. The next morning, they wake with rather different expectations about their future together.

Our culture is deeply split about sexuality. We raise our daughters to value themselves as whole people, and the media reduces them to bodies. We are taught by movies and television that sophisticated people are free and spontaneous while we are warned that casual sex can kill us. We're trapped by double binds and impossible expectations.

A 1990s study of teenagers in Rhode Island documented the confusion. Teens were asked to respond to questions about circumstances under which a man "has the right to have sexual intercourse with a woman without her consent." Eighty percent said the man had the right to use force if the couple were married, and 70 percent if the couple planned to marry. Sixty-one percent said that force was justified if the couple had had prior sexual relations. More than half felt that force was justified if the woman had led the man on. Thirty percent said it was justified if he knew that she had had sex with other men, or if he was so sexually stimulated he couldn't control himself, or if the woman was drunk. More than half the students thought that "if a woman dresses seductively and walks alone at night, she is asking to be raped." Clearly, most of these teenagers didn't understand that a man never has a right to force sex.

Our cultural models for ideal female sexuality reflect our ambivalence about women and sex. Men are encouraged to be sexy and sexual all the time. Women are to be angels sometimes, sexual animals others, ladies by day and whores by night. Marilyn Monroe understood and exploited this split. She was an innocent waif and a wildcat, a child and a sultry sexpot. Understandably, girls are confused about exactly how and when they are to be sexy.

Girls receive two kinds of sex education in their schools: one in the classroom and the other in the halls. Classroom education tends to be about anatomy, procreation, and birth. Students watch films on sperm and eggs or the miracle of life. (Even these classes are controversial, with some parents thinking that all sex education should come from parents.) Some schools offer information about sex, birth control, and STDs, but most schools' efforts are woefully inadequate. Most do not help students with what they need most: a sense of meaning regarding their sexuality, ways to make sense of all the messages, and guidelines on decent behavior in sexual relationships.

In junior high schools in the 1990s, it was considered a mark of maturity to lose one's virginity. Girls were encouraged by their friends to have sex with boys they hardly knew. Many girls desperate for approval succumbed to this pressure. But the double standard still existed. The same girls who were pushed to have sex on Saturday night were called sluts on Monday morning. The boys who coaxed them into sex at the parties avoided them in the halls at school.

At the Red and Black Cafe in Lincoln, where local teens danced to grunge bands, the graffiti on the walls of the restroom spoke to the confusion. One line read: "Everyone should make love to everyone." Just beside that line another girl had written: "That's how you die of AIDS."

Adolescent girls in the 1990s approached their first sexual experience with a complicated set of feelings. Sex seemed confusing, dangerous, exciting, embarrassing, and full of promise. Girls were aware of their own sexual urges and eager to explore them. They were interested in the opposite sex and eager to be liked by boys. Sex was associated with freedom, adulthood, and sophistication. Movies made sexual encounters look exciting and fun. But girls were anxious. They worried that they would be judged harshly for their bodies and lack of experience. They worried about getting caught by their parents or going to hell. They feared pregnancy, STDs, and a bad reputation at the same time as they worried about being sexy enough to please their partners. They had seen sex associated with female degradation and humiliation, and they had heard ugly aggressive words describing sex. So they were fearful of being emotionally and physically hurt. For the most part, girls kept their anxiety to themselves. It was not sophisticated to be fearful.

In the 1990s, over half of all young women ages fifteen to nineteen had sex, nearly double the rates of 1970. Five times as many fifteen-year-olds were sexually active in 1990 as in 1970. Twice as many sexually active girls had multiple partners in 1990.

My experience as a therapist suggested that junior-high girls were not ready for sexual experiences beyond kissing and hand holding. Girls this age are too young to understand and handle all the implications of what they are doing. Their planning and processing skills are not adequate to allow them to make decisions about intercourse. They are too vulnerable to peer pressure. They tend to have love, sex, and popularity all mixed up. And when they are sexual, they tend to get into trouble rapidly. They aren't emotionally or intellectually ready to handle the responsibilities that arise. The decision to have sex should be a North Star decision—that is, one that's in keeping with a sense of oneself, one's values and long-term goals. By high school, some girls may be mature enough to be sexually active, but the more mature and healthy girls often avoid sex.

I want to make a distinction here between intercourse and other sexual experiences. It's healthy for girls to enjoy their own developing sexual responsiveness and to want to explore their sexuality. It's possible to be sexual and be a virgin. But in the 1990s there was no established or easy way to stop a sexual encounter. Thus, some girls avoided dating and touching because they did not know how or when to draw a line. Ironically, the sexual license of the times inhibited some girls from even kissing.

As a graduate student in the 1970s, my first clinical work was to teach a sex-education class for delinquent teenage girls at a state institution. The girls were between thirteen and sixteen. All were sexually active. Two had been pregnant, one had been gang-raped, one had been involved in prostitution, and another was known as the blow-job queen of the institution.

As we sat around the table for our first group, I was struck by how young these girls were, how unsophisticated and utterly ignorant they were about sex. They swore like longshoremen, but they knew little about their own bodies, contraception, or pregnancy. One girl announced, "You can't get pregnant without oral sex cuz that's when the sperm goes into your belly." Another girl, who had been pregnant, said earnestly, "I really never had sex." Their sex education had come from movies, television, and the night streets.

The lack of physical information was bad enough. Worse was that these girls didn't have any guidelines for making decisions about sex.

They were barely aware of what they were doing and afterward often "forgot" that they had had sex. They didn't know they had the right to make conscious decisions about sex. They didn't know how to say no.

I developed a sexual decision-making course. We role-played seduction scenes. I role-played the seducer with lots of animated tips from them. They were their embarrassed and inept selves—they giggled, looked down, barely whispered their objections, and were easily cowed by small amounts of pressure. With lots of practice, they learned to deliver a loud, firm no. If the guy persisted, they learned to shout, push, punch, and escape.

Next, we talked about making decisions to be sexual and about how to communicate with another person about sex and intimacy. I explained that a girl's first sexual experience was important. It was a template for later experience. If she's fortunate, her first experience was with someone she loved who loved her and sex occurred in the context of an emotionally committed relationship. If she was fortunate, the lovemaking was gentle and passionate and deepened the caring between the two participants.

Almost none of the girls in that group were so fortunate. Their experiences had been confused, hurried, and impersonal. Intercourse happened *to* them. Most of them had been coerced into sexual encounters. None had had sex as the result of a conscious choice to share love in a relationship.

I helped them undertake imagery work. Until they could picture a good experience, I doubted that they could have one. Instead, I told them to have fantasies of good dates with respectful guys who were interested in where they wanted to go and what they wanted to do. The date should last all evening and include compliments, talk, and fun. At first, they found this impossible. They didn't think dates like that occurred, but gradually they could conceive of a decent date.

I taught this group to develop their own list of criteria. At first the lists were heartbreaking. One girl said, "The guy should spend money on me—you know, take me to McDonald's or someplace." Another said, "The guy should say he likes me."

We started where they were. Any criterion was a step in the direction of assuming responsibility for making conscious choices about sex. They learned that they could decide who was a worthy sexual partner. After a few weeks some of the girls developed slightly tougher criteria.

All girls need help making sense of the sexual chaos that surrounds them. As opposed to what they learn from the media, they need to be told that most of what happens in relationships is not sexual. Relationships primarily mean working together, talking, laughing, arguing, having mutual friends, and enjoying outings. Girls need to be encouraged to be the sexual subjects of their own lives, not the objects of others' lives. They need help separating affection from sex.

Girls want to be sexy but respected. They want to be cool and sophisticated, yet not jaded and promiscuous. They want to be spontaneous, yet not die of AIDS. Lizzie and Angela are examples of girls with typical problems with sexuality in high school in the 1990s. Lizzie was a good student; Angela was a dropout. Lizzie came from a strong family and Angela from a broken home. Lizzie was popular and well adjusted, mature for her age; Angela was immature and impulsive, with few close relationships. Both girls were casualties of our cultural chaos.

LIZZIE (17)

Lizzie was referred by her school counselor because she wanted to transfer to a different high school. Lizzie drove to my office for an after-school appointment. She was a curvaceous senior dressed in a plaid skirt and fashionable sweater. Early in the session she said, "I think I'm a healthy person mentally. I'm not sure I should be here. All my problems are in the real world, not in my head."

I asked what those real-world problems were.

"My friends," she said. "Or rather the people I thought were my friends. At this point, most of them aren't talking to me."

Lizzie was from a working-class neighborhood. As a girl, she fished with her father and bowled with her uncle. She had a loving grandmother nearby who taught her to cook. Her parents worked in a tire factory along with most of the parents of her friends. The children had attended the same schools, played on the same soccer and baseball teams, and hung out in the same parks and cafés. Lizzie had been a good athlete in elementary school, and in junior high and high school she was a cheerleader.

Her sophomore year she started dating Paul. She had known him since kindergarten, but they began dating after a church hayrack ride. For over a year it was a wonderful relationship. He was a handsome football player. All Lizzie's friends told her how much they envied her. Lizzie's parents liked Paul, and his parents liked her. Their junior year they were homecoming prince and princess. Everyone was sure that their senior year they would be king and queen.

Lizzie sent the summer after her junior year working at a camp in the Colorado Rockies. The kids were fun, the scenery was breathtaking, and she liked one of the counselors. At first, she and Jesse were just friends. They took walks in the mountains and canoed on the clear lake under the cold stars.

Jesse was from Chicago and on his way to Northwestern in the fall. He was everything that Paul was not—worldly, sophisticated, and new. Lizzie resisted falling for him, but he was around every day and, as she said, "It's easy to fall in love in the mountains."

One night after talking for hours under a blanket on the shore of a mountain lake, they began kissing. Jesse took off Lizzie's shirt and then her slacks. He was eager for sex and Lizzie, while not quite so eager, didn't say no. They became lovers that night.

The summer sped by. Lizzie answered Paul's weekly letters carefully. She told Paul that she missed him but was too busy to call or write long letters. She never mentioned Jesse. In late August she said goodbye to Jesse. He invited her to come visit Chicago, but he didn't believe in long-distance relationships and warned her that he would date other girls. Lizzie was hurt about this, but told herself that, after all, they weren't engaged.

When she returned home, Paul asked, "Did you sleep with anyone?" Lizzie looked stunned but didn't deny it. Paul interpreted that as an admission of guilt and he began to sob. They talked far into the night. Paul was hurt and upset, but communicative. He left saying he wanted to be friends.

The first few weeks of school were fine. Her friends were happy to see her and she was busy with cheerleading. She had some classes with Paul and his friends, which at first were comfortable, then awkward, then unbearable. Paul quit speaking to her. When she walked down the hall, Paul's friends called her names—slut or bitch—names she was surprised they would use, especially with her.

Lizzie tried to talk to Paul but he refused. His friends grew more belligerent and even warned her to leave him alone. She tried to wait it out, but time didn't seem to help. In fact, over time more friends chose sides. Most of the boys and several of the girls whom she'd known all her life quit speaking to her.

In October she was not invited to a big party for cheerleaders and athletes. She quit the cheer squad. She considered talking to her parents, but knew that they would be most upset that she had had sex. So she went to the school counselor's office.

Telling me about all this, Lizzie was sad and angry. She knew this wasn't fair. She knew she had a right to decide who she would date. She resented being called a slut.

At first, we managed the crisis. I encouraged her to cry, shout, and do whatever helped her express all her feelings. We talked about immediate practical problems: Who could she sit with at lunch? (There were a few friends who had remained steadfast.) What should she do when guys called her names in the halls? (She decided to look them in the eye and say, "I hope you never have to go through something like this.") How could she spend her Saturday nights? (She decided to work at a domestic violence shelter. That would help her feel less sorry for herself.) Ultimately, Lizzie decided to stay at her school. She didn't want to give Paul's friends the power to drive her out of her school in her senior year.

We talked about basic issues. I asked her, "What kind of people do you really want for friends? What do you have to give other people? What really makes you happy? What makes you feel proud of yourself? How do you set priorities and make good decisions about your time? How do you lead a life that truly reflects your values?"

Meanwhile, Jesse no longer answered her letters. He wrote three times after they parted, but each letter was shorter than the last. Lizzie admitted that the relationship was more important to her than it was to him. Having sex had also set her up to feel more pain when they separated. She felt some guilt about her decision. A part of her believed the boys who were hissing in the halls that she was a slut. Suddenly sex seemed fraught with peril.

Lizzie developed her own policies about sex. She decided to wait until she was in a long-term relationship with someone who cared for her at least as much as she cared for him. She wanted to discuss how sex would affect the relationship, and she wanted protection from pregnancy and STDs. She also decided that she would make her decisions to be sexual in the cold, clear light of day, not in the heat of passion on a date.

For now, Lizzie developed ways to treat herself after the long tough days at school—walks in Wilderness Park, issues of *People* and *National Geographic* from the library, and trips to the coffeehouse with a friend. She reminded herself that there was life after high school. Lizzie begin looking into college. Gradually things calmed down. Paul started dating another girl, and he and his friends lost interest in punishing Lizzie. Lizzie was not as popular as she had been her junior year, but popularity mattered less to her. She stayed close to two of her girl-friends since childhood and made some new friends at the shelter.

When she stopped therapy, she was dating a college student. They made out, but stopped short of intercourse. Lizzie had decided to wait for a while. She wasn't ready to handle the pain that followed losing a lover.

Lizzie was a strong, well-adjusted young woman, but like all teen-agers, she was caught between competing values when it came to sex. Her parents expected her to be a virgin when she married. Her boy-friend over the summer encouraged her to have sex, even though the relationship would be short-term. Her high-school friends were out-raged, not that she had had sex, but that she had had it with someone they didn't know. Lizzie learned to take care of herself and withstand disapproval. She learned to think about her relationship choices and to take responsibility for sexual decisions.

ANGELA (16)

I first met Angela when she was four months pregnant by Todd, her boyfriend of several months. She bounded into my office wearing a black leather skirt and a low-cut T-shirt that had SKID ROW printed on the front. In a matter of moments, Angela was spilling out her life story.

Her dad had had an affair when Angela was in eighth grade. Her mom left for Arizona with her younger brother and she seldom heard from them. Angela lived with her dad; his new partner, Marie; and Marie's three young children.

Angela complained that she seldom saw her dad alone and that the kids "stole her stuff" and were "spoiled and hyper." She had no privacy and her dad and Marie expected her to babysit so that they could go out on weekends.

I asked her about school and she wrinkled her nose. "I had to go to the learning center till I turned sixteen, but I hated it there. As soon as I had my birthday I dropped out."

"What did you hate?"

Angela sighed elaborately and stretched her white arms above her spiky red hair. "It was boring. I hated all the junk we had to take. The girls were snobs."

"Tell me about your parents."

She sighed again. "When I told my mom I was pregnant, she prayed, then she disowned me. She likes my brother best. He's too young to have sinned all that much."

She leaned back into the couch. "I get on better with Dad. He's more low-key. He's mad about my pregnancy, but he still loves me. He wants me to live with him and Marie till the baby is born."

"What about after the baby is born?"

"I want to live with Todd," Angela said. "But if I can't do that, I'll move into subsidized housing. I'm already signed up."

"Is Todd the baby's father?" I asked.

She giggled like the young girl she was. "Todd's great. He's so cute."

"How long have you been dating him?"

She held up her hand. "Five months. That's the longest I've stayed with anyone."

"Will he help you with the baby?"

"He wants to, but he's got one child already," Angela answered. "He has to pay child support and he has a car payment. He promised to go to the hospital with me. He's happy I'm pregnant."

I asked Angela for more details about her life after her parents' divorce and listened as she told me her story in a matter-of-fact, even chatty, way. I felt overwhelmed by so many problems facing someone who failed eighth-grade math. At the end of our session I asked her, "If you weren't pregnant, what would your goals be?"

Angela grinned and said, "I'd want to be an MTV star."

Our time was up. I handed Angela an appointment card. She chided me gently, "You didn't ask about the names."

I smiled at her.

"Alexandra or Alex, what do you think?" she asked.

"I think they are beautiful names."

After Angela left, I thought about her. Her cheerfulness in the face of her enormous problems was both endearing and unnerving. I liked her naiveté, optimism, and energy. I hoped she had enough to pull her through the next few months.

The next session we talked about Angela's social life. After her parents' divorce, she'd escaped to a video arcade that was a hangout for the lost and troubled kids in the north part of town. Nearby there had been drug busts, shootings, and several rapes. Angela couldn't have picked a worse place to land. Her third night there, Noah offered to take her for a drive in his truck. They drove to the country and he encouraged her to have sex.

Angela described the experience to me. "I thought Noah was cute, but I wasn't ready for sex. I hadn't really thought about it, but it happened. I didn't enjoy it much. I thought, What's the big deal?"

After Noah, she had a new boyfriend every few weeks. She'd be attracted to someone and go out with him, not on a date really, but cruising or to his apartment. Sometimes she had sex with guys who didn't even know her last name and vice versa. Angela always hoped the guy would become her boyfriend. Usually, though, early into the relationship, they broke up. Angela would be heartbroken for a few days and then meet another "cool guy." She had crushes just the way junior-high girls always do. The difference between her and girls twenty years ago is that she had sex with all her crushes.

Todd was a regular at the video arcade. He was tall and blond with a "bad boy look." Girls fell for him. Angela noticed him her first week, but he often brought his little daughter with him and Angela assumed he had a regular girlfriend.

Five months after meeting him and after she had broken up with yet one more crush, Todd approached her in the concession area and offered to buy her a Coke.

"He was so sweet," Angela said. "I told him I'd been dumped and he was sympathetic. He wasn't hustling me or anything, he just wanted to talk."

The next night Angela wore her best outfit to the arcade. Todd came over to talk to her again. After an hour he suggested they go to his place where they could have more privacy. Angela agreed and that night they had sex. Two weeks later she missed her period.

We ended that appointment with Angela promising to see a doctor for a checkup. I said I'd be happy to meet Todd if he could come with Angela.

Angela came to her next appointment in black tights with a white sweatshirt, her first maternity outfit. She carried a copy of *All About Babies* and told me immediately that she was depressed. Todd wouldn't come. He didn't "believe in shrinks."

She sighed and ran her hands through her hair. "I went to Birthright this week to try to get money. They made me watch their sucko film about fetuses. I've been to welfare about ADC and it's so complicated. There're piles of forms to fill out and you have to prove everything. The lady who interviewed me was a bitch. Plus, I'm trying to quit smoking."

"Have you been to a doctor yet?"

"We can't find a doctor who takes Medicaid. This week has sucked." Angela sighed. "Todd's being such a jerk. I've hardly seen him. He says he's busy at work, but he's been at Holly's house. She's the mother of his little girl."

Angela told me that Marie's kids had chicken pox. Her dad was bitching about money. Todd's car needed a hundred dollars in repairs and that made him crabby. She'd been throwing up in the morning.

I asked how she felt about having a baby, and for the first time that morning she smiled. "I'm happy about that. I'm glad I'll have someone to love."

We spent the hour talking about her pregnancy. Angela had a project that she was interested in—being a mother. She loved looking at baby clothes at Goodwill and talking about pregnancy with her friends. She no longer felt so inferior to girls who stayed in school. She had something they didn't have. I'm glad we had a happy session because the next time Angela came in Todd had broken up with her.

Angela's eyes and nose were red from crying when she told me the news. But by then she was mostly mad.

"How could he be such a jerk? He promised me that he'd stay with me. Then he called me last night and said that he was moving in with Holly."

She wobbled her head sarcastically. "They *need* him.

"I hate men," she continued. "All the guys I've dated have turned out to be assholes."

At the end of our session she reported some good news. "I found a doctor and I haven't had a smoke in six days."

We talked about relationships in later sessions. Angela realized that after her folks' divorce, she'd been looking for love. She fell for any guy who told her she was pretty. Because she gave herself so impulsively and easily, she was hurt frequently. She grew to expect rejection, and a part of her wasn't surprised when Todd left her.

"If you take a little time, maybe you could figure out other ways to feel less lonely. Maybe you rely more on yourself and girlfriends. But if you want to date, perhaps you can find someone who will stick around and make you happy," I said. "Could we at least set some criteria for what needs to happen before you have sex with a guy?"

"Like what?"

"You need to decide for yourself."

Angela looked skeptical.

"It takes some time to know if someone is honest and caring," I continued. "Jerks can fake things for a while. How long do you think you would need to be with someone before you knew the true person?"

Angela thought awhile before she said, "Probably at least a month."

"That's one criterion. Do you have any others?"

"That he have a job and a car. That he be fun."

"Let's write these down," I said.

I saw Angela through most of her pregnancy. We talked some about her long-term goals. We discussed the perils of looking outside oneself for salvation. I suggested that she needed to find a way to support herself and the baby and to establish some friendships that lasted.

Early one morning, Angela called me from the hospital to tell me that Alex had been born. He weighed just under six pounds and had blond hair like Todd's. Marie had been her birth coach. She sounded proud and happy. She said, "If you come up to visit, bring me some chocolate. I'm starving in here."

I last saw Angela a few months after that. I was shopping at a discount grocery and she strolled by with baby Alex. She looked her old self—a happy smile, apple-red hair, and black eyeliner. She handed me Alex, a chubby baby with spiked hair. He was dressed in a black leatherette jacket. I held him and he cooed. I cooed. I could tell by his good health and smiles that he was well cared for. As he wiggled in my arms, Angela told me about her current situation. She had a new boyfriend now, Carey, who actually met her criteria for a relationship. He worked as a TV repairman, owned a Jeep, and liked babies.

Angela was working on her GED. Her mother had never seen Alex and rarely called Angela, but Angela talked to Marie about her problems. She, Carey, and Alex ate Sunday dinner with her father and Marie.

She laughed as Alex held his hands out to her and she took him back quickly. "Isn't he great?" she said as she chucked him under the chin.

I pushed my cart down the aisle, happy that I had seen her and that things were going better than I would have predicted.

SEXUAL VIOLENCE

On Sunday mornings I wake early. Everyone in my family sleeps in and I like the time alone to read our local paper. One Sunday these were the headline stories: "The Nightmare Began with Goodbye" was about Candi Harms, a first-year university student in 1992. Candi lived in an apartment with her parents a mile from her boyfriend's place. Between 11:40, when her boyfriend walked her to her car, and midnight, when she was due home, something happened. Her abandoned car, with her keys and purse still in it, was found in a remote area north of town.

Another headline announced that domestic violence was at an all-time high. On an inside page of the Sunday paper, a new fashion line was on display. The photo showed skimpily clad models wearing high heels at a New York show. On their tight, short outfits, over their breasts and buttocks, were painted bull's-eyes. The caption of the fashion photo read: "Walking targets."

These stories about women and girls were being told in every paper in America. They had a chilling effect on all young women. Their confidence in their ability to navigate their world was eroded. Their fear spoke to the heart of the question, What is our environment like for girls?

I saw a bumper sticker on a young man's car that read: "If I don't get laid soon somebody's gonna get hurt." He was not alone in his philosophy. On any given day in 1994, 480 women and children were forcibly raped, 5,760 women were assaulted by a male intimate partner, and 4 women and 3 children were murdered by family members. Rape was the "tragedy of youth" because 32 percent of all rapes occurred when the victim was between the ages of eleven and seventeen.

These statistics glossed over thousands of sad stories. One of my students missed class many times because she was being beaten by her boyfriend. Another group of students presented a panel discussion that included the results of our classroom questionnaire about abuse. More than half the women students reported abuse in relationships. The last three times I had spoken at a high-school class, a girl approached me afterward to tell me she'd been raped.

Classes on self-defense were filled with women and girls who recently had been victimized. In my classes for college students, I asked what men did to protect themselves, and they reported that they did nothing. I them asked the women, who generated a long list of the ways they were careful. Fear had changed their behavior in a thousand ways—where and when they could go places, who they talked to, and where they walked, studied, and lived.

As a therapist during the '90s, I worked with many victims of sexual assaults, some recent, still bruised and in shock, others struggling to come to terms with assaults that occurred years before when they were children. The youngest girls I worked with were two sisters, three and five, who had been brutally assaulted by a stepfather. My oldest client was a woman in her seventies who told about a rape that occurred when she was a teenager. Fifty years later, she still had nightmares. Some days I left work thinking that every woman in America had been or would be sexually assaulted.

Long after the physical trauma of assault, victims must contend with emotional wounds. A number of factors influence the severity of the trauma that comes from sexual violence. Generally, the trauma is more severe if the victim is young, if the assaults occur with frequency and over a long period of time, if the assailant is related to the victim, and if the assault is violent. Violent assaults by a family member are the most damaging.

Other factors that are important include the reactions of the victims. The sooner girls tell someone what happened and seek help, the better. The more support girls have from family and others, the better. Finally, girls vary in their own resiliency and ability to handle stress. Some are capable of a quicker, more complete recovery than others. All victims of sexual assault are helped by post-traumatic stress work, either with family, friends, or therapists.

ELLIE (15)

The first appointment with Ellie and her parents was painful for everyone. Ellie sank into my big chair and curled up like a small child. Her dark eyes were filled with tears. Her dad, Dick, was so overwhelmed he could barely speak. Ronette, who was small and dark-haired like her daughter, did most of the talking. She began our session by saying, "I'm so shattered by this that I can barely speak."

Dick was a welder and Ronette ran a hair salon out of their home. They were hard workers who put their children first. Dick had an American flag flying in their yard and flag decals on all the vehicles. He'd been wounded in Vietnam and was president of his local VFW.

Ronette liked the country music at the VFW and was proud that she and Dick were good dancers. She was a bighearted woman who had run into few problems she couldn't solve. Both cared deeply about Ellie, who was the oldest of their three daughters.

Ronette took deep breaths and gave me an outline of events.

"Ellie acted up some in eighth grade. She argued about everything— her chores, the telephone, and her studies—but we weren't really worried about her. We knew kids acted that way. Her grades were pretty good, mostly Bs. She was on the swim team. We liked her friends."

Ronette sighed. "What worried us most was her disobedience. She skipped school several times and she slipped out at night with her friends. We were afraid she'd get hurt."

Ellie began sobbing as her mother talked, and Dick curled and uncurled his fists like a boxer ready for a fight. Ronette's face was tearstained and tense, but she continued.

"This last month she's driven us crazy. She's been insulting to us and mouthy at school. Yesterday she was called into the counselor's office because she pushed a kid in the hall. That's just not Ellie. Her grades dropped and she quit going out with her friends. We knew something had to have happened but we couldn't figure what."

Dick said, "We asked her what was wrong and she wouldn't tell us."

"Thank God Ellie told her school counselor," Ronette said. "Things were going downhill fast."

I asked, "I know this is difficult, but what exactly happened?" We all looked at Ellie, who buried her face in the chair.

Dick said, "We don't know many details. It's too hard to talk about."

Ronette said in a dull voice, "Ellie sneaked out to a bowling alley. She thought her friends would be there but they weren't. When she walked across the parking lot to come home, four boys pulled her into their car and raped her."

"I wish we'd known," Ronette said. "Ellie's not telling hurt us almost as much as the rape. We thought she trusted us more than this. We thought we had a good family."

"It's common for girls to keep these things secret," I said. "It doesn't mean that you don't have a good family."

"I can't believe this happened to Ellie," Ronette said. "I feel guilty that I somehow didn't prevent this."

"I want to die," Ellie whispered.

Dick said, "I'd like to kill those guys."

"What should we do now?" Ronette asked. "None of us can sleep. We can't eat. Dick has missed the last four days of work."

The whole family was in shock and would need treatment. No doubt the younger girls were also in great pain. I planned to do some family work, but first I wanted to see Ellie alone.

At our next session, she looked a little better—her dark hair was out of her face and her eyes were dry. We visited a few minutes about school and her last swim meet. Then I brought up the rape.

She hugged a couch pillow to her chest and grew silent. Her fingernails and the tips of her fingers were badly bitten. She wasn't ready to talk, so I told her stories about other kids who had been hurt and how they came to terms with it. I talked about the nature of trauma.

"When you cut your finger, it bleeds; you may not like blood, it's scary and messy, but fingers that are cut are supposed to bleed. That's healthy. If they don't bleed, something is wrong. What happened to you is horrible and you are going to feel a lot of pain. You won't like it, it's messy and scary, but it's part of healing. Burying the feelings will hurt more in the long run."

Ellie stared at me from behind the pillow; her dark eyes were filled with pain. I explained that certain things happen with trauma. She might have nightmares and trouble with sleep. She might be afraid to go out and afraid to be home alone. She might feel crazy and like she will never recover. She might feel it was her fault and that she should have been smarter and prevented what happened.

Ellie nodded in agreement and said softly, "I keep seeing those guys over and over."

I sat with her as she cried.

The next four sessions were similar to our second session. I read to Ellie or told her stories about other girls I had known who made it through experiences like hers. Ellie's fingers stayed red and bitten. She didn't want to leave the house without one of her parents. She had no interest in doing anything with her friends.

Then in our sixth session Ellie came in and said, "Today I'm going to tell you what happened."

She paused. "You get better if you talk about it, right?"

I nodded.

She picked up the couch pillow and told me the story. She had planned to sneak out and meet her friend for a Coke, but her friend's dad stayed up late that night and she was afraid to leave or even to call. So when Ellie arrived at the bowling alley, her friend wasn't there.

"I waited for an hour," Ellie said. "I wasn't feeling all that great; I had a headache and these high-school boys kept staring at me. I wasn't scared of them, but I was embarrassed being there all by myself."

Her voice grew huskier. "I left the bowling alley about twelve. I noticed those guys were leaving, but I wasn't worried. They pulled up beside me and offered me a ride. I didn't know them well so I said no. They circled the lot and returned. Then they stopped the car and two of them got out and pulled me in."

Her voice was flat now. "There were four of them. I couldn't see their faces very well in the dark car. Two of them held me down in the backseat and they drove into the alley behind the bowling alley. I started to cry and one of them said, "Let's not do this." But his friends called him a pussy and he shut up. I don't think he raped me though. Only three guys raped me."

Ellie stopped and looked out the window. Her eyes were dry but filled with pain. She caught her breath and continued. "The driver raped me first. His buddies pulled down my jeans and he jumped on top of me. He didn't kiss me or anything."

Her voice broke, but then she continued. "I never had sex before and I felt like I was being split open. When he finished, he encouraged the others to do it too. The two in the backseat took turns. I threw up. Later they used my shirt to clean up my puke."

Ellie was shaking now as if she were chilled. Her voice was flat and dead. "All the time they did this, they were laughing and joking. The driver said I must have wanted it or I wouldn't have been out alone. They treated me like an animal, like I didn't have feelings.

"Afterward, they dumped me out of the car and threw my shirt after me. I put it on so I wouldn't be topless and walked home. I was crying so hard I thought I might have a stroke or something, but I didn't go in the house till I stopped sobbing. I slipped in my window and lay in bed till morning. Then I took a bath and rinsed out the shirt."

Ellie looked at me. "I was amazed that the next morning my parents didn't notice anything. At breakfast they talked about my little sister's dental appointment."

Over the next few months I heard that story many times. At first Ellie told it without much emotion, but gradually she connected her words and her feelings and she sobbed as she told the story.

I asked her to write, but not send, letters to the guys who raped her, letters that allowed her to express all her anger. She scrawled letters beginning, "I hate you for what you've done to my life. You've ruined everything for me and my family. We'll never be normal again."

Dick bought her a punching bag and hung it in the basement. Nightly she went down and punched it. At first, she had trouble connecting with her anger as she punched, but I encouraged her to keep trying. I told her to visualize the boys, the car, the rape as she hit. Once she did this, she hit with a frenzy and yelled about the rape. Afterward she collapsed in a puddle on the floor, but she felt calmer. All that anger was out of her and in the bag.

Meanwhile, the court case against the boys worked its way through the system. This retraumatized Ellie in some ways. The police came by her house with further questions, and she had to tell her story at a deposition. The newspaper carried articles. Her name wasn't mentioned, but seeing the stories always caused her pain. The trial loomed in her future as a public exposure of her shame.

Dick and Ronette came in monthly to talk about their reactions to the rape.

Both of them were afraid to let their daughters out of the house. Neither could bear to read news of rape or violence against women. Dick had revenge fantasies that interfered with his work. He woke at night covered with sweat, the way he had during the war in Vietnam. Sometimes Ronette cried when she was working on her customers. She would wrap a towel around the person's hair and run out of the room.

Later, the younger sisters joined our group and talked about how Ellie's experience affected their lives. The middle sister swore she would never go out alone at night or hang out with boys her family didn't approve of. The younger sister wanted revenge. Since the rape she'd had trouble in school for acting up. Everyone agreed their family was different now. Other families talked about money, school, and ordinary activities. They were obsessed with the rape. They, like Ellie, needed a place where they could talk and cry.

Gradually Ellie recovered. Her fingers healed and her nails grew longer. She regained her enthusiasm for the swim team and school. She went out with her friends. She and her sisters signed up for a self-defense class.

We talked about the implications of the rape for her future. Ellie said that she felt vulnerable. She would always be more cautious and more anxious than her friends. For right now she was not interested in boys. She wanted to stay away from sex for a long time. She said flatly, "I've lost all my curiosity."

Ellie was relatively lucky in that she was not severely injured, didn't contract an STD, or get pregnant. She was also lucky that her parents brought her to therapy. Even so, Ellie was a different girl than she was before the rape. She was more cautious and dependent on her family. Just when she was beginning to explore the world, her wings were clipped. She's tiptoeing, not flying, through her adolescence.

Another common experience for girls is some kind of sexual assault by a friend or an acquaintance. These are especially damaging because they erode girls' trust in the world around them and make all relationships feel potentially dangerous. Because the assailant is someone the victim knows, often the case is more difficult to handle afterward. The victim tends to feel responsible and is less likely to report it. If she does report it, there's more likelihood the assailant will argue that the sexual experience was consensual.

One of my clients was raped while on a field trip with her biology class. A student who came into her tent to borrow a butterfly net held her down, choked her, and raped her. The next morning, she pretended it never happened. She denied the experience until a year later when she went camping with her family. She crawled into their tent and stopped breathing as memories flooded her. She told her mother what had happened and her parents reported the crime. The boy claimed consensual sex. After a year, it was hard to prove otherwise and my client dropped the case. She came to therapy because she wanted to be able to camp without having panic attacks. She wanted to be able to trust guys again.

A client doing volunteer work over the summer at a camp for inner-city children was cornered and assaulted by the minister in charge of the project. She didn't report it because she was sure that no one would think the minister capable of such an assault.

One of my college students told of being a Little Sister at a fraternity. She and a friend had attended the frat's Saturday night "testosterone party." A guy she liked pulled her into a bedroom and tried to assault her. She screamed and kicked and managed to escape, and she never returned to the fraternity. She got nauseated whenever she thought about that evening. When she told me about the incident, she asked, "Is that how men treat their little sisters?"

Rape and sexual assault are personal problems that cry out for a political solution. The solution to our cultural problems of sexual violence lies not only in the treatment of individual victims and offenders, but also in changing our culture. Young men need to be socialized in such a way that rape is as unthinkable to them as cannibalism. Sex is currently associated with violence, power, domination, and status.

Rape hurts us all of us, not just the victims. Rape keeps all women in a state of fear about all men. We must constantly be vigilant. One day in the winter of 1993 I was cross-country skiing along a jogging trail. A tall man dressed in a ski mask and a black jogging suit ran toward me. It was dusk in a busy residential neighborhood, but his size and shape frightened me. I began planning my escape and imagining what I should scream to attract assistance. As he approached, he said my name and I realized it was my own husband.

Men are fearful for their women friends and family and aware that women are afraid of them. A male student complained that he hated rape. He said, "When I walk across campus after dark, I can see women tense up. I want to reassure them I'm not a rapist." Another said, "I haven't dated a girl yet who trusts men. Every girl I've cared for has been hurt by some guy. They are afraid to get close. It's so much work to prove I'm not a jerk."

But mostly rape damages young women. They become post-traumatic stress victims. They experience all the symptoms—depression, anger, fear, recurrent dreams, and flashbacks. The initial reaction is usually shock, denial, and dissociation. Later comes anger and self-blame for not being more careful or fighting back. Young women who are raped are more fearful. Their invisible shield of invulnerability has been shattered.

The incidence of sexual assaults peaked in 1993. According to RAINN, by 2019, the incidence of sexual assault had dropped by 63 percent since that peak. In 1993, one in three women was likely to be raped in her lifetime. Now those numbers have dropped to one in six. Yet, one in six is not, ultimately, a statistic to celebrate. Rape is still an all too common problem and most assaults are perpetrated against girls between ages thirteen and twenty-two.

Many factors have contributed to this precipitous drop. Alcohol use in teens also peaked about that time and has dropped ever since then. Rapists are much more likely to be arrested and charged in 2019.

Assaults are more likely to be captured on video, in ways that can lead to convictions in court. The notion of consent has morphed from fuzzy with no clear rules, to "No means no," to, in 2019, "Yes means yes." Fewer teens are drinking and, in fact, fewer teens are even spending time together. In 1965 and 1994, roughly 90 percent of girls dated in high school. Now, less than half of all girls have a date in high school. The way teens relate has changed qualitatively. They are operating under a whole new paradigm.

Without a doubt, teens were confused and conflicted about their sexuality in 1959 and 1994. However, today, confusion about sexuality has intensified. In 1994, public schools offered rudimentary education on sexuality, but by 2019, twenty-six states had no curriculum for sex education. In this absence, online chats and pornography become the teacher. Teens may not be sexually active, but they are exposed to coarse online communication, pornography, and hookup culture.

Some girls see lack of intimacy as normal, and they arrange to meet someone someplace for anonymous sex. Not caring is seen as a benefit. No one will get hurt because there is no relationship. It is almost as easy to find a sexual partner online as it is to order a backpack. And it's about that romantic.

Direct communication is even more difficult than it was earlier. Because so much of teen social life happens online or via hookups, girls have real trouble embedding their sexuality in loving relationships. This disconnect between sexuality and face-to-face relationships leads to odd splits. Girls might engage in virtual meetups and be amorous online but never actually hold hands with a date.

"The idea of a date where a boy picks up a girl and meets her parents, then they go to dinner or a movie, that's unheard of," Kendyl said, wide-eyed, in one of our focus groups. "That whole notion is so old-timey."

"In my case, it'd be a *girl* picking up a girl," Marta added. "Can you imagine my girlfriend showing up in a fancy dress to ask for permission to take me to dinner? *Very* retro."

"My mom has told me about dating," Amalia added mournfully. "I wish we still had that." Still, she confessed, "If a boy actually asked me out to dinner or a movie, I'd be afraid to go. I wouldn't know how to behave."

Much of what girls of previous generations did face-to-face now has an online counterpart. Couples don't meet, they text each other. Flirting often involves posing for selfies in sexy clothes. Sometimes couples meet off-line, but often it's either to take pictures together or just hook up for sex. As Izzie said, "No one knows how to have a relationship anymore."

Until late adolescence, many girls only experience online dating and online breakups. A major component of a real relationship is trust and, in the digital age, trust is in short supply. Too many people tell secrets online. Natalie, who began dating during her junior year, said she waited until she was mature enough to accept responsibility for a real, in-person relationship. "Before that," she explained, "I only had relationships—and I use that term loosely—on my Android."

Natalie's first "real" relationship began with texting, but after a few weeks, Noah asked her out for coffee. They talked for hours about music, friendships, and their shared passion: politics. After that, they met for walks and concerts. They volunteered together on a City Council campaign. Natalie feels lucky to be in a good relationship.

More of our focus group girls felt like Jada, who said, "I am not interested in dating. I've watched people try it and become miserable."

"Guys are straight-up immature," Kendyl said. "They date just to be seen with a good-looking girl. They don't care about the girl's personality, sense of humor, or interests."

"I would want my parents to get to know any boy I was thinking of dating. I'd want him to do things with us as a family," she went on.

"My parents would want to get to know anyone I was going out with," Marta agreed. "Maybe they would invite her to dinner before our first date. It'd probably be awkward, but that's okay. I like my parents to be protective."

In 1959 and the early 1960s, boys were expected to meet a girl's parents and bring girls home at an agreed upon time. By the 1990s, parents generally had less say in dating; daughters neither wanted nor needed their approval. Today, once again, girls like their families to meet their dates.

Now it's rare for girls to be sexually active in middle school, and most high-school girls postpone sexual activity until later. Teen pregnancy rates have dropped. Most girls now believe that girls who are sexually active in their early teens are immature and likely to have mental health problems.

David Finklehor at the University of New Hampshire, who researches teens' sexual behaviors, notes that teens today are less likely to have had sex than teens in 1995. Furthermore, the age when teens become sexually active has steadily risen. Girls today proceed with caution into the world of dating and tend to value their parents' opinions on their romantic lives.

Many Christian girls believe they should wait for sex until marriage. But all kinds of girls, regardless of religious beliefs, react to junk sexuality and sleaze by formulating rules for themselves that are protective. Some girls avoid dating because they do not want to be sexual. Others girls don't feel ready for the emotional responsibilities of dating or they don't want to be hurt or hurt anyone by breaking up. Interestingly, the girls with the most self-knowledge and maturity were waiting. They could see all the confusion, complexity, and risk that came with sex.

"Some guys don't have boundaries and it's hard to know if they even like you or just want to have sex," Maddie told me. "Before I say yes to a date, I wait for a long time so I know the relationship is for the right reasons." She sighed and continued, "I'm the last of my friends to be a virgin. Some of my friends are encouraging me to just do it, but I know I'm not ready."

When we discussed attitudes toward sex in our focus groups, the girls could have talked for hours. They all felt pressured to be "hot" or "sex positive." They were also aware that double standards still existed. Boys still talked trash about girls who were "too easy."

"Promiscuous is a word used only for girls," Olivia said.

"Boys use words like bitch, whore, and pussy to describe others in a negative way," Jordan said.

"Most girls are sexting by seventh grade," said Olivia. "They're all competing for the attention of a few cool boys."

"I knew a girl whose nude photos were leaked," Izzie said. "She was ridiculed and slut-shamed to the point she changed schools."

Most of the girls in our groups had been harassed. Olivia said, "A boy in band with me was always touching me inappropriately. It was really uncomfortable, plus he was verbally assaultive. Finally, I went to the band teacher crying. I said I'd quit band if he didn't stop. The principal made the boy apologize and stop bothering me, but I was still really uncomfortable."

Several girls who attended the same high school were frightened of a creepy teacher. Amalia said, "We all know he touches girls whenever he gets a chance and he's always staring at our boobs."

Izzie said that several girls had gone to the principal's office to complain, but nothing had happened. A month after our focus group with these girls, the teacher was arrested for sexually assaulting a student. It made the front page of our local newspaper.

When the focus group girls talked about sex, they were animated and eager to share their stories. Clearly, they had strong feelings about their sexual environments. Jordan said that she and most girls she knew didn't want to date in high school. She told us that she and a boy in her chemistry class had really liked each other, but they decided they were too young to be dating and involved emotionally.

"I don't want to hurt anyone or be hurt," Amalia piped up. "I'm not going to have sex until marriage. That is what the Bible teaches, but I also believe that waiting makes for better relationships."

Many teens are exposed to pornography when they are twelve or thirteen. This is often their first exposure to sex and it's usually a deeply disturbing experience. It changes the way teens think of sex. Boys learn to be hypermasculine, even rough, and to view sexuality from a selfish, misogynistic point of view. Violent pornography breeds violent behavior that is based on simple misunderstanding of what a sexual relationship can be. Our culture couldn't teach teens a less healthy model of sexuality if we tried.

A 2010 study coded for aggression in pornographic videos. It found that almost 88 percent showed verbal or physical aggression against women, according to the article "When Porn Is Sex Ed," written by Maggie Jones for the *New York Times*. In 2011, an American Association of University Women study found that almost 50 percent of college-age girls experienced verbal or physical aggression or blackmail via social media.

Another effect of pornography and online activity is hookup culture. Teens sometimes meet for sex or have sex at parties with people they hardly know. Especially when teens are drunk, there is a high risk for sexual assaults. Sexual assaults and date rapes are still a prominent part of the adolescent experience, today with an added ingredient: social media.

ESPERANZA (18)

"Imagine the worst thing that could ever happen to you, an experience that dehumanizes you and destroys every feeling of happiness you've ever had . . . and then imagine that event was recorded on someone's phone and posted online for everyone you know—and everyone in the world—to see. That's what happened to me."

Esperanza's story could be the lead segment on a morning news show today. A bright, charismatic basketball player from a loving family, at sixteen she suffered a uniquely modern tragedy—the dual misery of a sexual assault and its subsequent broadcast on YouTube.

During a house party over one Halloween weekend, Esperanza tried beer for the first time and wound up drinking several cans; she also joined her girlfriends in multiple rounds of tequila shots. Late in the evening, sleepy from the alcohol, she made her way upstairs and lay down to rest.

Three of her male classmates noted her impaired state and followed her upstairs. There, one boy—wielding his iPhone camera—urged his buddies to rip off Esperanza's Wonder Woman costume and take turns mugging for the camera and groping her in a bedroom decorated with hockey posters. Only when his friends were done did the cameraman— a student council officer and National Merit Scholar—relinquish his phone, so that he could take a turn. The final moments of the iPhone recording idled blurrily on a pile of athletic shoe boxes, accompanied by a soundtrack of Esperanza's groggy protests.

It's hard to know how many people saw the video, which was posted online sometime after midnight, and then made the rounds at the speed of high-school gossip—which is to say, exceedingly quickly. By 10:00 a.m. the following morning—around the time that Esperanza and her parents left the police station, where she had several interviews and an initial counseling session with a victim's advocate—the video had been removed. Regardless, screenshots snapped by concerned classmates, together with the boys' internet histories, enabled police to assemble a solid legal case against the three young men, all of whom Ezzie had considered friends before that night.

"I literally thought I would die. Not that I wanted to kill myself; it was worse than that. I simply thought I would die from grief and humiliation and pain. Like, my body just wouldn't go on."

It took time, but Esperanza's body and heart did heal. With the help of therapy sessions and a break from school until the end of the semester—her teachers and school district allowed her to keep up with her classes from home—she worked through the initial paralysis of grief and emerged into a new state, one of anger and advocacy.

"I gave myself time to wallow. I deserved that," Ezzie said. "For a couple months, I wouldn't even see my best friends. I felt like everyone I knew had betrayed me. Everyone from the party, everyone at my school. Anyone who'd seen it, or heard about it . . . I felt like they were all my enemies."

"Did you spend a lot of time alone?" I wondered aloud.

"I would only see my parents and my little brother, Ernesto. I asked for a kitten and my mom brought home two. I let Ernesto name them and he picked Eyeball and Chugbit." She shrugged and managed a laugh. "Maybe I should have named them myself."

Inspired by Elizabeth Smart, whose book she read several times in the months following her assault, Esperanza decided that she would not let her worst moment define her forever. She joined a group at her church for survivors of violence and slowly invited friends back into her life.

It was a condition of their probation that the boys would not return to Esperanza's school; two transferred across town and one boy's family moved to another state. Despite that, Esperanza chose to enroll in a

Catholic high school for her senior year; she needed the freshest start she could manage in her small midwestern city.

The way we educate teenagers about gender, empathy, and sexuality is one cause of this kind of tragic event. Of course, action is both an individual choice and responsibility, but it can also be the result of lack of skills, miseducation, and ignorance. Assault and harassment are not just individual behaviors but are also cultivated by cultural norms, media, music, and the teaching of others. Historically, women have been taught to protect themselves and boys have been taught to be sexually aggressive; in other words, boys are instructed by our culture to be the people girls need to protect themselves from. Girls are praised for being nice, sweet, and good, while boys are praised for risk-taking, confidence, and manliness.

Unfortunately, today the internet teaches children about sex long before parents are even aware it's an issue. The majority of parents don't know their children have been exposed to pornography, and the rest are likely to underestimate the amount of pornography their kids see. This may be one of the first times in history in which children are more aware than parents of the darkest edges of their shared culture.

Parents need training in pornography literacy and they need to talk to their children *early* about pornography. We recommend that parents talk to girls about what they see online and view with them some of the online sexuality they are exposed to; this can run the gamut from sexualized social media content to straight-up pornography. This exploration with daughters gives parents both information and authority. Daughters, while uncomfortable at first, will be grateful their parents understand what they are dealing with. When parents do this, it's important not to ask for their daughters' personal information, but rather for general information, such as, "Have any of your friends accidentally come across porn online?" or "Can I look at Snapchat with you and see what it's like?" Let girls be the teachers.

Adolescents need sex education, honest discussions of the negative effects of pornography, and lessons in clear sexual communication. Ideally the next generations of boys will be freed from both entitlement and the shame they experience when they feel vulnerable. That shame has led to a great deal of male violence and even to groups such as Incel, whose members target women who have spurned them. By encouraging boys to be strong and express their emotions without fear, we help them become whole people; in turn, our culture will become a safer, kinder, and healthier place.

Boys can benefit from learning that manhood is not about domination and power *over*, but rather about kindness and power *with*. With new definitions of heroism, healthy role models, and new rules for boys, we can promote the growth of healthy, wholesome, bravehearted young men. Boys' education should include honest conversations about relationships and especially about how to handle the ups and downs of misunderstandings, rejection, and conflict.

Empathy and appreciation for others' points of view lead to respectful relationships. However, we know that since the advent of online technology, empathy scores have decreased. Our country could use a thousand new ways to help screenagers acquire empathy and understanding for others. Schools need to make a deep commitment to teaching respect and acceptance for all. In Toronto, this training begins in third grade with a wonderful program designed by Mary Gordon called Roots of Empathy. Mothers take their babies to school on a regular basis in order to teach children about nurturing, development, and individual differences. We'd like to see this program widely available in American schools.

Our policymakers could pass laws limiting the production and distribution of pornography to children. Many countries have controls on access to pornography. We need to explore how to accomplish this combination of censorship, screening, and education, and we recommend research studies to find out what works. Why would we allow a for-profit industry to market terrible lessons to our children without a serious cultural debate about what should be done? We believe in freedom of speech, but we also believe twelve-year-olds shouldn't be exposed to brutal and degrading sexual images.

On the bright side, young women are reacting to our hypermasculine, aggressive culture of misogyny by pushing back with girl power and a fresh interest in feminism. The #MeToo movement, launched and spread by young women from all socioeconomic, ethnic, and cultural backgrounds, has energized and empowered women to come forward about sexual harassment and assault.

Thriving communities, families, and peer groups help teens flourish in all ways, including their sexual development. Values protect girls as do positive role models. We adults can help by sharing our beliefs and insights, being positive role models, and being intentional in what we teach adolescents about sexuality.

Our daughters have always needed time and protected places in which to grow and develop socially, emotionally, intellectually, and physically. They need them now. They need quiet time, talking time, reading time, and laughing time. They need safe places where they can go to learn about themselves and others and where they can take risks and make mistakes without fearing for their lives. They need to be valued for their personhood, not their bodies.

FOURTEEN

What I've Learned from Listening

FOURTEEN-YEAR-OLD BRANDI WAS marched into my office by her mother, a tired-looking landscaper from a nearby town who insisted she come for at least one session. While Brandi rolled her eyes and grunted, her mother explained that Brandi had been sexually assaulted by an alcoholic neighbor.

Brandi interrupted her mother to say that the assault was "no big deal." She said that other problems bothered her a lot more than the stupid neighbor. She complained of her mother's nagging about chores and her father's strict curfews on school nights. She said her biggest problem was that her parents treated her like a little kid and she was sick of it.

I suggested that it might help to talk about the assault. She said, "Maybe some girls, but I'm not the type who spills my guts to just anyone."

I didn't expect Brandi would return for therapy but, to my surprise, she asked for another appointment. The next time she came alone with her stuffed panda. She curled up on my couch and told me the real story.

Shana sat on the couch between her two psychologist parents. She was dressed in jeans and a Jurassic Park T-shirt and looked much younger than her thirteen years. Her father, a big, bearlike man in a tweed jacket, explained that Shana wouldn't go to school. At first, she played sick, but later she just wouldn't go. They couldn't understand why—her grades were good, she had friends, and, as far as they knew, nothing traumatic had happened.

Shana's mother, a tall, confident woman who researched addictions, wondered about depression. Her father had killed himself and one of her brothers had been diagnosed bipolar. She noticed that Shana stayed up nights, slept all day, and had no appetite.

I asked Shana why she wasn't going to school. She thought for a moment and said, "I feel like I'll suffocate or stop breathing if I go in that building."

What is happening in that environment? I wondered.

When I first met clients, I searched for things about them that I could respect and ways in which I could empathize with their situations. Unless I could find these things, it was impossible to help. I didn't believe that analysis of the past was always necessary, but I was interested in the life circumstances of my clients. What were their daily routines? Where did they spend most of their time? How comfortable were they at home and away from home?

I preferred ordinary language rather than academic or pop psychology language. In general, I didn't like victim talk, self-pity, or blaming.

I believed psychotherapy should empower people, help them be more in control of their lives, and enhance their relationships with others.

I tried to be what psychologist Don Meichenbaum calls "a purveyor of hope." I didn't encourage negative labels, diagnoses, or the medical model. I was drawn to therapists who viewed families in more positive ways. I respected Michael White and David Epston, who taught that clients come to therapists with "problem-saturated stories." It was the therapist's job to help clients tell more powerful and optimistic stories about themselves. White and Epston stressed that the client wasn't the problem, the problem was the problem, and they preferred "solution talk" to "problem talk."

White and Epston believed that many families were in trouble because they told problem-saturated stories about themselves. They warned that often mental-health professionals contributed to these stories by asking questions about failure and conflict and ignoring areas in which the person or family was strong and healthy. White and Epston empowered families by helping them tell new stories about their own resilience. They took pathology and shame out of therapy and instead generated optimism, trust, and collaboration.

My general goals for all clients were to increase their authenticity, openness to experience, competence, flexible thinking, and realistic appraisals of their environment. I wanted to help clients see things in new ways and develop richer, more rewarding relationships. Psychotherapy is one of many processes by which people could examine their lives intelligently. It helped people steer, not drift, through life. Examined lives were indeed more worth living.

Working with adolescent girls and their parents pushed me to reexamine my training about families. Much of the writing in our field at the time viewed families as a primary source of pathology and pain. The language of psychology reflected this bias—words about distance were positive (*independence*, *individuation*, and *autonomy*), whereas words about closeness were negative (*dependency* and *enmeshment*). Indeed, psychologists were so prone to pathologize families then that one humorous definition of a normal family was "a family that has not yet been evaluated by a psychologist."

Years ago, Miranda and her parents came to my office. Three months earlier she had been diagnosed as bulimic and referred to a treatment center eight hours away from her hometown. While Miranda was in this program, her parents secured a second mortgage on their home to pay for her treatment. They called her daily and drove to the faraway center every weekend for family therapy. After three months and $120,000, Miranda still had her eating disorder and her parents had been diagnosed as codependent.

My first question to Miranda was, "What did you learn in your stay at the hospital?"

She answered proudly, "That I come from a dysfunctional family."

I thought of her parents; Dad was a physical therapist and Mom a librarian in a small community. They weren't alcoholics or abusive. They took family vacations every summer and put money into a college fund. They played board games, read Miranda bedtime stories, and attended her school programs. And now, with Miranda in trouble, they had incurred enormous debts to pay for her treatment. For all their efforts and money, they had been labeled pathological.

Miranda was quick to agree with this label. It's easy to convince teenagers that their parents don't understand them and that their families are dysfunctional. Almost all the girls I saw in therapy felt that their parents were uniquely unreasonable. When a professional corroborates their opinions, they feel vindicated, at least for the moment. But in the long term, it hurts most teens to undercut their parents.

My goal with Miranda was to restore some balance to her concept of her family. When I suggested that her parents deserved some credit for the efforts they'd made to help her, Miranda seemed confused at first, then visibly relieved.

Psychology's negative view of families began with Freud. He believed that character was fully formed within the family in early childhood. Because of the pathology of the parents, he felt that the character structure of most children was flawed. The goal of analysis was to save the client from the damage done by the family. It was still a common view in the 1990s.

My work with adolescent girls helped me see families in a different light. Most of the parents I saw loved their daughters and wanted what was best for them. They were their daughters' shelter from the storm and their most valuable resource in times of need. I respected their willingness to seek help when they were in over their heads. I was honored that they allowed me, temporarily, to be part of their lives.

Good therapists work to shore up family bonds and to give hope to flagging families. We strive to promote harmony and good humor and to increase tolerance and understanding between family members. Rather than searching for pathological labels, we encourage the development of those qualities that John DeFrain found in all healthy families: appreciation and affection, commitment, positive communication, time together, spiritual well-being, and the ability to cope with stress and crises.

We can help girls discover positive ways to be independent. We need to politicize, not pathologize, families. Of course, each family has its own history, unique problems, and blind spots as well as its own unique strengths and coping mechanisms. A worthy goal is to strengthen families and to give the daughters power and permission to be who they truly are.

Daughters can learn to recognize the forces that shape them and make conscious choices about what they will and won't endure. They need consciousness-raising therapy to help them become whole adults in a culture that encourages them to forever be the object of another's gaze. This kind of therapy teaches them a new form of self-defense.

Even with these general ideas about therapy, I found adolescent girls to be difficult in the 1990s. It was harder to establish relationships with them, and they were more likely to quit therapy without notice. Mistakes with them seemed more serious. They were much less forgiving than adult clients. Their surface behaviors were often designed to hide their deep-structure needs so that it was hard to discern their real issues.

Here's how the work actually went: On the first visit, girls radiated confusion and a lack of confidence. They moved uneasily in their bodies. They flashed me a kaleidoscope of emotions—fear, indifference, sadness, smugness, resignation, and hope. They signaled despair about their sexuality and loathing of their appearance. They were braced for rejection and ridicule. Questions formed and re-formed in their eyes: Did they dare discuss bad grades, bingeing, alcohol, sex, cutting themselves, or suicidal thoughts? Would I be judgmental? Unable to understand? Or, worst of all, would I smugly offer advice?

New clients often smiled at me in a way that signaled, *I want you to like me, but don't expect me to admit it*. With girls this age, relationships are everything. No work can be done in the absence of mutual affection and regard. The first step is helping the girl develop trust—for the therapist, for the therapeutic relationship, and for herself.

Girls have dozens of ways to test the therapist. The best way to pass these tests is to listen. Sincere, total, nonjudgmental listening happens all too rarely in any of our lifetimes. It's best to ask open-ended questions. How do you feel about that? What do you think? What did you learn from this experience?

I learned to resist the urge to offer advice or sympathy. It was more useful to help with sorting—what could my client control? What opinions were hers, what opinions were others'? What was most important in her story of the week? What could be a small move in the right direction?

The most important question for every client was, "Who are you?" I was not as interested in an answer as I was in teaching a process that the girl could use for the rest of her life. The process involved looking within to find a true core of self, acknowledging unique gifts, and accepting all feelings, not just the socially acceptable ones. It included knowing the difference between thinking and feeling, between immediate gratification and long-term goals, and between her own voice and the voices of others. The process included discovering the personal impact of our cultural rules for women and discussing the possibility of breaking those rules and formulating new, healthy guidelines for the self. The process teaches girls to chart a course based on the dictates of their true selves. The process is nonlinear, arduous, and discouraging. It is also joyful, creative, and full of surprises.

I often used the North Star as a metaphor. I told clients, "Imagine that you are in a boat that is being tossed around by the winds of the world. The voices of your parents, your teachers, your friends, and the media can blow you east, then west, then back again. To stay on course, you must follow your own North Star, your sense of who you truly are. Only by orienting north can you chart a course and maintain it, only by orienting north can you keep from being blown all over the sea.

"True freedom has more to do with following the North Star than with going whichever way the wind blows. Sometimes it seems like freedom is blowing with the winds of the day, but that kind of freedom is really an illusion. It turns your boat in circles. Freedom is sailing toward your dreams."

Even in the Midwest, where we had no large lakes, many girls had sailed. And particularly in the Midwest, girls loved images of the sea. They liked the images of stars, sky, roaring waters, and themselves in a small, beautiful boat. But most girls also felt uncertain how to apply this metaphor to their own lives. They asked plaintively, "How do I know who I really am or what I truly want?"

I encouraged girls to find a quiet place and ask themselves the following questions:

How do I feel right now?
What do I think?
What are my values?
How would I describe myself to myself?
How do I see myself in the future?
What kind of work do I like?
What kind of leisure do I like?
When do I feel most myself?
How have I changed since I entered puberty?
What kinds of people do I respect?
How am I similar to and different from my mother?
How am I similar to and different from my father?
What goals do I have for myself as a person?
What are my strengths and weaknesses?
What will I be proud of on my deathbed?

I suggested girls keep diaries and write poetry and autobiographies. Girls this age love to write. Their journals are places where they can be honest and whole. In their writing, they can clarify, conceptualize, and evaluate their experiences. Writing their thoughts and feelings strengthens their sense of self. In their journals, their point of view on the universe matters.

We talked about the disappointments of early adolescence—the betrayals by friends, the discovery that one is not beautiful by cultural standards, the discovery that smartness can be a liability, the pressure to be popular instead of honest and feminine instead of whole. I encouraged girls to search within themselves for their deepest values and beliefs. Once they discovered their own true selves, I encouraged them to trust that self as the source of meaning and direction in their lives. I encouraged them to stay focused and goal-oriented, to steer from their self-defined sense of who they were.

Maturity involves being honest and true to oneself, making decisions based on a conscious internal process, having healthy relationships with others, and developing one's own true gifts. It involves thinking about one's environment and deciding what one will and won't accept.

I encouraged girls to observe our culture with the eyes of an anthropologist in a strange new society. What were the customs and rituals? What kinds of women and men were respected in this culture? How were gender roles assigned? What were sanctions for breaking rules? It was only after girls understand the rules that they can intelligently resist them.

I taught girls certain skills. The first and most basic was centering. I recommended that they find a quiet place where they could sit alone daily for ten to fifteen minutes. I encouraged them to sit in this place, relax their muscles, and breathe deeply. Then they were to focus on their own thoughts and feelings about the day. They were not to judge these thoughts or feelings or even direct them, only to observe them and respect them. They had much to learn from their own internal reactions to their lives.

Another basic skill I explored with my clients was the ability to separate thinking from feeling, something that all healthy adults must be able to do. It is particularly difficult for teenagers because their feelings are so intense. They are given to emotional reasoning, which is the belief that if something felt so, it must be so. In our sessions, as we processed events, I asked, "How do you feel about this? What do you think about this?" Over time, girls learned that these were two different processes and that both should be respected when making a decision.

Making conscious choices is also part of defining a self. I encouraged girls to take responsibility for their own lives. Decisions needed to be made slowly and carefully. Parents, boyfriends, and peers might influence their decisions, but the final decisions were their own. At first the choices seemed small. Who shall I go out with this weekend? Shall I forgive a friend who hurt my feelings? Later the choices included decisions about family, schools, careers, sexuality, and intimate relationships.

Girls can learn to make and enforce boundaries. At the most basic level, this means they decide who touches their bodies. It also means they set limits about their time, their activities, and their companions. They can say, "No, I will not do that." They can make position statements that are firm statements of what they will and will not do.

Closely related to boundary making is the skill of defining relationships. Many girls are "empathy sick." That is, they know more about others' feelings than their own. Girls need to think about what kinds of relationships are in their best interest and to structure their relationships in accord with their ideas.

This is difficult for girls because they are socialized to let others do the defining. Girls are uncomfortable identifying and stating their needs, especially with boys and adults. They worry about not being nice or appearing selfish. However, success in this area is exhilarating. With this skill, they become the object of their own lives again. Once they have experienced the satisfaction of defining relationships, they are eager to continue to develop this skill.

Another vital skill is managing pain. All the craziness in the world comes from people trying to escape suffering. All mixed-up behavior comes from unprocessed pain. People drink, hit their mates and children, gamble, cut themselves with razors, and even kill themselves in an attempt to escape pain. I taught girls to sit with their pain, to listen to it for messages about their lives, to acknowledge and describe it rather than to run from it. They learned to talk about pain and to express it through writing, art, or music. Life in the 1990s was so stressful that all girls benefited from predictable ways to calm themselves. If they didn't have positive ways, such as exercise, reading, hobbies, or meditation, they found negative ways, such as eating, drinking, drugs, or self-harm.

Most girls needed help modulating their emotional reactions. I encouraged them to rate their stress on a one-to-ten scale. I challenged extreme statements. A girl who came in saying "This is the worst day of my life" likely needed help reframing her day's experiences and putting events in perspective.

Girls in the 1990s were socialized to look to the world for praise and rewards, and this kept them other-oriented and reactive. They were also vulnerable to depression if they happened to be in an environment where they were not validated. I taught them to look within themselves for validation. I asked them to record victories and bring them in to share with me. Victories were actions in keeping with their long-term goals. Once a girl learned to validate herself, she was less vulnerable to the world's opinion. She could orient toward true north.

Time travel was another survival skill. All of us have bad days, lost days. Sometimes on those days it helps to go into the past and remember happy times or times when problems were much worse. Sometimes traveling to the future helps. It reminds us that we are on course toward our long-term goals and that certain experiences will not last forever.

Traveling in time is just like traveling in space. Going somewhere different gives girls perspective on the experiences of the day.

Finally, I taught the joys of altruism. Many adolescent girls are self-absorbed. This is not a character flaw, it is a developmental stage. Nonetheless, it makes them unhappy and limits their understanding of the world. I encouraged girls to find some ways to help people on a regular basis. Volunteer work, good deeds for neighbors, and political action help girls move into the larger world. They feel good about their contributions and they rapidly become less self-absorbed.

As a therapist and teacher, I have found adolescent girls quirky, fragile, and changeable. I also have found them to be strong, good-hearted, and insightful. As I write this I remember certain clients: the girl with lemon-colored hair in the rock band Veal who was flunking out of school; the girl in forest-green Doc Martens who wore nose and lip rings; the eighty-eight-pound twirler who felt too fat; and the hearing-impaired girl who insisted on being sexually active to demonstrate her normalcy.

All these girls tried to figure out ways to be independent from their parents and stay emotionally connected to them. They explored ways to achieve and still be loved. They reflected upon moral and meaningful ways to express their sexuality in a culture that bombarded them with plastic, pathetic models of sexuality. They learned to respect themselves in a culture in which attractiveness was women's most defining characteristic. They tried to become adults in a culture in which feminine was defined as docile, weak, and other-oriented.

Working with adolescent girls changed me. I became humbler, more patient and respectful of families, and more aware of the difficulties that they encounter when girls are in adolescence. I became angrier and more determined to help girls fight back and to work for cultural change.

Today, social media has made it even more essential that girls follow their North Stars. It's vital to teach centering, setting and holding boundaries, and how to distinguish thinking from feeling. Girls still benefit from looking at their culture from an anthropological vantage point and they have even more to gain from spending time with people very different from themselves.

If I were in practice today, I would focus some on breathing and the body. I would encourage girls to explore tai chi or yoga and to get massages as often as they see therapists. I would help girls find and localize emotional pain in their bodies. And I would begin and end each session with a moment of silence.

If I were a therapist now, I would conduct more therapy outdoors, walking with clients or sitting in park to talk. I would assign my clients the homework of hiking on quiet trails or looking at the stars. Some teens in urban and suburban areas can't see the stars and don't feel comfortable outdoors. Many teens have never hiked or identified plants and birds. Yet wherever girls live, they can find ways to connect with nature. Learning to be at home in the natural world is a great skill. It soothes, informs, and opens girls' hearts to bliss and grandeur.

I would actively work to connect girls to each other in face-to-face situations. I would encourage them to have sleepovers and form clubs. I would suggest they spend time with older people and children. And I'd advise them and their parents to connect to a community of families who see each other once a week.

Therapists today report that girls still come in because they are fighting with parents or suffering through their parents' divorce. One positive change they note is that being smart is no liability. Girls are more stressed today than in 1994 about getting good grades, but they are proud of them. Many girls struggle with eating disorders or the trauma of assaults. However, the most common presenting problems are self-harm, suicidal thoughts, anxiety attacks, and depression. Often these complaints can be directly linked to social media.

Social media disrupts the most basic of functions, including sleep. Several psychologists have said that the girls they see are all sleep-deprived. This chronic sleep deprivation affects biorhythms and contributes to anxiety and depression. It also increases the risk of obesity.

Therapist Gillian Jenkins believes that the most important advice she can give parents regarding their children's social media use is, "Don't let them sleep with their phones." This approach allows girls to get their much-needed seven hours of sleep and unplug from peers and alerts.

"FOMO is a big deal," Jenkins said. "Although I think it is less FOMO than some sort of fear of not measuring up." In her experience, constant comparison is girls' biggest problem; the sheer volume and accessibility of photos and information is staggering, and a lot of unhealthy thinking is supported by smartphones.

All the therapists we interviewed for this update commented on their clients' isolation. Many girls almost never went out with friends. They liked staying home on weekends watching Netflix and texting their friends. Therapists said that girls often chose to deal with their stress with digital distractions rather than by talking to parents or going out with friends.

"Girls' use of social media is motivated by legitimate goals, such as desire for community and curiosity, but somehow these goals are not really met," one therapist said. "There is a real loneliness in girls today, much deeper than when we were teenagers."

Therapists have observed that social media makes girls dependent on superficial feedback for self-worth. They encourage girls to come up with their own views of themselves, regardless of social media. They help girls learn to say, "Facebook is not about the real me."

One therapist told me that with social media, girls have no sense of no context, no room for nuance, and no idea about subtleties, sarcasm, or humor. She said, "Girls get their feelings hurt all the time." She urges girls to wait for half an hour before responding to hurtful messages. She hopes they would consider taking the high road, assume positive intent, and remember that whatever they sent out could become a screenshot and passed around.

Clearly, therapists now spend a great deal of time discussing social media. They help girls decide how much time each day to spend on devices and offer suggestions for meeting their goals. One girl had the idea of asking all her friends to agree to not text after 10:00 at night. Then no one would feel left out. Another girl decided to turn off her phone when she was with her friends. Still another approached things differently. She simply set daily activity goals, such as playing basketball or calling her grandmother. Then, at least sometimes, she wouldn't be on her phone.

Many therapists look at sites during sessions. Their clients show them great stories, fan fiction, or poetry. They encourage parents to do the same. By ignoring the world of websites and social media, some parents are missing out on the opportunity for great conversations with their daughters.

At the same time that therapists help girls manage their devices, they empathize with how hard it is to control use and they encourage self-compassion. They know how much adults struggle with many of the same issues. One common recommendation is that everyone in the family put their phones in a lockbox at a certain time of night and keep them there until after breakfast.

Therapists believe in the essential beauty and promise of all adolescent girls. As one compassionate psychologist told me, "I have faith in both the immensity and resilience of the human heart."

FIFTEEN

Let a Thousand Flowers Bloom

JUNE (27)

The morning we met in my office in the 1990s, June had worked a double shift at the Kawasaki plant, gone out for breakfast, and driven across town. June was big-boned with a round, pockmarked face. She wore her hair short and was dressed in a gray sweat suit. She sank into my couch and propped one foot up on the coffee table.

June's language was personal, precise, and earthy. She talked about herself softly and carefully as if psychotherapy, like dentistry, might hurt.

"I'm here because I am dating someone for the first time in my life," she explained. "I'm twenty-seven and I've never been kissed. I thought I might need some coaching."

She'd been at Kawasaki for ten years. Her closest friend worked next to her on the assembly line. Dixie was a single parent, and June helped her with her kids. She pulled out their school pictures to show me and said they called her Aunt June.

"They're real good kids once you get to know them," she said.

June had met Marty at work too. He was the union representative for her group of workers. The last three Saturday nights he had dropped by with a pizza and a video. Last Saturday night he put his arm around June. That's when she decided to call me.

I asked her about her family and June sighed. "I was afraid you would bring them up."

"We can wait," I say gently.

"I might as well get it out," she said. "After you hear about my teenage years, you'll understand why I haven't dated much."

June's father was a farm laborer who "never had much to do with me." Her mother was a cook at a rest home. "She was hardworking and fun. She'd bring me treats from the rest home—cookies and crafts that the residents made for me. She showed them my pictures and kept them posted on my activities. Everyone at the home loved her."

June paused and looked at me. "She died at the start of my freshman year in high school. It was an awful time to lose her. I had just started my period. I was clumsy and had bad acne. I had been chubby but then I got fat. I was totally alone."

June blew her nose before continuing. "The year Mom died, I watched the Miss America pageant. I stared at those thin, perfect girls and knew I would never be like that. I had no looks and no talents. Only my mom had loved me as I was. I thought about giving up."

She rubbed her forehead as if to erase some memories too painful to consider. "I don't know how I made it through that year. Dad was never home. I had hardly any clothes. I did what housework and cooking was done and that was precious little. Dad almost never gave me money for groceries. I was fat and hungry at the same time."

I asked her about the kids at school. "They were terrible. Not so much mean as totally indifferent. I didn't exist for them. I was too ugly and too sad to even be part of the class. I ate by myself and walked to and from school alone. No one would be my lab partner."

She rubbed her face and continued, "One time a boy approached me in the cafeteria, in front of all the other kids, and asked me to go to a football game. I was such a goof that I thought he meant it. I thought maybe he could see past my appearance and like the real me. So, I said sure, if I could get Dad's permission. Then he started laughing. His buddies all whooped it up too. They'd dared him to do it for a joke. He collected ten bucks for just asking me out."

June sighed. "After that I steered clear of boys."

Her father married Mercene a year after June's mother died. They took a honeymoon trip to Sun City and brought June salt-and-pepper shakers for her hope chest.

"By then I had no hope," she said flatly. "My stepmother was tight with money. Once I cut my foot pretty badly when I was hoeing beans. She wouldn't pay for the doctor. I still limp a little because of that. She only let me wash my hair once a week. I needed to wash it daily it was so greasy, but she didn't want to pay for the water. My teeth were crooked and the school recommended braces. Mercene said, 'I've heard that can cost a thousand dollars. No way we'll spend that kind of money for straight teeth.'"

I worked hard to remain neutral as June talked, and June herself displayed no anger. She continued matter-of-factly, "I was the black sheep. Once my stepbrother asked me why I lived with his family."

I asked how she survived those years when she was rejected at home and at school.

"I thought about my mother and how she would have wanted me to behave. I decided that other people's bad behavior was no excuse for mine. I would do the best I could. At bedtime I talked to Mom in heaven. I always tried to have something I was proud of to report to her. I knew she had loved me and that helped me know I was lovable even though the people around me were too blind to see it."

She wiped her face with a handkerchief. "At the time I desperately wanted friends, but I learned to take care of myself. I got so that other people's rejection didn't faze me. I developed my own ideas about right and wrong.

"After high school my life really improved. I started working at Kawasaki. Immediately I felt more accepted. I worked hard and people noticed. Women invited me to eat with them. The men joked around with me. My supervisor took an interest in me. He encouraged me to get my teeth worked on and have my foot evaluated. I wear a brace now."

June smiled when she spoke of work. "I have a Halloween party every year for all the workers in my area. Fridays I bowl on the union team. I've earned merit raises every year I've worked there, so I make good money.

"I've forgiven Dad and Mercene. I'm happy, so what is there to be angry about now? I am happier than they are. I try to do something for them every weekend. I take over a pie or mow their yard."

I asked how she gets along with her father. "Dad can't forgive me for being fat. He really wanted a beautiful daughter."

I thought of June's life. She has a spirit as delicate and strong as a spiderweb. She is gifted at forgiving and loving. Because she is unattractive by our cultural standards, she has been devalued by many, including her own father. But somehow she has managed to survive and even thrive through all this adversity. She reminded me of those succulent desert flowers that remain dormant for so many seasons and then bloom lavishly when there is a smattering of rain.

I said to her, "Your father has missed an opportunity to love someone who is marvelous."

We talked about Marty. June laughed and described him as a bulky man who was prematurely balding.

"His looks don't matter." She shrugged. "I know how hard he works and that he doesn't put anyone down. He's not a complainer."

I suggested that daily she imagine herself successfully kissing him. I also encouraged her to keep her expectations for that first kiss low.

"Bells may not ring and the sky may not light up." I quoted Georgia O'Keeffe, totally out of context, "Nobody's good at the beginning."

I pointed out that the relationship was going well. Physical affection was only a small part of a relationship. She was already gifted at loving and forgiving, which were much more important qualities. I predicted that kissing would be easy once she was ready.

When I saw June again, she reported that kissing was great. She asked me if I thought she needed more therapy.

"No," I said. "I think you could teach me some lessons about strength through adversity and the importance of forgiveness."

June is a good example of someone who, with almost no luck at all, fashioned a good life for herself. Almost all our psychological theories would predict that June would turn out badly. But adversity built her character. What saved her was her deep awareness of her mother's love. Even though her mother was dead, June felt her mother's spirit was with her. That enabled her to feel valued at a time when she was rejected by everyone. June was determined to live in a way that would make her mother proud.

June had the gift for appreciating what was good in her life. Her life, which might strike some people as difficult or dull, was rich and rewarding. She had friends, money, a boyfriend, and the respect of her peers. She had no bitterness or anger because she was happy. She was a desert flower opening to the rain.

Early adolescence is when many of the battles for the self are won and lost. These are hard fights, and the losses and victories determine to a great extent the quality of women's future lives. While young women are in the midst of these battles, none of them look terribly strong. Surface behaviors reveal little of the deep struggles that are battles to hold on to true selves.

Alice Miller believed that strength in adolescence requires an acknowledgment of all parts of the self, not just the socially acceptable ones. Simone de Beauvoir thought that strength implies remaining the subject of one's life and resisting the cultural pressure to become the object of male experience. Carol Gilligan referred to resilience as "speaking in one's own voice," and bell hooks called it "talking back." Resistance meant vigilance in protecting one's own spirit from the forces that would break it.

Margaret Mead defined strength as valuing all those parts of the self whether or not they were valued by the culture. She encouraged the survival of the ten-year-old androgynous self that was competent and connected, and she emphasized the importance of developing innate potentialities and fighting efforts to limit value.

In America in the 1990s, even the strongest girls keeled over in adolescence. The lessons were too difficult and the learning curve too steep for smooth early mastery. Strong girls managed to hold on to some sense of themselves in the high winds. Often, they had a strong sense of place that gave them roots. Sometimes they identified with an ethnic group in a way that gave them pride and focus, or they viewed themselves as being an integral part of a community. Their sense of belonging preserved their identity when it was battered by the winds of adolescence.

Strong girls then and now know who they are and value themselves as multifaceted people. They have identities that hold up well under pressure. Talent allows girls some continuity between past childhood and current adolescent lives. Being genuinely useful also gives girls something to hold on to. Girls who care for ill parents or who help the disadvantaged have a hedge against the pain of adolescence.

Almost all girls today manage to stay close to their families and maintain some family loyalty. Even if they come from problem families, they usually have someone in the family whom they love and trust. Through all the chaos of adolescence, they keep the faith with this person.

Yet most girls have difficulty with their families. All girls do some distancing as part of their individuation process but healthy girls know that their parents love them and stay connected in important ways. They keep talking and seeking contact. Even as they argue with their parents, a part of them remains loyal and connected to them.

Often strong girls are aware that they're being pressured to act in ways that aren't good for them. The premature sexualization of their lives makes them nervous. They may be involved in cliques, but a part of them hates the snobbishness and actively resists hurting other girls.

It helps girls to believe in causes or interests larger than their own lives. Girls who have some special passions can call on something that is greater than their experiences in the halls of junior highs. Often their passions can give them some perspective and sustain them through the toughest times. Strong girls manage to avoid heavy alcohol or drug use and deal with pain in more adaptive ways. Often, they have healthy stress-relieving habits such as reading, running, or playing the piano.

In *Smart Girls, Gifted Women*, Barbara Kerr explored the experiences of girls who grew into strong women, and she found that they had in common time by themselves, the ability to fall in love with an idea, a refusal to acknowledge gender limitations, and what she called "protective coating." None of them were popular as adolescents and most stayed separate from their peers, not by choice, but because they were rejected. Ironically, this very rejection gave them a protected space in which they could develop their uniqueness.

Many strong girls have similar stories: They were socially isolated and rejected by peers. Their strength was a threat and they were punished for being different. Girls who were unattractive or who didn't worry about their appearance were scorned. This isolation was often a blessing because it allowed girls to develop a strong sense of self. Girls who were isolated often emerged from adolescence more independent and self-sufficient than girls who had been accepted by others.

Strong girls may protect themselves by being quiet and guarded so that their rebellion is known by only a few trusted others. They may be cranky and irascible and keep critics at a distance so that only people who love them know what they are up to. They may have the knack of shrugging off the opinions of others or they may use humor to deflect the hostility that comes their way.

Many girls may protect themselves by creating safe spaces for themselves. These can be created by books, interests, families, churches, and passions such as music or art. Girls who grow up adrift in mass culture with little protective coating and no private territory are the most vulnerable. This business of protected space is complicated, however. Too much protection leads to the "princess and the pea syndrome," girls who are hothouse flowers unable to withstand stress. Too little protection often leads to addictions and self-destructive behaviors. The same stresses that help some girls grow, cripple others.

All lives have ups and downs. For most women, early adolescence is a big dip down. Strong girls, like all girls, do crazy things in junior high. They feel unstable and out of control. It's important to look beyond surface behavior to understand what's happening. For example, a girl can be depressed in junior high because she's bright enough to recognize our girl-poisoning culture and to feel defeated by it.

CAROLINE (17)

Caroline asked to interview me for her high-school psychology class. I agreed, provided we could trade interviews. Caroline had recently moved to town from Alabama, and I was interested in talking to girls from other states. We met at my house and Caroline interviewed me first. I was struck by her poise and sensitivity. Dressed in a dark blue skirt-and-sweater outfit, she looked older than her seventeen years. She could have been a college student in a journalism class.

Caroline interviewed me, then we jokingly traded chairs and switched roles. I asked her about her family. Her father was a military man who was a drinker and womanizer. He considered Caroline ugly and lazy. He whipped her for the smallest mistakes. Once when he was calling her names in front of his buddies, one of them told him to stop. Usually, though, his friends were too drunk or too insensitive to care when he belittled his daughter. Caroline said of her father, "He would have been a good horse trainer. He had lots of ways to break a person's spirit."

She continued, "Fortunately, he wasn't around all that much. When he was around, I'd grab a book and head for my room. Mom couldn't get away from him and he destroyed her."

I asked about the abuse. "It happened at night after he'd been out drinking. He'd stumble in, slamming doors and cursing. Mom yelled at him and he called her names. Then he hit her and she cried. Later she came to my bed for the night. I stopped the abuse when I was twelve. I called the cops on him."

I must have betrayed my emotions because Caroline said, "It wasn't as bad as you think. I loved school. We moved a lot and I went to all kinds of schools—parochial, military, and integrated public schools. But wherever I went, I was the best student.

"I was always the teacher's pet. The kids liked me too. I sang, danced, played sports, was good at art. I could joke my way into any crowd. Even though my home life was hell, I had high self-esteem from all the praise I got at school.

"No one at school knew what my home life was like," Caroline continued. "I pretended my parents had rules for me, that I had birthday parties and dental appointments. When we had school plays, I explained that my parents were out of town on business. I was doing so well it was easy to fool the teachers."

She settled back into the couch. "My sixth-grade year my dad brought a girlfriend home and Mom tried to kill herself. I had to pull the gun away from her. But I was in a good school in Boston and I loved my teacher. She arranged for singing lessons and she let me sing lead in the school musical. I maybe should have felt worse about my family, but I didn't. I was living my own life."

Caroline paused, and when she continued, the happiness had vanished from her voice. "The next year my parents divorced and Mom and I moved to the south to live with her parents. Everything good in my life stopped happening.

"The schools were horrible. Everyone with money went to private schools, and the public schools were broke. My social studies text was twenty years old, and our science labs didn't have microscopes. Once I had to go home and change clothes because I'd fallen in human poop in the schoolyard. Another time I was cut by a broken beer bottle.

"That school sent us the message that we were nothing, we were dirt. Most of my classmates bought it. They gave up their dreams and planned to get factory jobs as soon as they could quit school.

"I was an outsider, a northerner. I pretty much quit talking for a while.

"Meanwhile, my home life was miserable, Mom was a permanent invalid. My grandparents were well-meaning, but they didn't know how to help."

"What saved you?" I asked.

She dug into her purse and pulled out a picture. "Sandra saved me, or rather we saved each other. I met her early in my eighth-grade year.

She sat beside me in English. I noticed that she knew the answers to the teacher's questions. One day I asked her if she'd like to meet for an ice cream after school.

"Right from the first we understood each other. Sandra's dad was an alcoholic too. Her mother worked at the box factory and we had both raised ourselves.

"By the end of that first meeting we agreed to fight the system together. We promised each other we wouldn't do drugs or get pregnant. I'd traveled with my parents and I knew there were better places to be. Sandra loved to hear me talk about those places."

Caroline put Sandra's picture away. "We pushed each other to achieve. We knew that our one way out was education. We memorized vocabulary words. We asked for a list of the classics from a librarian and read those books. We went to every free lecture we could. We were determined. By tenth grade, Sandra and I were straight-A students. We sang and were in the student government. We had transcripts full of activities that showed we were well rounded. Then last year we moved here."

"How did that happen?"

"Sandra's aunt and uncle said she could move in with them and have her senior year at a good school. She wouldn't come without me. We share a bedroom. We're closer than sisters."

Since Caroline was a young girl, she had been determined to be the best at whatever she did. She had remarkable survival skills. Her experiences left her responsible, achievement oriented, and able to take care of herself in any situation.

Often in stories of teenage girls, the relationships between girls were ugly and destructive. Caroline's story was different. She and Sandra helped each other survive and eventually escape their stormy environments.

Both June and Caroline lacked what we call today "emotionally available parents." June's mother was dead and her father insensitive. Caroline's father was absent and her mother was mentally and physically ill. This absence of parental support made it clear that, from the beginning, they had only themselves to depend on for happiness. That's a lesson all girls must learn.

Both girls had a focus that carried them beyond the painful days in junior high. June wanted to behave in a way that made her mother proud, and Caroline wanted to make something of herself academically. Even in their darkest times, they were preparing in their own ways for brighter futures.

MARIA (16)

Maria was late to our meeting at the coffeehouse. She rushed breathless over to my table and plopped her book bag and sheaf of flyers on the spare seat. Maria was a tall young woman with straight dark hair and serious eyes. She explained that her VW, with its two hundred thousand miles and painted flowers, had just died.

I bought us Italian sodas. As Maria drank hers, she told me about the previous day's march against the death penalty. Her talk reminded me of my friends from the '60s and I couldn't resist asking her if she was a Grateful Dead fan. She loved the Dead, with their wild abandonment and their community of fans. Maria wished she had been a teen in the '60s when people were idealistic and free. She hated corporate America and our town's emphasis on money.

Maria was the second child in a Hispanic family. Her father was a social worker and her mother a landscaper. She had a brother, Alberto, two years older than she, and two younger sisters. Both her paternal and maternal grandparents lived in town and Maria spent time with them almost daily. "Family first" was the family motto.

Maria's family had a long tradition of social activism. In the late 1960s, her maternal grandparents had fled for their lives from El Salvador. Her great-uncle had been shot for his political activities. Her mother was an ardent feminist and active in her Catholic church's social justice committee. Maria said, "All of us were raised with the idea that we should work to make our society a better place. No one gets away with being indifferent. Even Alberto, who is a skateboarder, helps with sanctuary work."

Maria felt especially close to Alberto. As children they rarely fought. "He could make anything out of cardboard. We played all kinds of games that he invented," Maria said. "We made movies together and sang duets. He let me play with his friends. I was never left behind."

Maria sipped her drink. "I loved elementary school. Every now and then I'd be called a racist name, but Alberto was there to protect me. Until fourth grade my class was close. That's when cliques formed. My friends got together for cheerleading practice and I wasn't asked to join them."

She pushed her hair out of her eyes. "I wanted to fit in. I desperately tried to raise my coolness quotient. I even bought some Guess jeans, but they didn't help. The problem was my skin color.

"Mom encouraged me to fight the pressure to be a certain way. She hated racism and elitism. Later I did fight, but in sixth grade I was a chicken."

I asked her about junior high.

"The first day was awful," Maria said. "It was a big school and I kept getting lost. I ripped my shorts in gym, and I got called racist names in typing class. I came home sobbing."

She frowned at the memories. "My family said I'd make friends quickly, but I didn't. I didn't like most of the kids. The girls tried to hurt each other and their talk drove me crazy. I spent time with my brother and his friends."

She ran her finger around the rim of her cup. "I was lonely and mixed up for a while. I thought there must be something wrong with me, but Alberto and my mom kept saying it wasn't me. They talked me into joining Amnesty International so I'd have an outside interest.

"I got interested, all right." She smiled. "The people were great. Their friendship saved me in junior high.

"In Girl Scouts, we had a unit on self-esteem. I took it seriously. I tacked up a list of positives about myself on the mirror. I asked myself at the end of each day what I had done that I felt proud of. That work on self-esteem helped me in junior high."

Maria continued, "In high school I found 'my people.' I started a chapter of Amnesty International."

"Are the kids at high school different?"

"Alberto is there and I like his friends. Some of the girls seem trustworthy. My school is the biggest school in town and I'm meeting more Hispanics and African Americans."

"Have you dated?"

"Because of Alberto, I have high expectations," she continued. "I don't like macho guys. I like guys who can talk about their feelings and who respect women. In high school, not that many guys are that way."

Some friends of Maria's came in and she waved at them. "Another thing I don't like is competition. I love sports, but not competitive sports. Alberto's the same way. I think we learned that from our folks. They both try to set things up so that everyone wins in our family."

When I asked about the future, Maria said, "I'm dreading Alberto's graduation this year. He plans to go to Iowa and study writing. I'll feel lost without him. Someday I want to be a political scientist. I am excited about graduation, but also scared.

"I will miss seeing my grandparents every day. They have helped me through things and now they are getting old. One of my sisters starts junior high the year I go to college. I wish I could help her through it."

I thanked Maria for our interview and told her I thought her "coolness quotient" was quite high. She rolled her eyes and laughed. When I said good-bye, Maria handed me a flyer for the protest against the situation in the Balkans and offered, "Maybe you would be interested in this."

The preceding accounts tell the stories of three fighters: June, Caroline, and Maria. June fought back by talking to her mother's memory. Caroline fought her way out of an environment that could easily have trapped her forever. Maria forged her own self-definition independent of peer pressure. Properly faced, adversity builds character.

Unlike Ophelia, most girls recover from early adolescence. It's not a fatal disease, but an acute condition that disappears with growth and maturity. While it's happening, nobody looks strong. Even the girls in this chapter were miserable in junior high. From the vantage point of high school, they can tell their stories, but in junior high they had no perspective. That is impossible in the midst of a hurricane.

No girls escape the hurricane. The winds are simply too overpowering. Fortunately, by late high school, the winds of the hurricane are dying down and trees begin to right themselves. Girls calm down. Girls' thinking matures and their feelings stabilize. Their friends become kinder and more dependable. They make peace with their parents. Their judgment has improved and they are less self-absorbed.

The resisters and fighters survive. When it's storming, it feels like the storm will never end, but the hurricane eventually does end and the sun comes out again.

Today, girls are more sheltered than were girls in 1994. They aren't as likely to be exposed to drunk driving, sexual assault, or teen pregnancy. On the other hand, some girls today—like June and Caroline—struggle to make good choices in tough situations. Somehow, in spite of everything, they manage to be true to themselves and kind to others.

Other girls are quiet heroes who care for ill family members, work long hours to financially support their families, or counsel other teens through their problems. Still others are engaged in regular acts of kindness. Amalia visits a blind neighbor every day and reads to her. Maddie watches children on Sundays at her church. Jada adopts and rehabilitates abandoned animals whenever she finds one.

Today we are seeing a resurgence of girl activists. Not since the 1960s have so many girls been engaged in protests, campaigns, and advocacy work. In the wake of police shootings of unarmed blacks, anti-Muslim crimes, school shootings, and the demonization of refugees and immigrants, girls are organizing for Black Lives Matter, Sí Se Puede, and gun control. The students of Marjory Stoneman Douglas High School in Florida are examples of this powerful new activism. Malala Yousafzai, an activist for girl's rights in Pakistan and around the world and winner of the Nobel Peace Prize, has inspired many girls globally to work for human rights. Perhaps more than any time in modern history, girls are embracing their unique perspectives and advocating for change and equality.

GREER (16)

"I was allowed to do whatever I wanted at home—paint my nails, wear dresses—but when we went out, I would be 'Boy Greer.' That worked for a long time."

Greer and I met over Skype on Christmas Eve. Newly sixteen, with glossy curls and flawless eye makeup, Greer projected confidence from every pore. She appeared to be the quintessential adolescent fashionista; she was also born biologically male.

"Was this in elementary school? Did you already *know* when you were that young?"

"I didn't know what I knew." Greer laughed. "From a young age, I was drawn to girl stuff. Other boys liked sports and play-fighting and I wanted nothing to do with that. Even in preschool, I always dressed up as princesses.

"My mom was a great problem solver. It was her idea that I could be myself at home, but then we'd keep things more subdued outside the house. But by the time I started to go through puberty, I was ready to transition, and my parents were supportive of my decision."

Greer decided to fully transition to living as a female during the summer between middle school and high school. That way, she reasoned, people could get their gossip out over the summer instead of during the school year. Her instincts turned out to be prescient.

"How was your first day of high school?" I asked.

"Honestly, it was easy," she replied. "Only the principal and my guidance counselor knew, and of course, my close friends. But I started high school as a girl and that's how I'm known. I'm passable, so I had no trouble using the girls' bathroom. I felt an immediate weight lift off my shoulders because I was finally *myself.*"

"And your parents were by your side through everything?"

"More than that, they embraced who I am. I think they knew before I did; growing up, once in a while my mom would ask me if I thought I was a girl. She has always loved me for who I am. Same with my dad. Once I told him that I wanted to learn to wear makeup, and that weekend he took me to CVS and bought me everything I needed."

Greer tossed her hair out of her eyes and continued, "By the time I announced I was ready to transition, my parents were expecting it. I didn't feel nervous; it wasn't like any of us were bracing for impact. It was a calm conversation.

"I know I'm lucky. Most transgender people struggle coming out to their families and friends. But I've still had terrible experiences. At a dance performance, I was denied access to the girls' changing room and was forced to change in the guys' locker room. That was really terrible and scary. But that bad experience gave me perspective, so ultimately it was good for me."

"Do you feel a responsibility to represent and support other transgendered people?" I asked.

"I want to understand what other people in my community are going through. I volunteer at a center for LGBTQ youth, but I don't view myself as an activist, just a normal girl. I do carry the term *transgender* with pride, but I don't always want to lead with that."

"What does transitioning look like in terms of your physiological growth and development?"

"Two weeks after I came out as trans, I started puberty blockers," Greer explained. "I was on the cusp, and I didn't want to start puberty and get an Adam's apple or a deep voice. We didn't take this decision lightly; my parents and I did our research and discussed all of my options. Honestly, I'm so lucky I started then; it made the physical transition much easier. A month ago, I started estrogen. It's made my voice higher, but it has also made me more moody and emotional."

Greer laughed. "The mood swings are definitely not my favorite aspect of womanhood." She straightened her shoulders. "Of course, I want to have *the* surgery. It'll make me feel more complete as a woman."

"Now that you're fully living as a girl, do you notice that you're treated differently?"

"Mostly in the realm of dating," Greer replied. "I get a lot of attention from guys, and then when I tell them, they tend to lose the romantic interest. I suppose that's not surprising. Sometimes they want to stay friends or sometimes they run in the other direction. I'm like any other girl; when guys aren't interested in me, it takes a toll on my confidence. Once I dated a guy whose parents wouldn't let me step in their house because I was trans. Sometimes it's hard to decipher who really cares about me and who's into me for the novelty."

"Who do you turn to for support?"

"I have an amazing circle of friends," Greer replied, smiling. "We're all ethnically diverse, gay and straight and bi. I want to surround myself with people different from me and learn from them."

"How else are you similar to your peers?" I asked.

"It doesn't matter who you are, if you're a teenage girl, you have body issues." Greer sighed. "I'm naturally slender, so people assume I'm anorexic. Last week, a customer at my job said, 'You're so skinny,' and gave me a $20 tip to go buy a sandwich. Girls say they wish they were skinny like me, and I feel like I'm feeding the stereotype that pretty is skinny. I hate that.

"I believe we should embrace all body types. I've had promoters of diet products reach out over Instagram admiring my figure and offering to pay me for product endorsements. But pills and tea aren't what made me skinny. My attitude is, if you believe you're pretty, you're pretty. It will show in your aura."

I chuckled at her use of aura, but at the same time I understood: Greer did radiate an aura . . . of strength, confidence, and her own unique beauty.

"What are you proudest of?" I asked.

"My confidence skyrocketed when I transitioned," Greer said thoughtfully. "I've taken the built-up years of not being me and fully embraced my true girl self. I speak my mind. I stand up for myself and others. It really gives me hope, because when other girls accept themselves like I do, we can take all that energy and launch the Industrial Revolution of girl power."

Social media has contributed to a skyrocketing number of girl activists. Twitter and Facebook can be used to inform, organize groups, plan events, and spread the word about meetups and peaceful protests. These and other sites allow teens to stay connected to one another and build upon one another's successes.

Meantime, a new cadre of (s)heroes is stepping up to support girls during adolescence and beyond. Singer P!nk speaks out about body image and confidence. Alessia Cara's song "Scars to Your Beautiful" has become an anthem for body positivity. Amy Poehler's Smart Girls campaign, model Ashley Graham's candor about the fashion industry, Jameela Jamil's "iWeigh" Instagram presence, Beyoncé's *Lemonade* album, and actress Kristen Bell's public conversations about depression and anxiety are all examples of a new generation of activist celebrities in action.

While public figures' embrace of social change is crucial for our culture, plenty of girls are blazing their own trails without any fanfare or celebrity. Megan and Ina are shining examples of activism as a means of self-empowerment and global change.

MEGAN (16)

"Right after the Parkland shooting, I heard David Hogg and Sarah Chadwick giving interviews. I realized that a lot of students at my school feel like they do but don't have a platform. I felt they were calling us to action," Megan told me over the phone, a couple months after the highly publicized 2018 school shooting at Marjory Stoneman Douglas High School in Parkland, Florida.

A student at Firestone High, a predominantly black school in Akron, Ohio—and the best school in the district, in her opinion—Megan has long held an interest in politics. A member of student council and an advanced placement government student, she spent only a few days digesting the events in Parkland before she approached her favorite teacher with an idea.

"I said, 'Let's have a meeting. I want to organize our students to protest school shootings,'" Megan explained. "I posted the meeting announcement on social media and asked a really popular kid to post it on his Snapchat.

"We filled a room with thirty or forty people with just one day of planning," she noted with pride. At that initial gathering, Megan and other students created a safe space in which students could talk about their fears and anger, before moving into a discussion about goals for their new group. In short order, the students decided to stage a walkout in solidarity with the Parkland students and the nascent #NeverAgain and March for Our Lives movements.

"We didn't have a structure; we weren't yet a formal club. A senior class officer and I worked hard for a month. We tried to delegate to other people but we were on such a short timeline; a month wasn't a lot of time to prepare. I was at school from 7 a.m. to 6 p.m. working with my teacher and our leadership group. My mom made a spreadsheet for gathering contact information because I wanted this to go beyond the walkout. I didn't want this to be a one-and-done situation."

Initially, Megan and her peers experienced some pushback from administrators. Her principal, while supportive, declared that any students who participated in the walkout would be suspended from school for three days. The activists lost a number of students from their group after that information became public, but a number of students committed to proceeding with the walkout.

By now, planning meetings were standing room only. The local school board announced that it was up to the discretion of individual administrators to determine how to manage walkouts at their schools. Following that decree, Firestone's principal lifted the threat of suspensions.

"The day came, and we remained outside for just over seventeen minutes," Megan said. "Everyone was peaceful and respectful. Some students gave speeches, some read poems, and we held a moment of silence for Parkland students."

The event received positive coverage from the local media and positive feedback from the school board and principal. Approximately five hundred Firestone students walked out.

Since then, Megan and her peers have become an official school group, the Student Coalition Against Violence. She and several others testified before the Akron Board of Education with a list of demands. They requested a written statement from the board saying it doesn't support arming teachers with guns; increased access to school counselors; increased training programs for emergency situations that school staff attend regularly, and specific escape plans for each room in the school.

"We the students do not have all the answers, yet the same can be said for the adults. We must find the answers together," Megan noted in her remarks before the board. "With your help, we can change this situation and the fear that we face."

As winter melted into spring, Firestone students spoke at city and state marches, and Megan and several friends traveled to Washington, DC, for April 2018's March for Our Lives.

"It was inspiring beyond belief," Megan said. "We stood next to some Parkland survivors. They knew the murdered kids, that was their story. It was amazing."

The Student Coalition Against Violence continues to organize around a broad range of issues. They regularly write letters to their elected officials. They planned a Positivity Day for the entire student body, featuring positive notes and activities designed to get diverse groups of students talking to one another.

"I've always been outspoken about what I believe. I was political, but maybe not an activist," Megan said. "I didn't use that word as much before March for Our Lives happened. But then Parkland survivors stood up and said 'Enough is enough.'

"All of our group have parents who have raised us to stand up for what we believe in. I think that's why adults are listening to us now. We're realizing that even if we aren't getting very far with our national government, we can affect things locally."

She continued, "You have to understand, Columbine happened nineteen years ago, and I'm sixteen. I've done lockdown drills for my whole life. I've always gone to school and thought, 'What if?' We're perpetually in that state of fear eight hours a day, five days a week. When Parkland happened, all of us knew what the Parkland students were going through. We knew what they meant when they said that there can't be even one more school shooting.

"One thing I want to mention is that social media has a bad

reputation. Parents think it's ruining our generation and sucking our time away. But if you look at the #NeverAgain movement, social media is how we make things happen. It's how we keep our classmates updated and communicate with other students around the country."

Now that she's found her calling, Megan isn't looking back. Her reasons are political and they are also personal.

"My dad just had my new baby sister," she told me, "and that motivates me even more. She is three months old. I want her to grow up into a safer culture."

INA (17)

"I was harassed during my first years of high school. I was heavily involved in many academic activities—which had more boys than girls—and that unfortunately created problems. The fact that I was successful in those activities affected how I was treated within those groups. I'd hear from my team members that I shouldn't be doing them because I was a girl, or that I was only succeeding because 'people felt bad for me.'

"The comments progressed to social media, and most were centered around the theme of gender; they were triggered by the fact that I was a girl. This and my other past experiences inspired me to start this project."

Ina is a tour de force in her hometown of Lincoln, Nebraska, and is a shining example of a young woman empowering herself by empowering others.

"Hostile gossip about me spread to different schools and even my parents, friends, and teachers heard it. I hit my breaking point," Ina told me as she commuted from her high school to the class she was taking at the local university. "My father said, 'You're fortunate to have a strong family, a support network, and the resources needed to get you through such situations. Many girls and boys don't; you need to do something about it.'"

And she did. Ina came up with an idea for a program that would help young people—especially girls—contend with gender-based discrimination and bullying. She researched how and why this bullying occurs and learned that gender-based stereotypes develop among children as young as six.

"I had the idea of initiating a program that would combat these stereotypes when they first manifest," Ina explained. "Many programs focus on older youth who are already empowered and therefore don't affect the people who struggle with these issues the most. I was confident that if we started empowerment programs at elementary and middle schools, we could help teach kids that these stereotypes shouldn't affect how they live their lives. I want all youth to be empowered to dream and know that they have the capability to achieve what matters to them."

When Ina met with the director of secondary education at her school district's office, he was almost instantly supportive.

"He knew nothing about me, and yet there I was, asking to start a districtwide program." Ina laughed. Nevertheless, the administrator told Ina she could pilot her program at one elementary school. She chose her alma mater and created a curriculum for a six-day empowerment program.

"Originally, just two students enrolled, which was devastating," Ina admitted. "Then I realized we could still have a significant influence on those two girls. On the second day of the program, the two girls brought their friends and soon our pilot program had grown to include ten girls. We discussed times they had felt oppressed or disempowered because of their gender. The conversations with elementary girls were absolutely unbelievable.

"They told us about their P.E. teachers holding them to lower standards, their mothers doing more housework than their fathers, or how they were the ones who are asked to set the table at dinner. We discussed how their brothers were told to 'man up' and not to cry. We took what we learned from them and conducted activities to teach them to combat those situations."

Ina's pilot project received excellent feedback. She took her results back to the district administrator, who encouraged her to offer similar programs districtwide. The following school year, she launched "Like a Girl" programs at ten elementary schools and two middle schools. High school students served as program leaders; some of the early recruits were Ina's friends, but within a few months, more than 120 high schoolers had come on board as volunteers.

"The beauty is that it's all youth run; there is no adult involvement," Ina explained. "High-school students lead the elementary- and middle-school programs, develop curriculum, work with administrators to gain permission to run the programs, and also partner with the United Nations Foundation's Girl Up Campaign, which is dedicated to advocating for girls around the world."

Ina specifically chose to partner with Girl Up because of its focus on girls in developing countries. She believes that bringing global awareness to students in Nebraska helps them understand that gender discrimination knows no borders. She also believes that a key way for both her peers and younger students to empower themselves is through empowering others, both locally and around the world.

Lincoln Public Schools' Girl Up chapter is the first in Nebraska and has already become the largest of over two thousand chapters that operate globally. Volunteers are split into nine specialized teams that tackle everything from fund-raising to advocacy. Students meet regularly with their elected officials and have already hosted events focused on women refugees, sexual assault and safe spaces, and International Day of the Girl.

Now a junior in high school, Ina has created a sustainability plan to ensure there will continue to be students prepared to move into the program's leadership positions. In addition to her local work, Ina has been appointed an adviser to the United Nations Foundation's Girl Up Campaign. She's hoping to use this platform to expand similar programs in the Midwest, raise more awareness about gender-based stereotypes, and increase her involvement with the UN.

"How has this work changed you?" I asked.

"Without a doubt, it has raised my self-confidence," Ina replied. "I've been empowered personally, but it's also nice to know that there are others who share similar experiences. By working together, we can solve the injustices we face every day.

"It also gives me hope about what our future holds, from our current political situation to what we face in our personal lives. In less than a year, hundreds of us have come together to work for something we strongly believe in—gender equality and empowering youth. There are many people who want to make a difference and that gives me hope that we will soon see global gender equality."

Since 1994, America has become increasingly diverse, and social problems and political and economic polarization are more pronounced. Digital technology has contributed to our social problems, but also to social solutions. Strong girls today are often outsiders or from marginalized populations. This gives them a broader point of view and lots of practice at dealing with challenges.

SIXTEEN

A Fence at the Top
of the Hill

ON A MISTY Monday night in 1994, Sara and I sat on the floor of the Georgian Room at the YWCA in Lincoln. It was a lovely room with high ceilings, peach carpeting, and a grand piano. Baskets of dried flowers and an ancient grandfather clock adorned a marble fireplace. The room was designed for tea drinking by ladies wearing hats and gloves, but on that night twenty of us, dressed in sweat suits and tennis shoes, were there to learn self-defense.

There were several mother-daughter pairs, a trio of adolescent sisters, some college students, and middle-aged women. Our teacher, Kit, alias Kitty Kung Fu, asked how many of us had hit another person, and two of the teenagers raised their hands.

Kit was aware of our self-consciousness about the training, and she kept the tone funny and relaxed. She handed out materials on prevention, showed us whistles and Mace, and warned us to read the instructions before we were attacked. She taught us the vital points of the human body and how to punch, kick, break a stranglehold, and escape when grabbed from behind.

We paired off and practiced. Under crystal chandeliers, we attacked one another and struggled to break free. At first, we were wimps. We giggled and punched the air with gentle womanly moves; we apologized for our accidental aggression. We had to be reminded to scream, to go for the groin and the eyes.

Gradually we stopped being ladylike and learned power moves—the Iron Cross and the Windmill. We marveled aloud that these moves might really work. As we practiced, Kit walked among us, correcting, coaxing, giving us something we hadn't been taught earlier—instructions on fighting back.

After our self-defense training, we sprawled on the floor and watched a film on date rape. I had happily been married for decades and was unlikely ever to go on another date. This film didn't hold my attention, so I looked at the fresh faces reflecting light from the television screen. These young women were the granddaughters of the ladies who curled manicured fingers around china cups in this room. Their grandmothers never had lessons in how to bite, kick, scream, and scratch. Perhaps some had needed these lessons, but most had led violence-free lives. These girls were growing up in a world where one in four women would be raped in her lifetime. I allowed myself to hope the class would improve their odds.

There was something eerie about teaching our daughters how to fight off rapists and kidnappers. We needed classes that taught men not to rape and hurt women and also workshops that taught men how to be gentle and still feel manly.

As I sat there, I remembered a poem about gender differences from my nursery school days. Little boys were made of "snips and snails, and puppy dogs' tails." Girls were made of "sugar and spice, and everything nice." I didn't know then that poems could become self-fulfilling prophecies.

I remember another story from the 1990s, a time when my friend

Randy listened to a group of sixth graders identify what living creature they would like to be. The boys all wanted to be predators: wolves, lions, grizzly bears, and pumas. The girls chose soft and cuddly animals: pandas, koala bears, bunnies, and squirrels. One girl said softly that she'd like to be a rose. When I heard that choice, I thought that the damage had already been done. Roses can't even move, and, while beautiful, they don't experience anything.

To keep their true selves and grow into healthy adults, girls need love from family and friends, meaningful work, respect, challenges, and physical and psychological safety. They need identities based on talents or interests rather than appearance, popularity, or sexuality. They need good habits for coping with stress, self-nurturing skills, and a sense of purpose and perspective. They require quiet places and times. They need to feel that they are part of something larger than their own lives and that they are emotionally connected to a whole.

One girl was saved by her love of books, by long summer afternoons when she read for hours. Another was saved by thinking of faraway places and people. One was saved by her love of music, another by her love of horses. Girls can be saved by a good school, a grandmother, a caring teacher, or a creative project.

In the years prior to the 1990s, many young women were rescued by conversations and support from a beloved neighbor, a kindhearted aunt, or a nearby grandmother. Many women reported that when they were adolescents, they had someone they could really talk to, who encouraged them to stay true to who they really were. In the 1990s, with our more chaotic, fragmented world, fewer girls had that option available. Therapists often filled this role. They were the calm outsiders girls could trust with the truth of their experiences.

Certain kinds of homes help girls hold on to their true selves. These homes offer girls both protection and challenges. These are the homes that offer girls affection and structure. In these homes, parents set firm guidelines and communicate high hopes. With younger children, rules are fine, but with teenagers, guidelines make more sense. With older girls, there will be more negotiating. It's important to remember that rules, in the absence of loving relationships, are not worth much. Almost anyone can figure out how to break rules. What holds girls' lives in place is love and respect for their parents.

Parents can help by listening to their daughters, who need as much parent time as toddlers do. Teenagers need parents available when they are ready to talk. Usually girls want to talk when it's most inconvenient for their parents.

It's good to ask questions that encourage daughters to think clearly for themselves. When listening, parents should listen to what they can respect and praise in their daughters' talk. Whenever possible, they can congratulate their daughters on their maturity, insight, or good judgment. It's important to validate girls' autonomous, adult behavior.

When teenagers temporarily lose their heads, which most do, they need an adult to help them recover. When daughters have problems, it's important not to panic. It's a tough world for daughters. At times, girls from strong, healthy families can experience serious problems. Panicky parents make things worse.

It's important for parents to watch for trouble and convey to their daughters that, if it comes, the daughter and the family will be strong enough to deal with it. Helpful parents manage to stay reasonably calm through the storms. They have a direction and order to their own universe. They can be reassuring. Mr. Fred Rogers was a good role model. He said things like, "Tomorrow is another day," "Nobody is perfect," "Everyone makes mistakes," or "Nobody is liked by everybody." A soothing voice helps girls to calm down in the short term. In the long term, girls internalize these soothing words and say them to themselves when they are upset.

It's important for parents not to take things too personally or to be too hurt by rejection from adolescent girls. Girls' moodiness and irritability are usually related to problems outside the home, problems with school or friends. It's okay to have consequences for disrespectful behavior, but it's good to have a sense of humor and not "make a federal case" out of cranky remarks. Good parents ask their daughters what is wrong when they are particularly temperamental. Instead of consequences, they may need help.

Janet Reno said, "Growing up as a child today in America is even more difficult than raising children." That thought may help parents stay patient. Another thing that may help is recognizing "hot cognitions." Parents can learn to catch themselves before they react. For example, the thought that a daughter is selfish can be reframed: all adolescents are self-absorbed. It helps to remember the difference between the deep and surface structure of a daughter's behavior. When a girl says, "I hate my mom," it doesn't necessarily mean that. It can mean, "I'm trying to find out who I am."

One important reason to stay calm is that calm parents hear more. Low-key, accepting parents are the ones whose children keep talking to them. Successful communication with teenage daughters encourages rational thought, centered decisions, and conscious choices. It includes discussions of options, risks, implications, and consequences. Parents can teach their daughters to make choices. They can help them sort out when to negotiate, stand firm, and withdraw. They can help them learn what they can and can't control, how to pick their battles and to fight back.

Thoughtful parents model the respect and equality that they want their daughters to experience in the outside world. This takes work. All of us have been socialized to behave in gender-stereotyped ways. Parents must think about what their behavior teaches their daughters. Having a home with true equality between the sexes may be an impossible ideal, but it helps girls to see that their parents are working toward this. They will respect the effort.

Many parents worry about rigid sex-typing when their daughters are small. They carefully dress their girls in blue and buy them toy tractors. That's okay, but the time to really worry is early adolescence. That's when the gender roles get set in cement, and that's when girls need tremendous support in resisting the cultural definitions of femininity.

Parents can help daughters be whole by modeling wholeness. Good fathers are nurturing, physically affectionate, and involved in the lives of their daughters. Good mothers model self-sufficiency and self-care and are responsive, but not totally responsible for their family members.

It's important to discuss alcohol, drugs, violence, social pressure, and appearance. If these topics aren't coming up, parents are missing out on what's important to their children.

When girls talk about their drug and alcohol use, it's important to ask about how often, how much, and when and where the use is occurring. Is it experimental, the result of peer pressure or boredom, curiosity or a need to escape reality? Parents can also discuss what needs drugs or alcohol are meeting in their daughter's life and ask how she could meet her needs in healthier ways.

Parents can encourage their daughters to have friends of both sexes and to resist sexualizing relationships. As a therapist in the 1990s, I suggested parents view boy-girl relationships in junior high as friendships. It was not a good idea to tease girls about boyfriends. Treating male-female relationships in a matter-of-fact way promoted relaxed, open behavior between the sexes. When parents asked if they should allow their junior-high daughters to date, I recommended they say, "We want you to have friends of both sexes. Invite your friends over anytime for games or movies with our family." This brought boy-girl relationships into the realm of the everyday.

As a critical human dimension, appearance should be downplayed. It's healthy for daughters to have other things to feel proud of beside their looks. Parents can resist their daughter's focus on appearance and weight. While it's fine to empathize with how important looks are to students, it's also important to stand firm that in any decent value system they are not all that important.

One of the best things that can happen to a girl is that she has well-adjusted friends. Parents have some power to influence this by who they invite on trips and what activities they encourage. Money spent on pizzas and lemonade for a daughter's friends is money well spent.

Girl can learn by traveling during their adolescent years. Camps, international exchange and study abroad programs, and long summers with faraway relatives are great opportunities for growth. It gives girls a break from family. It helps them gain some perspective on their lives, something almost all adolescents need. Jobs are useful too. Of course, work hours need to be reasonable and job sites safe, but jobs allow girls to learn lessons from the real world and to see something outside peer culture.

It's good to remind girls that junior high is not all of life. There are other places—the mountains and beaches, the corner café, the family cabin on the lake, or the neighborhood clubhouse. There are other people—neighbors, relatives, family friends, old people, and babies. And there are other times. They will not always be trapped in teenage-hood; people do grow up. Along with this reminder, it's good to encourage volunteer activities that help girls to stay in contact with the nonadolescent portion of the human race.

Plato said that education is teaching our children to find pleasure in the right things. Parents can share their own pleasures with their daughters by introducing them to the natural world and the world of sports, books, art, or music. They can take them backpacking and teach them to fly-fish, tune up engines, collect political buttons, play cello, knit scarves, or go skydiving. Especially during this turbulent time, families need to find regular ways to have fun.

But even as I encourage parents to help, I admonish them to be gentle with themselves. Their influence is limited. Parents can do only so much, and they are not responsible for everything. They are neither all-knowing nor all-powerful. Parents can make a difference in the lives of their daughters only if their daughters are willing to allow this. Not all daughters are. Daughters have choices and responsibilities. Friends will have an impact. The culture will have an impact.

While parents can do some sheltering, we need to change our institutions. For example, most of what girls read in schools is written by men and about men. We need more stories of women who are strong, more examples of women in a variety of roles. History needs to include the history of women; psychology, the psychology of women; and literature, the writing of women.

Girls benefit from the limelight. Girls' schools, clubs, and groups allow girls to be leaders. Girls' art shows, literature festivals, and athletic events give girls' lives dignity and public importance. Girls need to see reflections of themselves in all their diversity: as workers, artists, and explorers.

Inclusive language helps girls feel included. One client of mine in the 1990s said, "My aunt is a mail carrier. It's been hard to know what to call her—'mail person' didn't sound right and 'mail woman' sounded like something from the circus. I'm glad we have a word now for lady mailmen." Another noticed that artists are generally referred to as "he." She said, "That makes us say 'women artists,' which doesn't sound like they are real artists."

Schools often ignore what is happening socially to students as they are herded from one class to another. Between the ages of eleven and fourteen, students' issues are relationship issues, and their problems are personal and social. Academics take a back seat to urgent developmental concerns. Schools could foster groupings organized around talents, interests, and needs rather than cliques. They could offer students the clarity they desperately need—supervised activities in which adolescents work and relax together, conflict-resolution training, and classes in which guidelines for alcohol and drug use and sexual decisions are discussed. They could offer awareness training in areas such as lookism, racism, and sexism. They could take responsibility for helping adolescents structure all the social and emotional turmoil they are experiencing.

Schools could offer clear sexual and physical harassment policies that protect students and establish norms for conduct toward the opposite sex. They could offer guidelines for appropriate sexual behavior and teach students how to say no.

"Manhood" needs to be redefined in a way that allows women equality and men pride. Our culture desperately needs new ways to teach boys to be men. Via the media and advertising, we are teaching our sons all the wrong lessons. Boys need a model of manhood that is caring and bold, adventurous and gentle. They need ways to be men that don't involve violence, misogyny, and the objectification of women. Instead of promoting violence as a means of solving human problems, we must strengthen our taboos against violence. Some Native American cultures have no words in their language for hurting other humans. What do those cultures think of us?

Much of the horrible behavior that now happens between the sexes comes from ignorance of proper behavior and lack of positive experiences with the opposite sex. We adults can provide that by working together in volunteer activities. Or we can host teen events. For example, in Lincoln in the 1990s, the Red and Black Cafe was opened by adults who wanted their teenagers to have a safe, cheap place to congregate. It stayed open late and hosted local bands. Teens loved it.

As a culture, we can use more wholesome rituals for coming of age. Too many of our current rituals involve sex, drugs, alcohol, and rebellion. We need more positive ways to acknowledge growth, more ceremonies and graduations. It's good to have toasts, celebrations, and markers for teens that tell them, "You are growing up and we're proud of you."

Our society teaches that sex, alcohol, and purchasing power lead to the good life. We really do know better. We need to rebuild our society so that its values are more congruent with what we know about the true nature of happiness.

My grandfather liked a poem about a town that had people falling off its cliffs. The city elders met to debate whether to build a fence at the top of the cliffs or put an ambulance down in the valley. The poem summarizes the essential differences between treatment and prevention of social problems. My work as a therapist was ambulance work, and after years of ambulance driving, I was aware of the limits of the treatment approach to major social problems. In addition to treating the casualties of our cultural messages, we needed to work for cultural change.

I believe, as Miller, Mead, and de Beauvoir believed, that pathology comes from failure to realize all one's possibilities. Ophelia died because she could not grow. She became the object of others' lives and lost her true subjective self. Many of my clients suffered from a thwarting of their development, a truncating of their potential. As my client described it—they are perfectly good carrots being cut into roses.

Adolescence is a border between childhood and adulthood. Like life on all borders, it's teeming with energy and fraught with danger. Growth requires courage and hard work on the part of the individual, and it requires the protection and nurturing of the environment. Some girls develop under the most adverse conditions, but the interesting question is, "Under what conditions do most girls develop to their fullest?"

Long-term plans for helping adolescent girls involve deep-seated and complicated cultural changes—rebuilding a sense of community in our neighborhoods, fighting addictions, changing our schools, promoting gender equality, and curtailing violence. The best "fence at the top of the hill" is a culture in which there is structure and security and tolerance for diversity and autonomy. Then our daughters can grow and develop slowly and peacefully into whole, authentic people.

I quoted Stendhal in chapter 1: "All geniuses born women are lost to the public good." Some ground has been gained since he said that, but not enough. Let's work toward a culture in which there is a place for every human gift, in which children are safe and protected, women are respected, and men and women can love one another as whole human beings. Let's work for a culture in which the incisive intellect, the willing hands, and the happy heart are beloved. Then our daughters will have a place where all their talents will be appreciated, and they can flourish like green trees under the sun and the stars.

Thriving in the Age of Disruption

THE SUGGESTIONS in the last chapter still ring true. In 2019 as in 1994, girls come of age in a culture that defines them by their appearance and sexuality. Middle schools continue to be spirit-crushing environments. They are filled with hormonal, immature kids eager to fit in. Most are large, underfunded, and short-staffed. They can feel like factories manufacturing humiliation and meanness. Girls still do best with parents who model respect for each other, and they thrive on authentic friendships with people of all ages.

However, family relationships are generally much improved. Parents need less advice on how to deal with their own hurt feelings. Conflict is no longer a constant and dramatic problem. In 1994, girls were rebellious and distancing themselves from parents. Now girls rebel less and report feeling affection for their parents. They tend to stay close to home and mature more slowly. They aren't dating at thirteen or even in many cases at seventeen.

This prolonged childhood can be a blessing unless it comes at the cost of readiness for life outside the family. Adversity builds strength.

Lack of risk and challenge can lead to teens unprepared for reality. We see evidence of that when teens graduate from high school and face college or the world of work. We see it in their need for comfort animals and trigger warnings, and in their high rates of depression, anxiety, and binge drinking.

Growth is always the result of stress. When girls are given opportunities for calibrated challenges, they become confident and skillful. Sara's friend Robin recently told a story about her fourteen-year-old daughter, Genevieve, who spent the first half of her summer vacation flouncing around the house, bored and restless. Finally, fed up, Robin barked, "Figure out how much money you have in your bank account, find a cheap plane ticket, and go somewhere!"

While Robin's suggestion was born of frustration, it worked wonders for Genevieve. She excitedly tallied her babysitting money, searched online for travel deals, and ended up spending a week in the Colorado Rockies with her favorite cousins. She navigated her first solo flight and was proud to fund her vacation with her own earnings. Robin was surprised, and thrilled, to realize that when she offered her daughter independence, everyone won.

Our culture has made progress in many areas. Violent crime and sexual assault rates have incrementally decreased. Teen drinking, drug use, and criminal activity have all declined. Divorce rates are lower and gay marriage is now legal. Schools celebrate increased ethnic diversity, and more students are engaged with the issues of our times. I sincerely congratulate all of us—all of *you*—who worked to make these things happen.

Raising healthy children has always involved protecting them from what is noxious and connecting them to the good and the beautiful. No matter the era, thoughtful parents help teenagers develop a strong sense of self and connect to others with love and empathy. They help their daughters mature into people who are kind, authentic, and competent.

By now, online activities have altered teens' emotional growth, social behavior, nervous systems, body chemistry, and attention spans. We may rue the day smartphones were invented, but we can't put the genie back in the bottle. Technology companies could work to make their products less addictive, but that is unlikely to happen without strong consumer demand and new laws regulating their products.

Meantime, our culture is changing at an accelerating pace. Now girls have new needs: to spend time off devices, to experience face-to-face interactions so they learn to converse, and to negotiate and have fun with real people.

Families who don't implement any controls over digital use are likely to have docile children and little overt conflict, but their teens are most certainly missing important developmental experiences. Families with strict limits, consistently enforced, generally experience well-adjusted teens and limited conflict. Unfortunately, very few of these families exist—it's just too difficult in our current cultural context.

Most families are stuck in the middle. Parents want more control but can't figure out how to get it. Teens are unhappy and upset about limits. Adolescents are likely to hide some of their digital use by claiming they are reading or studying. Parents know they don't know what's going on. Yet good parents persist with limit setting. They carve out space for family meals, card games, or breakfasts together before everyone leaves for the day.

Rather than offer specific rules about technology use, we suggest families convene meetings in which all members discuss and then agree upon what feels fair. We recommend postponing girls' launch into the world of social media as long as possible, but practical issues may make cell phones necessary and most girls want phones when their friends start using them. Families can make group decisions about issues such as how to handle smartphones in bedrooms or during meals, rides to school, or on family holidays. Parents and their daughters can decide together what degree of transparency is reasonable and revisit their guidelines regularly.

One family I know has only one email address for the whole family. Another has a technology "fast day" every Sunday. Still another family has agreed that all devices will be turned off by 9 p.m. every night and left charging on the kitchen counter until morning. Parent groups are forming nationwide around the phrase "Wait Until Eighth." They collectively agree not to give their children cell phones until at least eighth grade, so that no child feels left out or different from her peers.

We recommend that parents make time to join their children online and take an interest in their teenagers' online activities. This helps them understand their children and the world of social media and gives them more authority when they talk to their kids about their devices. They might also be surprised that they enjoy certain online games or social media sites, and finding common ground with their children benefits everyone.

Organizations such as Common Sense Media and the Center for Human Technology advocate for sensible use of digital devices, but we need more advocacy and research on preventing addiction to social media. We need to develop a network of support groups similar to Alcoholics Anonymous for teens and adults who are hooked on screens. All high schools should offer classes in media education, social media education, stress management, and communication skills.

What is abundantly clear is that the more time they spend off-line, the happier teenage girls are. Off-line time can be spent jogging, practicing clarinet, or playing chess with siblings. It can be giggling in clothing stores with friends, baking gluten-free cupcakes, or swinging on too-small swings at the local playground.

All pathology originates from disconnection to our true selves. If our culture's newest problem is the social media–produced disconnection to our hearts, bodies, and one another, then the cure is reconnection. Let's work together to foster a culture that turns screen-agers back into teenagers.

Parent-child conversations can focus on the deep structure and meaning of girls' lives. What does the daughter most want for herself? Is it five hundred Twitter followers or a sense that she is respected and appreciated for who she truly is? Is her highest aspiration social acceptance or does she strive toward a deeper purpose? Is she happiest online or when she is jogging with her dog on snowy mornings? What does she want her epitaph to read?

We can help our teens reflect upon their passions, talents, virtues, challenges, and long-term goals. We can share our thoughts on our own passions, challenges, and goals as well. We can talk about how to get along well with other people and demonstrate by our own behavior what kindness in action looks like.

In this hurried world, the best gift parents can give children is their attention. We can offer our daughters the gift of slow time and the gift of presence. Parents and other role models can also encourage activities that offer girls what we call deep time—geological time, celestial time, solar time, seasonal time, and animal time. Horses and dogs have not sped up in our modern area. Their biorhythms remain as slow as they have been for hundreds of years, which is one reason that animals are so restful and peaceful for humans. Activities such as hiking or camping take families out under the night sky, where they can hear the tumbling of water over rocks, the wind in the trees, or the calls of an-cient birds.

Parents can encourage children to spend time with extended family and neighbors. They can organize Wednesday nights at the beach or Friday night spaghetti dinners. They can engage with their communi-ties via mother-daughter book clubs, choirs, or cycling teams. They can plan and attend family reunions or take vacations that broaden their perspectives on the world. It doesn't matter what families choose;

there exists an endless buffet of activities that expand girls' points of view, discourage narcissism, and promote maturity.

Authentic adults are created by authentic experiences. Children greatly benefit from opportunities to express themselves creatively. Indeed, creative self-expression builds identity. Almost all girls have some creative passion—music, art, writing, theater, dance—that can be nurtured.

Activism also broadens perspective and helps girls become deeper, truer versions of themselves. As we saw in our interviews with activist girls, parental support was a great predictor of their nascent interest in advocacy. Many parents today are involved in volunteer work at middle and high schools. Others work to provide safe and welcoming spaces for marginalized, troubled, or homeless teens or any youths who need a positive place to hang out. This kind of work helps parents truly understand the many social and cultural worlds their daughters navigate.

Most states offer leadership camps and organizations that foster personal and social growth in girls. Parents and their daughters can look for local chapters of national organizations such as Girl Up, Girls Inc, #BuiltByGirls, or Girls on the Run. Beyond these, many communities have savvy young women who have established their own organizations; social media can help parents and their daughters find local outlets for girl-focused empowerment.

Girls yearn to be respected, relaxed, bold, kind, and free to grow. They want to fully experience their emotions and also attain good emotional control. They want to explore the world yet feel safe. They want their lives to be meaningful and useful and they want to be loved.

Since the beginning of humanity parents have wanted their daughters to grow up and be healthy, happy, productive members of the tribe. Our desires are no different in 2019, except in our new electronic village, our tribe now includes seven billion people. We must raise our daughters with this message: you have many talents and gifts, you are special to us and to those who know you, but you are on a crowded planet with many people in need. We want you to grow into all you can be and we want you to help heal this troubled world.

Recommended Reading

Brill, Stephanie and Kenney, Lisa. (2016). *The Transgender Teen: A Handbook for Parents and Professionals Supporting Transgender and Non-Binary Teens.* Cleis Press.

Damour, Lisa. (2017). *Untangled: Guiding Girls Through the Seven Transitions into Adulthood.* Penguin Books.

Ehrensaft, Diane and Spack, Norman. (2016). *The Gender Creative Child: Pathways for Nurturing and Supporting Children Who Live Outside Gender Boxes.* The Experiment.

Favilli, Elena and Cavallo, Franchesca. (2016). *Good Night Stories for Rebel Girls.* Timbuktu Labs, Inc.

Freed, Richard. (2015). *Wired Child: Reclaiming Childhood in the Digital Age.* CreateSpace Independent Publishing Platform.

Khan-Cullors, Patrisse and Bandele, Asha. (2018). *When They Call You a Terrorist: A Black Lives Matter Memoir.* St. Martin's Press.

Miller, Kelsey. (2016). *Big Girl: How I Gave Up Dieting and Got a Life.* Grand Central Publishing.

Normandi, Carol Emery and Roark, Lauralee. (2008). *It's Not About Food: End Your Obsession with Food and Weight.* TarcherPerigee.

Nye, Naomi Shibob. (2005). *A Maze Me: Poems for Girls.* Greenwillow Books.

Page, Elisa Camahort, Gerin, Carolyn and Wilson, Jamia. (2018). *Road Map for Revolutionaries: Resistance, Activism, and Advocacy for All.* Ten Speed Press.

Price, Catherine. (2018). *How to Break Up with Your Phone: The 30-Day Plan to Take Back Your Life*. Ten Speed Press.

Reynolds, Eliza and Reynolds, Sil. (2013). *Mothering and Daughtering: Keeping Your Bond Strong Through the Teen Years*. Sounds True, Inc.

Sales, Nancy Jo. (2017). *American Girls: Social Media and the Secret Lives of Teenagers*. Vintage Books.

Simmons, Rachel. (2010). *The Curse of the Good Girl: Raising Authentic Girls with Courage and Confidence*. Penguin Books.

Simmons, Rachel. (2018). *Enough As She Is: How to Help Girls Move Beyond Impossible Standards of Success to Live Healthy, Happy, and Fulfilling Lives*. HarperCollins.

Single, Jesse. (2018). "Your Child Says She's Trans. She Wants Hormones and Surgery. She's 13." *The Atlantic*. July/August 2018, p. 88.

Tribole, Evelyn and Resch, Elyse. (2012) *Intuitive Eating: A Revolutionary Program That Works*. St. Martin's Griffin.

Twenge, Jean M. (2017). *iGen: Why Today's Super-Connected Youth Are Growing Up Less Rebellious, More Tolerant, Less Happy—and Completely Unprepared for Adulthood*. Atria Books.

Walker, Sarai. (2015). *Dietland*. Houghton Mifflin Harcourt.

West, Lindy. (2017). *Shrill*. Hachette.

Index